WORLD

Film retains its capacity to beguile, entertain and open up windows onto other cultures like no other medium. Nurtured by the growth of film festivals worldwide and by cinephiles from all continents, a new generation of directors has emerged in this environment over the last few decades.

This new series aims to present and discuss the work of the leading directors from across the world on whom little has been written and whose exciting work merits discussion in an increasingly globalised film culture. Many of these directors have proved to be ambassadors for their national film cultures as well as critics of the societies they represent, dramatising in their work the dilemmas of art that are both national and international, of local relevance and universal appeal.

Written by leading film critics and scholars, each book contains an analysis of the director's works, filmography, bibliography and illustrations. The series will feature film-makers from all continents (including North America), assessing their impact on the art form and their contribution to film culture.

Other Titles in the Series

YASH CHOPRA

Rachel Dwyer

Qui dono novum libellum?
Thomas and James

First published in 2002 by the
BRITISH FILM INSTITUTE
21 Stephen Street, London W1T 1LN

The British Film Institute promotes greater understanding of,
and access to, film and moving image culture in the UK.

Cover design by Ketchup
Text design by Ketchup
Set by D R Bungay Associates, Burghfield, Berks
Printed in England by The Cromwell Press, Trowbridge, Wiltshire

British Library Cataloguing-in-Publication Data
A catalogue record for this book is available from the British Library

ISBN 0–85170–875–7 (pbk)
ISBN 0–85170–874–9 (hbk)

CONTENTS

FOREWORD

For me, singing a song for Yashji comes easier than penning my thoughts on him and there are so many songs that have embellished our long and memorable association. Over the years, our relationship has transcended the music we created together and has developed into a deep bond. I am 'didi' (elder sister) to him and when he addresses me so, I know it comes straight from the heart , just the kind of filmmaker and person that he is ... straight from the heart!

His films have entertained generations of film-goers and are unforgettable for their emotional content, their grand canvas and the aesthetic visuals he so painstakingly creates. While no film of his fails to tug at our hearts, each of them is still a balm for frayed nerves ... no wonder then, that Indians the world over, watch his films over and over again.

I first sang for *Ek Hi Raasta* (1956), in which he was an assistant, followed by *Sadhana* and then *Dhool ka phool*, his directorial debut. Ever since Yashji turned producer with *Daag*, I have sung in every film made by him, each one unique in its own way, each one among India's all time great films. My personal favorites among films directed by him are *Kabhi kabhie*, *Silsila*, *Chandni*, *Lamhe*, *Deewar*, *Trishul* and of course the film in which he launched his son, Adi, as a director, *Dilwale dulhania le jayenge*.

Recording for Yashji is always a pleasure. While I am at the mike, I watch him enacting the song, lost in his own world, visualizing his heroine through his lens, even dancing if the song is such...and this helps me bring more expression to the song.

After the *gaana* (song), its *khaana* (food) ... he loves good food and he relishes even more watching others enjoy what he has laid out for them ... and Pam bhabhi, shares his passion for films, music and food in equal measure ... and with the food Yashji serves up, yet another passion ... nostalgia ... we go down memory lane, recalling all the times we have shared ... the song ends up sumptuously!

Yashji and I almost share a birthday – he is born on 27 September while I, on 28 September. Both of us pride ourselves in being Librans. His balanced nature, his sense of fairness, his soft and emotional side, his sensitivity towards others and his love for beauty are all hallmarks of his star sign and each of these traits are so vividly reflected in his films.

Yashji has truly lived up to his name, Yash (fame) Raj (reign). He has towered over the industry like a colossus and yet his continued success and popularity have not affected his ideals and his simple values in life. Even at the pinnacle of his career, he is still God-fearing and respectful towards his elders and never fails to acknowledge all the people who contributed towards his stellar achievements.

I am glad that this book by Rachel Dwyer will provide you with an insight into Yashji, the celebrated film-maker and the person I have had the privilege of knowing so closely.

I wish him many more years of good films and a long and happy life.

Lata Mangeshkar
February 2002

ACKNOWLEDGMENTS

I should like to acknowledge my brief but fulsome thanks to the following:

My friends in India who have provided me with warm hospitality, sound advice on so many levels – in Bombay; Shaad and Murad Ali, Shyam and Neera Benegal, Anurag Chaturvedi, Pamela Chopra, the late Michel d'Costa, Shobha Dé, Imtiaz, Anil and Ayesha Dharker, Reima and Owais Husain, Adil Jussawala, Udita Jhunjhunwala, Maithili Rao, Amrut, Rekhi, Asim, Monisha and Sonal Shah, Farooque Shaikh; in Delhi; Muzaffar and Meera Ali, Suzanne Goldenberg, Rohit and Rashmi Khattar, Ashis Nandy, Ranjana Sengupta, Radhika Sinha, Patricia Uberoi, and Ravi Vasudevan; in Calcutta; Bhaskar Mukhopadhyay, Devdan and Pauline Hawthorn-Sen.

Those who provided materials and other information: Jerry Pinto; Khalid Mohamed and the staff of *Filmfare*; and the late Iqbal Masud.

The people who gave me their advice and often extended interviews: Yash and Pamela Chopra, Aditya and Uday Chopra, Kiddy and Beena Chadha, Joginder and Suneeta Sanger; the staff of Yash Raj Films (especially Sally Fernandez, Sahdev Ghei, Avtar Panesar and Mr Vakil); Vikram Chandra; Shobha Dé; Kirit and Meenal Trivedi; Javed Akhtar, Dev Anand, Amitabh Bachchan, Juhi Chawla, B.R. Chopra, Shiamak Davar, Madhuri Dixit, M.F. Husain, Jatin-Lalit, Karan Johar, Anil Kapoor, Rishi Kapoor, Shammi Kapoor, Shashi Kapoor, Aamir Khan, Salim Khan, Shahrukh Khan, Khayyam, Kiron Kher, Dilip Kumar, Manish Malhotra, Amrish Puri, Gulshan Rai, Rajiv Rai, Rekha, Sadhana, Javed Siddiqui, Sri Devi and Uttam Singh.

SOAS Research Committee for funding most of my fieldwork, supplemented by the British Academy for the beginnings of this project in 1997.

Paul Fox and Glenn Ratcliffe for their photographic work.

Christopher Shackle for his advice on the Urdu lyric at the end of the book.

Andrew Lockett for his editorial suggestions.

Those who invited me to present this work and contingent papers at conferences and seminars, for their advice and hospitality: Mihir Bhattacharya at the University of Jadavpur, Lawrence Cohen at the University of California at Berkeley, Harsh Dehejia at the University of Bombay, Nicholas B. Dirks at the University of Columbia, Kathryn Hansen at Rutgers University, Philip Lutgendorf at the University of Iowa, Purnima Mankekar at Stanford University, Jim Masselos at the University of New South Wales, Francesca Orsini at the University of Cambridge, Gurharpal Singh at the University of Hull.

My colleagues for their continuing support, criticism and encourage-ment: Daud Ali, Dipesh Chakrabarty, Faisal Devji, Ron Inden, Sudipta Kaviraj, Uday Singh Mehta, Francesca Orsini, Chris Pinney, Madhava Prasad and Christopher Shackle.

Former and present students who have witnessed much of this work in progress, and given me helpful comments and suggestions, in particular Kaushik Bhaumik, Jessica Hines, Anna Morcom, Ambika Samarthya and Kush Varia.

My family and other friends, especially Michael.

Images courtesy of Yash Raj Films Pvt and Gulshan Rai, Trimurti Films Pvt. Chapter 6 builds on a chapter from Dwyer 2000a and a paper I published in *West Coast Line* (Dwyer 2000d).

PREFACE

This book is the first research-based academic study of a contemporary top
Indian director. It examines the life and work of a major film-maker, Yash
Chopra (1932–), one of the most powerful people in the Hindi commercial
film industry.[1] He has been a leading figure in the movie business for over 40
years as a director, and has been a major producer since 1973, consolidating
his success in the 1990s with a series of box-office hits. As such, he is a public
figure, not only in the film industry but also as a representative of the industry
to the wider world. His name has come to represent a certain style, not only in
film-making but in Indian culture itself, where his name is synonymous with
romance, glamour and beauty. A 'Yash Chopra wedding' or a 'Yash Chopra
outfit' needs little further definition. The public and the private person are
hidden behind these filmic representations, hence it is a discussion of these
various manifestations of 'Yash Chopra' which forms the core of this book.

I had not initially set out to write a book about Yash Chopra but was teach-
ing and researching on Indian cinema when I first saw him on television,
talking about films of the 1990s and the rise of a new anti-hero. This
programme was made in 1993, although it was not until 1995 that I saw it, at
the time he released his hit *Darr/Fear* (1993), the story of a woman stalked by
an obsessive. I had enjoyed this film enormously, especially its music (by
Shiv-Hari), the performance of Shahrukh Khan, and its style. Three
moments, all song sequences, were particularly striking and seemed to me to
be new expressions within the established language of Hindi cinema.

One was the song *'Chota sa ghar/*Our house is quite small', in which an
engaged couple fantasise about their life together, dreaming of the flat in
which they will live. It suddenly becomes furnished, the couple switch from
being young lovers to models of domesticity, then step through a picture of a
landscape into a Swiss idyll where they enact the traditional erotics of the
Hindi film in song and dance, bypassing the bedroom as a location of eroticism, although the chorus *'Darwaza band kar lo/*Shut the door', shows their

need for private space. The idea of the lovers' fantasy in the face of the reality of the average house, the disregard for real space and time and the banality or universality of the lyrics counterpoised with the picturisation of the song were striking in their brilliant use of the idioms of the Hindi film.

The other two moments were more sinister, involving questions of invisibility and anonymity. The second was the opening scene, which showed the heroine running around her college, looking for the invisible singer, whose song '*Tu haa kar, ya naa kar, tu hai meri Kiran*/Whether you agree or not, you are mine, Kiran', states the stalker's intention and the film's focus on the limits of desire. The third was a Holi party when the stalker had warned the heroine he would put colour on her (*rang dena* 'to colour' has overt sexual connotations). She is tense but the family celebrates Holi as usual. However the stranger gains entry to their garden, disguised as a musician and he achieves his intention of playing Holi with the heroine. Apart from this manipulation of the medium of Hindi film, what interested me about *Darr* was its dangerous attraction. The performance by the then rising star, Shahrukh Khan, as anti-hero was disturbing because, although he was clearly a psychotic stalker, like the rest of the audience, I was on his side by the time of his confrontation with the hero.

I was surprised to realise that Yash Chopra, whose recent film *Chandni* was one of the first Hindi movies I ever saw, was in his 50s or 60s and yet making innovative films. He was also understated yet authoritative, shy but forceful and in spite of a thick Punjabi accent, highly articulate in English. I disagreed with his view that this was 'a boy who loved too much and did not know where to stop' but was intrigued by his argument. After the interview, I realised who this film-maker was. Not only had he made great films such as *Waqt/Time* (1965), *Deewaar/The Wall* (1975) but he was also the 'king of romance'. I resolved to interview him on my next visit to Bombay in connection with my research on romance, which led to *All you want is money, all you need is love*,[2] but also developed into the idea of writing a book on the man himself.

I first wrote to Yash Chopra in March 1996 requesting a meeting. He did not reply. When in Bombay, I called and, since he kept an open office at that time, he agreed to meet me for an hour. In the flesh Yash Chopra did not fit with the image I had of him from his films or from the gossip magazines. Instead he seemed more of a businessman, a producer, ensconced in a palatial office. He was polite, but seemed a completely different person from the persona ascribed to him in popular imagination. Correct, quiet and thoughtful, yet totally 'unromantic'.

We met again that summer in Leicester Square then I returned to Bombay in February 1997 with a research project in mind, but he remained entirely the businessman, always making and taking telephone calls, giving little attention to what I thought were important conversations. I was very disappointed, and began to abandon my idea of a book about him. It was only when I accompanied him to his film sets that I saw an altogether different person, a high-spirited, hard-working creative film-maker, interacting with his stars and staff. We continued in this vein for four months, our only non-work conversations being about food and other films. Subsequently we have had many further meetings in the UK and in Bombay, while staying in touch via fax and phone. We became friends, in a strange way, comfortable and entertained enough by each other, close yet by no means intimate. Writing a book about someone one disliked would be a very perverse activity. Yash Chopra has declined to read my work ahead of publication and has made no attempt whatsoever to influence it.

The major source for this study are the dozens of interviews I recorded over the years with Yash Chopra. These were in English, with the occasional digression in Hindi/Urdu. He speaks Hindi on occasion when he complains his tongue is weary from English or if there is any likelihood of confusion. Then he repeats himself in the other language. The interviews took place in Yash Chopra's office, home, on sets, in the car, in Bombay, in London, and locations. Yash Chopra's use of English is fascinating, a mixture of old-fashioned government school English, modern English and American slang, phrases translated directly from Hindi and Punjabi, and his own idiosyncratic expressions which have entertained me, his family and friends, ending up as part of our own lexicon.[3] However, I was unable to keep this rich language in my book, finding transcribed material wandered, was interrupted – mostly by the telephone and streams of visitors– and lacked the spontaneity and savour of its Punjabi pronunciation. However, I have kept very close to Yash Chopra's own words, editing rather than rewriting his words.

The key question this book asks is: Who is Yash Chopra? I see not one, but several Yash Chopras. One is the professional and public person, the film-maker–director, producer, storywriter, the person who has created the 'Yash Chopra' film, image, story, lifestyle etc. In writing about this Yash Chopra, I need to tie together Yash Chopra, the creative person, with Yash Chopra, the businessman. This is a multiple story, about the interaction of Yash Chopra the person with external forces and people. This is largely based on interviews with him and his colleagues, but also on external sources such as trade and gossip magazines and so on. In these contexts, I shall consider the idea of the 'auteur' in the context of Hindi film-making. The second is the Yash Chopra in the film texts themselves, where I consider his relations with the ideas of authorial experience that are seen within the lives of the screen characters. This does not imply that I find the texts autobiographical but they are nonetheless important because they reveal much about one or more Yash

Yash Chopra

Chopra. Thirdly, there is Yash Chopra the private person, whom I have got to know in a range of situations. I intend to tie these various Yash Chopras together to give some wider portrait of the person and the films, while structuring my narrative chronologically around his cinematic output. How does one connect the quiet man and the boisterous Punjabi, the devoted family man, the great romantic, the hard-headed businessman? What has driven him to take such risks and to achieve such success?

I have found this book unusually difficult to write. I continue to find Yash Chopra elusive and changing both in terms of his film-making and in the broad range of personae he adopts in his public and private life. Compounding these problems, there is a scarcity of primary documentation and an absence of a critical discourse around figures in the Hindi film industry. I have tried to deal with these concerns in writing this book, but am aware that some of my findings remain preliminary and somewhat inconclusive. Although these lacunae could allow me to postpone writing, I hope that this work will lay a foundation for further discussions around the many topics that it raises, in however unpolished a form.

Author's note

There is a great problem with referring to people. The use of surnames is common but has an air of the British public school, whereas first names can easily sound 'matey' and Mr or Mrs X sounds almost comically Victorian. This problem is compounded in India where there are many more systems of address, some people in the film industry being known only by one name. Almost everyone in Bombay calls Yash Chopra, Yashji. –ji is an honorific, which I use when talking to Yashji, but since it looks rather 'toadyish' in print, I've stuck to Yash in the book, with no disrespect intended. I have done this with others too – so Amitabh, Shashi, Dilip, Rekha etc. I hope they will understand that this is a dilemma which I have resolved logically, if not always formally or politely.

All unacknowledged quotes are taken from interviews I conducted between 1997 and 2001. All unacknowledged translations are my own.

One
Yash Chopra: Cinema and Biography

Biography

India has a long history of 'lives'. Some Sanskrit texts describe the nature and behaviour of gods and goddesses in order to explain the cosmos, while others narrate the lives of heroes and heroines, often members of royal dynasties, in terms of ideals and exemplary characters, within the tight conventions of Sanskrit poetics.[1] The medieval *bhakti* (devotional) movement gave rise to hagiographic lives of the *sants* (saints), which are still narrated to gatherings of devotees as examples of devotional, although not always exemplary, lives.[2] Texts produced in the Mughal and other courts of medieval India recount the lives of the kings and their courtiers, many for the glorification of the institutional office which that person held. Nineteenth-century lives are fascinating as these various traditions of 'lives' are elaborated by new ideas about the person/individual/self, and I suspect there is a wide gap between texts of lives and the imagination of what a life or a person is, even in the individual, let alone in wider society.[3]

How can one leap from this type of biography, of 'great men',[4] to the world of cinema? One cannot, yet one must, given that there has been so little attention paid to the life stories of the 'great' men and women in the Hindi cinema industry, who are thought of as 'commercial' rather than 'creative'. There are lives of Ray and other 'art' film-makers and of those in the Hindi film industry who are regarded as more artistic[5] and hence more capable of being 'auteurs'.[6] Hence it is not surprising there is no official 'life' of Yash Chopra, who works within the paradigm of mainstream Hindi cinema. Many of these recent biographies are reminiscences, by the author or by people who knew the person, tied together by unstated ideas on work and the person on loosely-conceived romantic ideas about the creative artist. They can for the most part be viewed as extensions of the gossip circulated by film magazines.[7] Since Yash Chopra, though well-known and powerful, is not a star, less gossip attaches to him than to his actors. Although this gossip is held to be true, it remains unproven and I have chosen not to follow it up.

The debates on questions of authorship are long-running and inconclusive, as the balance swings between material determinism (economic, technological, ideological) and conflicting ideas on subjectivity.[8] I remain undecided. As Hollywood directors, notably John Ford, were admitted as auteurs to the pantheon of the great, so Yash Chopra could be regarded as an auteur. However, the idea of the director as author is so overburdened with ideas of romantic creativity and infatuation, that I should prefer to avoid its use. In the everyday world, Yash Chopra is regarded as a force, whether as a stylist, as the expositor of a genre (the romance), or simply as a brand name.

Lives in films

Yash Chopra creates lives in his films and it is to these indirect expressions of his attitudes I now turn. The only complete life story in a Yash Chopra film is shown in *Deewaar*, which was based on a bound script,[9] where childhood shapes the (anti-)hero's life, as he is branded a criminal with the tattoo *'Mera baap chor hai'/*'My father is a thief'. We follow his life until his death.

Yash Chopra's films show a belief in the force of destiny or fate, in particular in love, where the couple are made for one another. This is seen clearly in his most recent film, *Dil to pagal hai/The Heart is Crazy* (*DTPH*) (1997), where the hero and heroine are linked by a series of coincidences even before they have met.

Most of the films are set around the key moments of love and romance. The romantic couple meet, they often have to face a dilemma arising from previous commitments or family duties, then are reconciled to the wishes of their families. Throughout the films, the clear message is that love and fun are located in family and in relationships.

Although I have disavowed a search for Yash Chopra within his films, there are some performances or characters which are designed as reflections of him as a person. The hero often manifests features of Yash Chopra the man. For example, Shahrukh told me that he took the stammer in *Darr* from Yash Chopra's own stammer; Shahrukh's emotional outburst in *DTPH*, when he quarrels with Madhuri over her inability to perform as he wishes, is strongly reminiscent of Yash Chopra's behaviour. Although I could give more examples of this, instead I will consider one film, *Kabhi kabhie/Sometimes* (1976) in which I believe two of the heroes are more clearly autobiographical.

One case where Yash Chopra seems to have drawn on a real life story is in *Kabhi kabhie*, where the character of Amit draws on the life and poetry of Yash Chopra's close friend, Sahir Ludhianvi, who wrote all the lyrics for Yash Chopra's films from the first film in 1959 until his death in 1980. Before Yash Chopra came to Bombay in 1951, he was a fan of Sahir's as a college student in Jalandhar and said he used to walk around with a book of Sahir's poetry. On arriving in Bombay, his brother, B.R. Chopra, who was already established in the film industry, thought Yash Chopra might be excited to meet some stars. Yash Chopra says he wanted to meet Sahir more than anyone. They became friends straight away, and that friendship remained close until Sahir's death 30 years later. Yash Chopra never lost his admiration for his friend, accepting without judgment his personal problems and his depression. Sahir had written the lyrics for Guru Dutt's *Pyaasa/The Desirer* (1957), where the role of the hero, the poet Vijay, is said by many to be based on Sahir himself. Sahir also wrote the lyrics for *Kabhi kabhie*, in which Amitabh Bachchan plays a poet who gives up his poetry to become a businessman in self-defeating sorrow after the marriage of his beloved, writing only one bitter version of his most famous poem, dedicated to her, after their separation. It is only in the closing scenes that he writes an optimistic version of an earlier, sad poem, and the happy ending of the film is ensured. The character played here is the poet as Yash Chopra would wish to see him, his unhappiness stemming his creativity, which returns as he achieves happiness. There certainly seems to be an element of Yash Chopra's desire to be a poet in this portrayal. Yet many people have remarked how the character played by Shashi Kapoor, who married Amitabh's beloved, is so like Yash Chopra, an energetic, cheerful man but a frustrated poet. His open and frank relationship with his son in the film prefigures Yash Chopra's relationships with his own sons, who were very young at the time of the film, and indeed with young people in general. The film's ultimate solution lies in the pragmatic, non-romantic acceptance of one's spouse and family, whatever their merits.

The private view

Yash Chopra finds it hard to tell his life story, although he is happy to recount anecdotal stories of incidents in his life.[10] Although he has written stories for his films, Yash Chopra never writes about himself; but there are two autobiographies by men from similar backgrounds whose lives followed different trajectories. These are fellow Punjabi Khatris, and fellow Arya Samajis who were displaced by the Partition, actor Balraj Sahni and civil servant Prakash Tandon. Their books shed much light on the social milieu of which Yash is a product.

Balraj Sahni (1913–73) was known for his commitment to the political theatre movement IPTA (Indian People's Theatre Association) and for film acting, where he often played the role of the displaced peasant, and/or the victim of Partition. In Yash Chopra's first colour film, *Waqt/Time* (1965), he played the father of three boys whose family was separated by an earthquake. It requires little imagination to read the family's displacement from the Punjab to Delhi and its final reunion in Bombay as a metaphor for the Partition. Sahni, like his younger brother, Bhisham,[11] was also a writer. Balraj wrote first in English but later in Punjabi. Although he lived in Bombay for much of his life, his heart remained in the Punjab. His later writing was in Punjabi and he used to go to Punjab for his holidays and toured villages with a theatre group. Before his death he was planning to return to live in Punjab. Sahni's age is close to that of Yash Chopra's elder brother, B.R. Chopra. Like B.R. Chopra, he had studied English Literature at Government College, Lahore and shared with the elder Chopra a commitment to social change through the arts. His autobiography, *Balraj Sahni by Balraj Sahni* (1979), is very external, containing little about his feelings, even those on the death of his first wife. His time in London with the BBC is rather glossed over. This is a book about the individual, the creative person, a close-up rather than a wider shot. It is nevertheless important in giving us insights into the way that life stories – even of a person whose psychological awareness was evident in his acting – are not easy to verbalise in writing, for reasons we can only imagine – was interiority seen as a breach of privacy? Did he simply lack descriptive skills? He clearly saw his life story as linear, valuing his childhood memories for nostalgic reasons, for being his first memories rather than because of the emotional significance of childhood, or because they showed how he moved away from the lifestyle and values of his Khatri, Arya Samaji origins, similar to those of the Chopras.

Prakash Tandon's *Punjabi Century*[12] is the work of a great descriptive writer who became a successful businessman and bureaucrat. His nostalgia for his youth, his historical awareness and his ability to connect the specific and personal with wider social events make this a fascinating insight into a Punjabi childhood. He includes the personal and the interior in this narrative, making it both specific to him as well as representative of the life histories of many. He deploys western literary narrative techniques and makes his life story flow smoothly, in a continuous chronicle. This is the work of a skilled writer not just recollections.

Clearly, Yash Chopra would not see his life nor tell it in an identical manner to these two authors, but I think their attitudes are informative. Tandon in particular fills a number of gaps in Yash Chopra's story of his family background. Yash Chopra does not keep a journal, but he writes occasionally, mainly verse, that he later destroys without sharing with anyone. Verse is his preferred medium for thinking about the individual, as he often uses verse to recollect moments in his life or recapitulate his thoughts. One of his great regrets in life is that he is not a poet. He reads little prose apart from the English-language press, which he devours avidly, while his favourite poet is still Sahir Ludhianvi.

Friends and relations

Yash Chopra tells his life story in fragments which I have pieced together. There is only one point which he asked me to emphasise, namely certain key relationships. Not those with his parents, but those he has with his older brother, B.R. Chopra, his lyricist, Sahir, his friend, Kiddy and with his family.

'Family, films and food', is his motto. Yash's absolute priority is his nuclear family, his wife, Pamela and his two sons, Aditya and Uday. He is not a

Yash and Pamela Chopra on set

demonstrative person, and his relations with them can appear formal to an
outsider, yet it is clear that there is a great deal of communication between
them all. Yash rarely talks about Pam in public, as is traditional, but says she
has always been the ideal wife. She runs the household with a firm hand, dealing with staff, business colleagues, family and friends. She organises the
whole of Yash's life, from what he wears to what he eats. The only time I have
ever seen Yash dispirited was when she was seriously ill. He immediately
cancelled all work and flew with her to New York, where he stayed during her
treatment. He was very emotional when it proved successful:

> Pam is my dearest friend, we are so close. She knows me inside out, my
> weaknesses and my strengths. When she had cancer I was so miserable. The
> fear of losing her was terrible. The three of us supported her emotionally,
> did what we could, because we can't do anything without her. We're disorgan-
> ised, we're dependent on her, we're spoilt. She's a fantastic girl. The way she
> looked after me when I was sick, I can do anything for her. She's made me

very happy, but I don't know if I've made her happy. I'm ready to do anything for her. She bowled me over, I'm floored. She is so organised, my work is because of her. The way she looks after our units when we're abroad is unbelievable. She's intelligent, smart and a good wife. She can do most things better than me.

Aditya's relations with his father are partly professional, and it can seem that he is the one in charge. Aditya is tense, focused and obsessive about films and cricket, whereas Uday's nature is very relaxed, apart from in regard to his fitness training. They are very respectful to their parents, elders and guests and spend most of their time with a small group of friends, many of whom are also involved with films or were with them at school or college. The family is very close-knit and they prefer to spend as much time together as possible.

Yash's great friends in the 1970s were Deven Verma, who has had small roles in many of Yash's films, and Shashi Kapoor who acted in Yash's films for 20 years. Yash still has good relations with them, but his great friend Kiddy Chadha is like family. They met when Yash was in the UK for the release of *Waqt* in 1965 and have been close ever since. They speak on the phone every day and always stay with each other in London or Bombay. Kiddy, like Yash, is from Lahore, and emigrated to the UK about 40 years ago. He is a very wealthy businessman, with no intellectual pretensions, but like Yash, enjoys money in a detached manner, and is also very family-oriented. Kiddy and Beena's house in Hampstead is the Chopra's home from home. Kiddy and Yash enjoy playing jokes on each other and on their other friends, Gangu Valrani who lives in Muscat and Joginder Sanger in London and eating out and relaxing at home.

> There is no reason for friendship, it's just chemistry. There is no reason you fall in love with a girl either. Kiddy is not in films, but our habits are the same. He is my best friend, my dearest friend. We don't do any business together but I can tell him anything and he'll never say no.

Yash has many close connections in the business world but he always says about others, 'No-one in the film industry is your friend or your enemy for long.' In recent years, his status is such that few talk to him as an equal and an air of hierarchy is clearly present. Sanjeev Kohli has been entrusted with much of the administration of Yash Raj Films, while Mahen Vakil has been working with Yash for nearly 40 years. His other long-standing collaborations were with his cameramen, K.G. Goregaonkar and Manmohan Singh,[13] Pran Mehra,[14] Sahir Ludhianvi,[15] and Lata Mangeshkar.

Yash says of his day-to-day life:

> I have a maximum of half a dozen friends after all this time in this field. I feel happy if my friends come home. I don't go to parties. I'm happiest when it's just us four.
>
> I also like poetry. When I'm alone I like to write then tear it up. Then I feel on top of the world. I write Urdu but prefer Hindi script. I don't read much as I'm lazy, but I have a good memory especially my visual memory.
>
> I don't like English music – the blues and things. I don't understand opera, for instance. I'm not familiar with western, classical music.
>
> God has been so kind, so kind, it's not even funny. I didn't even have money to see a film when I was young. Getting all this success is still like a dream.
>
> Ambition is a driving force to go further. I must make a fantastic film. Ideas are there but I have to have finances to make more.

Yash Chopra remains a middle-class Punjabi of his generation at heart, yet also young and modern in many of his attitudes, and flexible enough to respect others' views and behaviour. A simple illustration: Yash Chopra does not even drink tea or coffee, let alone alcohol. Yet he provides drink for others even in his home, and shows women drinking in his films often as part of a joke, without any condemnation or even comment on their conduct. I think this is also the key to his success as a director, namely his unchanging core of 'Indian values', which exists alongside a flexible attitude to changes around him and a delight in the new.

The family's roots
Yash's social background is unremarkable. He comes from a middle-class family of Punjabi Hindu Khatris, who are members of the Arya Samaj.

Punjab, defined by its geography as the land of the five rivers, has its own history and a distinctive culture. The British brought it under their control entirely in 1849, after the two Anglo–Sikh wars, and quickly set up colonial institutions – administrative, social, educational and military – almost a hundred years later than Eastern India.[16] The Chopra family was deeply affected by these social changes and the encounter with colonialism. Yash's father joined the British government service, while B.R. Chopra was educated at one of the new British-style universities, where he studied English literature, before joining the print media which were part of this new social dynamic. A new middle class emerged in India in the colonial period, the Chopra family being typical of this group which entered the British administrative service then took up its educational opportunities for further advancement. Yash Chopra's family background is very middle class and he argues that even today, when he is financially among India's elite, that he is still middle class:

> I don't waste, in that I'm very middle class. Class does not make a difference, nor does money. I may be loaded with money but I'm not going to join that class. I like to meet people from different walks of life. I'm not stuck-up.

Delhi had faded into relative obscurity after the 1857 uprisings, and Lahore flourished; again in 1921, not long after Delhi became the capital of British India, it was separated from the Punjab administration and Lahore became the political and cultural centre of the Punjab. Although Lahore was situated in West Punjab, which was mainly Muslim, unlike the East, mainly Hindu, its culture was largely composite, for it had been a key city under the Mughals and was later the centre of Ranjit Singh's Sikh kingdom, established in 1799. The Chopras moved around Punjab, although their base was near Jalandhar (Jullunder), in East Punjab, an area of mixed Hindu and Sikh population. From 1870 it was linked by rail to Lahore and Amritsar and hence to Karachi, Calcutta and Bombay.

The Chopra family was also deeply affected in a direct manner by later changes in the Punjab's history, in particular the Partition, which divided East and West Punjab on religious lines in 1947. The West went to Pakistan, the East to India, and the Chopra family moved to East Punjab and to Bombay.

The British regarded the Punjabis as a 'martial' race, an ideal which the Punjabis themselves have taken to heart. They see themselves as down-to-earth, while others often regard them as crude, and their alleged stupidity makes them the butt of jokes in India, in particular the 'Sardarji' (Sikh) jokes, which, like jokes about the Irish in the UK, can be offensive. Although they form a large urban population, they are seen typically as rich peasant farmers, who have profited enormously since independence from the 'Green Revolution'. They are famous also for their music, in particular the *bhangra* dance which has been re-exported to India in a new form developed by British Punjabis; their food, which has become the standard 'Indian' cuisine around the world; and their clothes, the *salwaar khameez*, also known as the Punjabi suit, which has been adopted by women throughout India since independence. Punjabis have also dominated India's cinema, a topic to which I return later. Yash's own identification with Punjabiness is unequivocal:

> Punjabi? I'm proud of being Punjabi. I was brought up as a typical Punjabi. Jalandhar is not a big town. I was in Punjab before I came to Bombay, I know its culture or atmosphere better than any other, its music, costume and so on. I'm fond of robust food. I like its characters.
>
> The Punjab is a state of five rivers, *panch ap*, the people are robust, healthy and extrovert. The land is fertile. It's not the Punjab now; two rivers are on that side [in Pakistan]. Its culture is great, its music mind-blowing – romance, passion and beat are there. Punjab has kept its culture. Now it's disco, so-called *bhangra*, *vilayati* ('foreign') disco *bhangra*. They like food. They live beyond their means. Punjabis have few inhibitions. Boys and girls from good families didn't come [into films]; Punjabis were the first to shed barriers: Kamini Kaushal, Prithviraj [Kapoor], K.L. Saigal. They are very enterprising. They don't need much. Now they have Maharashtrian heroines, South Indian dances. Bengal is a very artistic state [draws fingers across forehead].

Punjabiness is not a language issue with Yash Chopra. He says Punjabi, which is his first language, is an intimate language, yet although he speaks it to his brothers, friends and his Punjabi colleagues, he speaks Hindi to his wife and to his children. His wife, who speaks Punjabi to her relatives and her Punjabi friends, says that when they met they had a formal relationship and began to speak to each other in Hindi, since Punjabi felt too informal. They have continued to speak to each other in Hindi, with the result that his sons, raised in Bombay, speak only Hindi and English. He converses in Urdu with Muslims, and prefers to speak English to foreigners (even if they understand Hindi), unless he is tired. He speaks Hindi for much of his work, although, like the rest of the film industry, he uses English for written documents, in speech he mixes the two freely. He reads and writes English, Hindi and Urdu.

The Chopras belong to the community of Khatris, a group which prospered under the British rule of the Punjab as petty government officials as well as their usual occupation as small traders. Nowadays, the Khatris provide, if there may be said to be such a thing, a dominant caste in the post-independence film industry. Khatri names include Chopra, Dhawan, Kapoor, Khanna, Malhotra, Puri, Sahni, Talwar and Tandon, among others. However, Yash Chopra does not find the term 'Khatri' particularly meaningful in his own life, as one would expect of a member of the Arya Samaj, a nineteenth-century socio-religious reform movement.

The Arya Samaj,[17] founded by Swami Dayananda, as part of its return to 'Vedic values', rejects caste (*jati*), but not social hierarchy or the dominance of high castes, arguing for the *varna* system, that is the division of society into four major classes: Brahmins, warriors, merchants and labourers. Its other major emphasis is on social reform, for although it criticises the Other (mainly Muslims and Christians), it admires European discipline and individualism. Although founded by a Gujarati, the Arya Samaj flourished in northwest India, where it is the dominant form of caste Hinduism. The Arya Samaj was also a proto-nationalist movement, and took an active role in stirring up anti-Muslim feeling during Partition, through its association with the RSS (Rashtriya Swayamsevak Sangh/Association of National Volunteers) and with the move to 'reconvert' Muslims. However, these political associations do not resonate with many of its followers today, who regard it simply as a 'modern' reform version of Hinduism which emphasises a Vedic Golden Age.

The Chopra family

Yash can hardly recall any older relatives apart from his mother's father, so I begin the family history with Yash's father, Lal Vilayati Raj Chopra. Yash says he was called Vilayati ('British, foreign') because he was fair-skinned and looked like an Englishman. He was born in Rahon, near Jalandhar, at the family's ancestral home, 'Rajvilas'. He studied Persian and Urdu, which helped him gain admission into government service, as an officer in the Public Works Department. This work took him around Punjab, moving several times between Lahore, Firozpur, Amritsar and Jalandhar. He was based in the state capital, Lahore at the time Yash Chopra was born, then moved to Amritsar before going back to Jalandhar. After his retirement Vilayati went to work in Bengal, where he died in 1946 in an accident in Asansur. Yash recalls that B.R. arrived too late to carry out the last rites, while Yash himself was very ill with a fever and for several days was unaware that his father had died. Yash has few clear memories of him, although he occasionally mentions his habit of early rising was instilled by his father:

> My father used to say, the person who rises before sunrise has so much time, so much advantage over all others. I get up every day at six o'clock. I do something. I walk for one hour and while walking, walking the sun has started coming up. You feel so much peace, that I feel you are so creative at that time.

Yash also says that he was brought up in 'a very nice atmosphere', where actions spoke louder than words:

> You should not preach, you should set an example. My father was like this. You should copy the ideal of your parents, not their lectures. You give freedom of expression, we don't lecture and give *bhashans* [lectures].

Yash's father's place seems to have been taken largely by B.R. Chopra, who at 18 years his senior must have been very much a paternal figure, although always addressed as 'Bhai sahib' ('Brother'), and referred to as 'Mr Chopra', his wife, being referred to as 'Bhabhi' ('sister-in-law').

Yash's mother, Draupadi, who died in 1979, was clearly a more important figure in his life. She did not know English, and could read only a little Hindi. However, she had a photographic memory and was a great storyteller:

She came once or twice to Bombay to stay with Bhai sahib or me, but when we went to Jalandhar, we saw how popular she was. We had a very big house, but there was no room for people. She was a queen there: here she was nobody. She sat on the verandah with the door open and every passer-by greeted her. She would give if people needed but they never had to ask. Goodness, I have not seen a more unselfish person in my life. She never spoke against anyone or me. There she is an all powerful person. If I die today I don't think I'll have such a following. Her goodness to people is there. There is no single word against her.

Vilayati and Draupadi's oldest child, Hansraj (1902–64), seems to have been the black sheep of the family, and Yash forgot to mention him to me until I heard about him from B.R. Chopra. In a family of achievers, he did not matriculate, and after his first wife died, leaving five children, he had a 'love marriage'[18] to a Bengali woman. The next brother, B.R. (Baldev Raj), born on 20 April 1914, excelled at his studies, so became the family patriarch, providing guidance to the rest of his siblings. While Kuldeep Raj (1916–) became a banker, and the only girl, Vimla (later, Vimla Bhalla) (1920–) married an engineer, the other three were connected with the film industry, moving within B.R.'s orbit. Dharam Raj (1924–) came to Bombay with B.R. soon after Partition, while Rajkumar (1928–) became a film distributor presumably with his older brother's assistance. The youngest, Yash Raj (27 September 1932–) lived mostly with B.R. Chopra until he was nearly 40 years old, when he left home against his brother's wishes. It is to B.R., the key figure in Yash's early life, that I devote much of this chapter.

B.R. Chopra

Typical of his generation of Punjabis, B.R. Chopra studied in an Urdu-medium school. He began his high school in Jalandhar, where he also learnt Hindi and Sanskrit then went to Lahore in the eighth standard, taking his MA in English Literature at the prestigious Government College. This college was the training ground for others who later became prominent figures in the Hindi film industry, including B.R.'s classmates Chetan Anand and

Balraj Sahni, while Kamini Kaushal's father, Shri Ram Kashyap was the vice-principal.

As a member of the somewhat puritanical Arya Samji, the young B.R. was not allowed to see films, but he disobeyed his father, once going to see Valentino in *Son of Sheikh* (G. Fitzmaurice, 1926).[19] He began creative writing during his college days, writing short stories, including one he remembers, called 'The truths', the only copy of which he left in Lahore in 1947, along with a notebook in which he wrote synopses of all the books he read. He also wrote articles for film magazines, including *Varieties* (Delhi), *Movies* (Calcutta) and *CineAdvance* (Karachi). Unfortunately, I have not been able to trace any of these articles, but B.R. Chopra informs me they were mostly criticism of the film producers, who, in his opinion, were wasting their time with comedies and mythologicals, dancing and songs, thus avoiding dealing with any serious social issues.

When B.R. finished college, he wanted to join the ICS (Indian Civil Service), but he fell ill and was unable to complete his exams. He was offered a position as an income tax officer which he declined on the grounds that he would feel inferior to his college friends who would be more prestigious ICS officers. His film writing had been noticed, and in 1938, B.R. was offered the editorship of a new film magazine, the *Cine Herald*, based in Lahore. The magazine was highly successful, distributed in Calcutta and Bombay, and ran until 1946.[20] After six months as editor, B.R. went to Bombay for a special edition, after which he revised the contract in his favour, taking total control of the paper and increasing his share of profits so that he made enough money to live a comfortable life.

B.R. developed good relations with the producers in Lahore. Lahore, now the centre of the Pakistani film industry,[21] was one of the major centres of the Indian film industry before Partition, along with Calcutta, Bombay and Madras. (The Great Eastern Film Company, which produced silent films such as *Prem Sanyas/Light of Asia* [Franz Osten, 1925], had been the only major Delhi-based company.) Lahore's producers, drawn mostly from the elite families of the city, found a ready supply of trained actors, musicians, singers and dancers, while Punjabis were regarded as having the kind of beauty required for the film industry. Lahore also had many (non-native)

B.R. Chopra

Urdu-speakers, who were able to act in talkies. Lahore was the capital of
Punjab, but Punjabi films were not as popular in Lahore as Hindi-Urdu
films, the first Punjabi talkie, *Sheila* or *Pind di kuri* (K.D. Mehra, 1935) being
made in Calcutta.

Key figures in the Lahore film industry were Roshan Lal Shorey, who had
trained in cinema in the US, and Roop K. Shorey, whose Kamla Movietone
produced films such as the Punjabi hit *Mangti/Plea* (R.K. Shorey, 1943), starring Mumtaz Shanti among others. They migrated to Bombay in 1947 where
their hit film *Ek thi larki/Once There Was a Girl* (R.K. Shorey, 1949)starred
Meena Shorey, who became known as the 'Lara lappa girl' after her performance of the song 'Lara lappa'. Dalsukh M. Pancholi from Karachi, who had
learnt film-making in New York, imported American films to show in his
Empire talkies in Lahore. He later became a film producer, launching stars
such as Pran, but his films were most famous for their music which introduced
Ghulam Haider, Noorjahan and Shamshad Begum. The latter became a star in
Pancholi's *Khazanchi/Treasurer* (1941), an all-India hit, after which the
'Khazanchi Competition' was named, which Lata Mangeshkar won in 1945,

thus launching her singing career. B.R. continued working with some of these producers in the 1950s, when they had migrated to Bombay, notably Gulshan Rai who joined B.R. as a financier in 1957, and was later Yash's producer in the 1970s. A.R. Kardar, who had founded the United Players' Corp in Lahore in 1928, made the first talkie *Heer Ranjha* (A.R. Kardar, 1932), in Hindi and Punjabi later founded Kardar Studios in Bombay where B.R. shot his first home production *Ek hi raasta/Only One Way* (1956).

B.R. knew many of the film-makers from Lahore, and also interacted with the visiting film people from Bombay. He recalls being present at the *muhurrat* ('auspicious inauguration') of Sohrab Modi's *Pukar/The Call* (1939)[22] and meeting B.N. Sircar on his visit to Lahore in 1938, along with P.C. Barua. Mehboob Khan came to B.R.'s office when he was scouting for new faces in Lahore, eventually hiring as his star Arun (real name Gulshan), father of the current star Govinda, as the hero, and they continued to work together when B.R. later moved to Bombay.

It was not surprising, therefore, that B.R. began to take a more active role in the movies, working as a publicity officer for Northern Indian Film, a Punjabi film-making studio. He even helped produce *Seti Murad* (B. Mehra, 1941) where he made Rs 20,000.[23] In 1946, he joined two of his father's friends who had opened a newspaper agency called Thapars who were making a film. B.R. was to be the assistant director, but the film was cancelled because of the riots in the city. The film did not sink forever, since B.R. later made it as *Chandni Chowk* (1954), and it was also remembered as the film from which Khayyam (who later achieved great success as the music director for films including *Kabhi kabhie* and *Umrao Jaan*, [Muzaffar Ali, 1981]) drew his first salary of Rs 50 as Chisti's assistant.

Yash's childhood and education

During the 1930s, the Chopra family was based in Amritsar, and as B.R. had to live with his family, he commuted by train between the two centres, keeping a bicycle at either end. He married Prakash, the daughter of a session judge in 1940 and settled in Lahore. Yash, then aged eight, lived with them and went to primary school, only returning to live with his mother in 1944/5 when the family moved back to Jalandhar.

Yash remembers little about this time, although B.R. still laughs when he remembers Yash's favourite pastime was eating and how much Yash liked an advert for Sunlight Soap, which he could not pronounce, saying 'Sunligka'. Yash often got into scrapes, and B.R. remembers him falling and cutting his face on a table, and being more concerned with avoiding being told off than with his injuries.

Recollections of childhood tend to differ markedly between India and the west. Probably as a result of the all-pervasive 'therapies' and ideas derived from psychoanalysis, many of us think of childhood as the critical years in a person's life, which structure their desires, emotions and ambitions. Yash does not see the individual being shaped in this way, so sees childhood as a less important part of his life, at least in the context of this book, than his later years. However, it is curious that he likes to regard himself still as a child, as many youngest children in large families do.

Yash has fond memories of his childhood, remembering his schooldays with affection, as he does his time at the Doab College, Jalandhar,[24] living a typical middle-class lifestyle, studying agriculture and Sanskrit among other subjects.

> I'm a very middle-class boy. Before my BA I didn't wear trousers, only shorts and half pants [shorts]. I didn't have shoes, I wore only *chappals* [sandals]. Even now I can't wear suits and ties. I'd never been in a car, I went everywhere on foot or I borrowed a bike. A bicycle was the luxury of life.

> I didn't see films at school – I wasn't allowed to by my father. It was only after he died and I was at college. On Saturday mornings there were English films, on Sunday mornings there was one show. I saw mostly Hindi films, since there were three or four shown a day, although there were English films every Sunday. I used to see two films a week. I remember Mehboob Sahib's and Raj Kapoor's films, but I don't remember seeing Bimal Roy's films in college. I only saw them and Guru Dutt's films later. Raj Kapoor was a favourite, since I saw *Aag*. I loved his passion, I could see it in his films. He puts his last shirt on a film. Very nice, decent, wonderful films. All romantic, not action. He had a communist feeling – mixture of Charlie Chaplin and Christian ideas with the Indian way. He did it very well – mixing orthodox and traditions.

The Arya Samaj promoted Hindi as its major language. Yash spoke Punjabi at home (see above), but at school he also studied Urdu, which was then the preferred language of culture in the Punjab, its script used also for writing Punjabi. Yash was fond of both Hindi and Urdu, but as a fan of poetry, especially romantic poetry, read more in Urdu.

Yash says there was little chance of romance in those days. Yet when I pressed him about the elusive, unattainable woman in his films he said:

> I may have left someone in the college or schooldays, before I joined films. We were good friends. In my eyes, she must have been beautiful. After all, beauty is not printed. Either it's there or it's not there. Actually, I knew I couldn't get her. She must have gone somewhere else. She must have married and settled down. That feeling may be unconsciously coming in my films, but it's not a conscious effort on my part. It comes out when I plan a film, thinking about a boy who isn't getting a girl.

This happy family life came to an end when riots broke out in Jalandhar in 1946. Yash Chopra remembers:

> I remember everything. I have vivid memories about this time. I remember seeing killings, looting, burning – so much killing, the whole of a train being butchered. During the riots, there were bodies everywhere. People would stop the train, killing people. There was a strange fever against the other community. A strange hatred came to my mind.

Nonetheless, for a young boy it was an exciting time and his memories are vivid, often of the pranks he played. Like many Arya Samaji boys, Yash was a member of the RSS, a Hindu nationalist group founded in the 1925 by Keshav Baliram Hedgewar. This is regarded as a paramilitary, fascistic movement by some,[25] while others, including Yash Chopra, saw it at the time as a sports club (akhara), a kind of boy-scouts, where they played kabaddi and drilled with lathis (bamboo staves) and performed yogic asanas. He also enjoyed the brotherliness and the discipline, a quality he admires in other contexts today. This innocence was shared by others at the time, one other member saying, 'I was attracted because I had a natural inclination to have a good physique, a healthy body, a healthy mind and healthy ideals.'[26]

Presumably as part of the RSS efforts, Yash Chopra made petrol bombs, for use in riots, which he stored in his sister-in-law's *tandoor* ('clay oven'), forgetting to tell her, so when she lit it, she nearly blew up the whole house. He once joined a band of looters, and stole a tray of watches from a shop. His mother, Draupadi, found the watches, beat Yash soundly then made him take them back to the shop owner to apologise. At this, she decided that Yash was running wild in Jalandhar, so sent him off to his sister and brother-in-law, who were living in southern Punjab, around 50 miles from Delhi. Yash recalls:

> My brother-in-law went to Rohtak, to take charge from a Muslim engineer who was leaving for Pakistan. I went to his house in a car. On the way the car broke down and we started pushing. People said we'd be killed but we reached the Dak Bungalow. I stayed for one month during which I couldn't go anywhere, couldn't get food, and we had only *dal*. In the morning I'd go out, all the fields were empty, everyone had fled because this was a Muslim area. I picked mushrooms. There was nothing else. I still have a passion for mushrooms. The bungalow was safe, but we couldn't go out. There was no-one there but my sister, my brother-in-law and two or three servants. I used to walk around all day for three months as there was nothing else to do.

The Partition does not seem to have left deep scars on Yash, but he says that he has avoided anything to do with politics ever since (although the mark on his fingernails at election times show that he, unlike many younger people in the industry, still casts his vote). He says:

> I don't believe in politics and bloodshed in the name of religion. You should not kill, but they have only one reply to every argument: kill him! You have to take sides. I don't want to make a political film where you have to comment. I thought of making a Hindu-Muslim film [in addition to *Dharamputra*], until Mani Ratnam made *Bombay* [1995], and everyone would think I copied him.
>
> In Jalandhar we had Muslim friends. We are not against others. Killing is not the end of an argument.

Yash still cherishes the idea of making Sahir Ludhianvi's anti-war poem, *Parchhaiyan/Shadows*, into a film, but feels that people now are pro-war and the film would be inappropriate.

If there had been no Partition – no politics – the industry would have been richer in music, writers (the language is the same), the girls are pretty. There would have been more talent – and that is only Punjab. [Pakistani] television is good but their films are cheap.

The Partition had a greater effect on B.R. Chopra because he was living in Lahore until 1947 and because he was older (33), and had a family to protect. Despite the riots in Lahore, and the increasing difficulty he had even travelling to the office, B.R. and family hoped to stay on, until a riot which B.R. estimates involved 5,000 people broke out on the main road near their house. B.R. thought they were unlikely to escape as the slogan-chanting mob approached their small colony, and his wife fled barefoot with the two children to a safer place in the colony, where they were saved by the police. The next day, 2 August 1947, B.R., Prakash and the two children left for the family home in Jalandhar. They have never returned to Lahore.

We haven't been back but would like to go. My people are calling me. The principal (of Government College) called them – Balraj Sahni, Chetan Anand, Manmohan Krishen. We wanted them to go for centenary but it was 1965 and the war broke out. She has bad arthritis and is scared to go.

Vilayati Ram had already died, but the brothers, apart from Yash, were still at home, where around 25 people, including B.R.'s father's sister and his father's mother were living. B.R. settled the family in the house and went straight to Bombay to look for work, where he spent 15 August, Independence Day, 1947, alone.

Two
From Assistant to Director

The Bombay film industry, in the late 1940s and 1950s; migration from Punjab

A high proportion of the film industry's Muslim personnel left Bombay for Pakistan, including key figures who would be critical to the growth of the Pakistani film industry – such as the singing-star Noorjehan and the music director, Ghulam Haider.[1] The major effect of the Partition on the film industry was that many people arrived in Bombay during the years preceding and following independence, most of whom were from the Punjab, like the Chopras, who brought about an increasing 'Punjabification' of the industry. Some of these migrants, like B.R. Chopra, were refugees from Lahore, while others who were already working in the industry and could no longer return 'home', settled permanently in Bombay. This latter group included the Anand brothers and Balraj Sahni. The industry retained the Muslim workers who chose to stay on in Bombay, whether they were stars, such as Dilip Kumar (Yusuf Khan), or worked at the lower levels such as technicians. Some people migrated later, for instance the writer, Manto moved from Bombay to Pakistan and the actor A.K. Hangal from Karachi to Bombay,[2] as the border between the two countries remained open for some years. We know less about how Muslims fared, but there does not seem to have been any victimisation of Muslims in the film industry, which has always prided itself on its secular stance compared to other sections of society.[3]

Changes in the film industry were also the result of India's participation in the war effort, as industrial activity was stepped up, especially in iron, steel, cement and cotton production. The undocumented black economy is said to date from this time, and tax evasion spread into the film industry at all levels. More films were made, even though stock was rationed, and producers had to make one in three of their films for the war effort. In fact the cinematic output was such that there were not enough theatres to exhibit the films, and this need was met by a new system of distributors and exhibitors which remains in place to this day.[4] Stars became the major selling-point for these distributors and exhibitors, and also for the new independent producers, whose methods of production were to contribute to the decline of the studio system of the 1930s and 1940s. During the 1950s, many producers set up their own studios (A.R. Kardar, Raj Kapoor, V. Shantaram and others), but these were not to be the same fixed units as in the pre-independence era. Other film producers also launched production houses but these only included production staff, while the remaining personnel, the actors, music directors and even directors, were hired for particular films. The stars were released from the need to sing as changing technology allowed playback singing to became the norm, with professional singers, such as Lata Mangeshkar, Mohammed Rafi, recording songs to which the stars would mime, with the singing stars becoming rare.

During the 1950s, a new ethos swept the industry, concerned with the making of a national cinema, new films for a new country, but this manifested itself in more subtle ways within the film texts themselves.

B.R.'s story gives a good idea of the loose networks, contacts and interaction involved in film finance and production in the aftermath of Partition. After leaving Lahore and going to Bombay, as many others also did, B.R. travelled between Bombay and Punjab until 2 February 1948, when he brought his wife, Prakash, their son, Ravi, and B.R.'s brother, Dharam, to a huge bungalow he had found in Versova, which then lay outside Bombay.

In Jalandhar B.R. met up with Mohanlal Sibal and Harkishanlal Sibal, friends of his father from government service before they had moved into business, becoming partners in Sri Gopal Papers in Rawalpindi. Just before Partition, they moved to Jalandhar and then to Delhi. They were keen to start a new business and also to invest in the film industry, starting up a company called Sri Gopal Pictures, along with another partner at B.R.'s old magazine, *Cine Herald*, Shahjilal Handa, and D.P. Berry, formerly of *Screen World*. Sri Gopal Pictures financed B.R. Chopra to produce a film, directed by B. Vedi, but his first effort *Karwat/The Turn* (1949), the story of refugees from Pakistan who came to India, was a dismal flop. B.R. had to sell some of

Prakash's jewellery and use all his connections to get the film screened, but in the end the financiers recovered enough money through the distributors to continue their old business in Delhi.

B.R. was very dispirited and thought of returning to journalism. He contacted his Uncle Durgadas, an editor of the *Hindustan Times*, who agreed to help him, but advised B.R. to continue to struggle to make a film. B.R. contacted his old friend Mehboob Khan who said to him, 'Films may fail, but you have to keep trying.' B.R. then met another old friend from Lahore, I.S. Johar, and narrated a story based on Marie Corelli's *Vendetta*. B.R. wanted to make a film based on Johar's script idea so he bought the story for Rs 500 and began to look for a financier. Like other aspiring hopefuls, B.R. hung around in Parisian Dairy (later Talk of the Town) on Marine Drive, where he ran into Govardhan Das Aggarwal, a producer and financier he had met in Lahore, when he was making a picture, *Dak Bungla/Dak Bungalow* (M. Sadiq, 1947). B.R. had gone to see it as a film journalist and had made several criticisms; the film had flopped and Aggarwal said B.R. had been vindicated. B.R. narrated Johar's story to him, which Aggarwal liked, so they arranged to meet him the next day.

> Because of the delay I didn't think it would happen. I am a very tense and pessimistic man. I thought the next day I would face shame because he would not be there. I went late, but he was there and he provided *pakodas* etc. He said it was an extraordinary story. Let's get down to cast, credits but I will only finance it if you direct it. I tried to refuse, but he insisted and he gave me a cheque for Rs 50,000.

Around 15 fellow journalists from Delhi were in Bombay, all of whom tried to persuade B.R. that his skills lay in journalism, and he should not make a fool of himself but hire a host director. B.R. felt indebted to Aggarwal, so went ahead and, having changed the story from Johar's original, he made the film, *Afsana/Story* (B.R. Chopra, 1951), produced by Sri Gopal Pictures.

B.R. wanted Ashok Kumar to play the hero. Ashok Kumar had come to Bombay in 1934 to work for Bombay Talkies, where hits such as *Acchut kanya/Untouchable Girl* (F. Osten, 1936), *Kismet/Fate* (Gyan Mukherjee, 1943) and *Mahal/Palace* (Kamal Amrohi, 1949) established him as a

sophisticated hero. He had also taken part in production and direction at
Filmistan and had helped in winding up Bombay Talkies. In 1951, he also
starred in *Deedar/Sight* (Nitin Bose). B.R. Chopra had not been introduced
to Ashok Kumar so arranged a meeting at Ashok Kumar's house in Worli
through a Mr Trivedi, the Chairman of Bombay Talkies after Devika Rani
left, who now had an office at Eminent Studios in Andheri. Ashok Kumar's
first question was to ask B.R. if he was a refugee from Lahore. B.R. said he
was, and had produced a flop film and needed a hit.

> Ashok Kumar said, 'How can you direct a film? You will appreciate that I am on
> top and don't want to risk my career with someone with no experience.' I said.
> 'I understand, but I feel sorry because you are the best man for the role.'
> However, he somehow felt impressed or maybe touched. He said. 'You come
> with me to Bombay Talkies.' I narrated the story to him. He sat down for two
> minutes and then said, 'I am very much impressed. If you can tell it the way you
> have narrated it.' I said, 'I don't know about on the screen.' He agreed to do it.

Ashok Kumar suggested a few amendments to the script, which B.R.
accepted. Once the shooting started, he realised B.R. knew very little about
direction so gave him advice and took him to see the shooting of Gyan
Mukherjee's *Sangram/Struggle* (Gyan Mukherjee, 1950).[5] However, B.R.
was a fast learner and after several arguments between the two men, they
developed a deep mutual respect, working on 13 pictures together. This film
was a great success, as B.R. says:

> Picture was superhit. The fool stayed. I was able to stay in the industry. This is
> the beginning of my career.

The film, *Afsana*, was a convoluted crime story of twins, Chaman and Ratan,
both played by Ashok Kumar, separated in a storm in childhood. Ratan loses
his memory, and is brought up as Ashok, becomes a magistrate and marries
Leela, while Chaman, who inherits the family money, loves Meera, who is
still in love with Ratan. Chaman, falsely accused of murder, flees to
Mussoorie, where he meets Ratan, who has left his wife after finding she has
been having an affair. Chaman and Ratan become friends, Chaman pre-
tends to be Ratan, but is killed in a road accident. People believe that Ratan

is dead, and Ratan is taken for Chaman. In the end Ratan is cured of his amnesia by Meera; Leela commits suicide and Ratan starts a new life with Meera.

B.R. then directed two pictures for Hira Films: in 1953, he made *Shole/Embers*, starring Ashok Kumar and Bina Rai, and in 1954 *Chandni Chowk* a Muslim historical, starring Meena Kumari. After this B.R. set up his own production company, establishing himself almost immediately as a major producer.

The founding of B.R. Films

In 1955 B.R. Films was founded, taking the motto of *Cine Herald*: *Ars longa vita brevis* 'Art is long: life is short'. It was financed by Mr Puri, the proprietor of the Thompson Press, which owns *India Today*, who also financed R.K. Films and Mehboob Films.

B.R. Films' first movie was a jubilee hit (i.e. ran for more than 25 weeks), 1956's *Ek hi raasta*, as were his next two films, *Naya daur/The New Era*, 1957 and *Sadhana* 1958 (both directed by B.R.). These films established the banner of B.R. Films and its style of film-making.

B.R. liked to work with a regular team. He generally used the same lyricist, soon replacing Majrooh Sultanpuri with Sahir Ludhianvi from *Naya daur*, although his music directors varied, perhaps because of Sahir's insistence he be paid more than the music director. As someone with a literary background, it is not surprising that B.R.'s films were narrative-driven. B.R. had a 'story writing department' for his films which included Kamil Rashid, F. A. Mirza, C. J. Pavri, Akhtar ul-Iman, Dr Rahi Masoom Reza, Satish Bhatnagar, Hasan Kamaal, while he took stories from outsiders such as Pandit Mukhram Sharma (*Dhool ka phool*, Yash Chopra, 1959 and *Ek hi raasta*). Each film dealt with a specific social problem: *Ek hi raasta*, widow remarriage; *Naya daur*, industrialisation; *Sadhana*, prostitution and so on. This was a feature of much Indian literature of the 1930s when socialist realism was at its height, especially in the writings of the Progressive Writers' Movement and in the work of the Indian People's Theatre Association (IPTA), of which many of the Chopras are life-members. Chopra's religious background, as a keen Arya Samaji, made him anxious to address issues of social reform as a form of religious duty. This emphasis on stories with a purpose remained true of B.R. Films from then to the present day. Although arguing for social reform, the films always uphold the sanctity of the home, embodied in the wife. Other films in the 1950s were also experimenting with melodrama and realism to tell of social problems but they were rarely as issue-driven as the films of B.R.

As well as being popular for these stories and good music, the banner was also known for its organisation, its ability to make films quickly by having a firm script and careful advance planning. B.R.'s literary background soon allowed him to emerge as a spokesman for the film industry and he was clear about the kind of film-making he admired, namely the more realistic cinema of V. Shantaram, Mehboob Khan and Bimal Roy.

B.R. was not one to avoid controversy when he felt he had a principle to follow, as was the case with his big 1957 hit film, *Naya daur*, released in the same year as such classics of Hindi cinema as *Mother India* (Mehboob Khan, 1957), *Do aanken barah haath/Two Eyes, Twelve Hands* (V. Shantaram), *Nau do gyarah/Nine, Ten, Eleven* (Vijay Anand), *Pyaasa* and *Tumsa nahi dekha/I've Not Seen Anyone Like You* (Nasir Hussain).

Akhtar Mirza (father of Saeed and Aziz Mirza) wrote the story for *Naya daur*, a drama about a villain Kundan, who brings modernity, in the form of an electric sawmill and cars, to a remote village, already crippled by pre-modern problems of caste and religion personalised in the relationship between Shankar and Krishna's contest for Rajani. A competition between the villagers, led by Shankar and Kundan, involves building a road for a race between a bus and a tonga. Through this story, the film argues for a new humanism over both modernity and feudalism and for a collectivist approach to the new technology.

Mehboob Khan, S. Mukherji and S.S. Vasan rejected this story, saying it would make a good documentary. When B.R. took the story, Dilip Kumar refused to even hear it, let alone sign it. B.R. then approached Ashok Kumar who felt he looked too urbane for the role of a villager, but he spoke to Dilip Kumar on B.R.'s behalf. Dilip Kumar was eventually persuaded to take the role, and by doing so, inadvertently contributed to the film's great notoriety.

After shooting for a couple of weeks at Kardar Studios, the unit, comprising several hundred people, was preparing to leave for a two-month outdoors' schedule near Bhopal, when Madhubala's father refused to allow his daughter to go with the unit. This was said to be because he disapproved of the alleged relationship between his daughter and Dilip Kumar. The Chopras took Madhubala and her father to court, arguing that the film needed to be shot outdoors, which was not always the practice in Bombay films of the 1950s. Dilip Kumar supported the Chopras, even appearing as a witness where he had to declare his love for Madhubala. The Chopras won the case, but asked for it to be withdrawn so Madhubala would not face criminal charges. Madhubala was replaced with Vyjayanthimala.[6]

Mehboob kindly gave ten weeks he had booked at Liberty cinema for *Mother India*, which was running late, to what he called B.R.'s *'Tangewala ki kahani'/*'Story of a tonga-driver'. He was worried that B.R. would lose money, so advised him to book this prestigious cinema for just five weeks. When the film had its silver jubilee (that is, ran for 25 weeks), he telephoned B.R. and asked if he could be the chief guest at the celebrations.

Yash Chopra comes to Bombay

While B.R. had been establishing himself in the film industry and Dharam had become his cameraman, Yash had been studying for his BA in Jalandhar, which he completed in 1950. Yash visited B.R. in Bombay, where he must have enjoyed the lifestyle and meeting people associated with the industry. It was not surprising that although B.R. wanted to send Yash to London to train as an engineer,[7] Yash wanted to be part of the film industry. Yash joined when B.R. was making *Shole*. B.R. thought that Yash should learn the ropes with another team and asked I.S. Johar to train him. After a month, a Mr Jeevan, a specialist in negative (or villainous) roles, said that Yash would learn more with B.R. and so Yash was paid his first salary on *Chandni Chowk*. Yash worked with B.R. on *Ek hi raasta*, and all his films subsequently. Yash was never B.R.'s chief assistant, but always the third assistant, although he was keen for a promotion.

B.R. told financiers that three out of his four films had been big hits, so asked if his brother, Yash, his assistant for seven years, could have a film.

They agreed, provided B.R. guided him. Yash was given his first feature to direct, *Dhool ka phool.*

Dhool ka phool (*Blossom of Dust, Love Child*, 1959)

B.R. planned for Yash to direct the film jointly with another of his assistants, O.P. Bedi, but Bedi left B.R. Films, so Yash directed it on his own. For his work as a director on this film, Yash was paid Rs 500 per month, by the time of *Waqt* this had increased to Rs 2,000. The two brothers developed a new working relationship, with B.R. as producer and Yash as director. B.R. took charge of the story and the business side of things, giving Yash leeway with direction. As Yash says:

> Once the story and the dialogues are in my hands, then I can sit with him as a director and say, 'Get this song written. I want Sadhana, I want Sunil Dutt.' I can say I want these stars, but if the star wants money, we have to ask the boss. So, anyway, this selection of subjects, selection of the stars, questions of money, everything is finally up to him. He never used to come on the sets. I direct, see to the art direction, costumes, the making of a film. He did not stop me from making the kind of films I wanted to make.

B.R. decided that Yash and he would not direct films at the same time but would each make a film in turn. This was in keeping with the work culture at B.R. Films, which ran as a well-organised company, making films quickly, to tight schedules, using largely the same production team. During the time that Yash was working as a director at B.R. Films, the films B.R. directed himself were *Kanoon/Justice* (1960), *Gumrah/Abandoned* (1963) and *Humraaz/Confidant* (1967).

B.R. wanted Yash to make social issue films with strong stories. Yash says:

> Mr Chopra has the best sense of story. His stories appeal to people. He makes very socially relevant films and always wanted to say something in a film. Even when he directs himself, there is the B.R. story department. Four story editors, Mr B.R. Chopra Sahib and myself, we used to work all together. If Mr Chopra makes a film, I used to work with him. When I made a film he used to work with me.

A well-known writer, Pandit Mukhram Sharma, who worked with Mohan Segal and Mahesh Kaul, wrote the story for *Dhool ka phool*, the title of which was suggested by Kavi Pradeep. The story begins with an affair between two college students, Mahesh (Rajendra Kumar) and Meena (Mala Sinha). He abandons her when his father insists he marry an heiress, Malti (Nanda). Meena, who is pregnant, is driven out by her 'aunt' and 'uncle' who did not love her, her only protector being her maid, who helps her give birth. In a moment of fear, Meena abandons the child, but returns a moment later, to find him gone. Abdul Chacha, an elderly Muslim, raises Roshan, believing the child he has found to be a gift from God.[8] Roshan's dubious origins earn him censure from his own Muslim community and also from the Hindus and he falls into bad company. When Roshan is accused of theft, he appears in court where the magistrate is his natural father, while his defence lawyer is Jagdish (Ashok Kumar), who has married Meena, who in turn is acting as a witness. In the end, Abdul hands Roshan over to Meena, while Mahesh is denied access to Roshan.

The star cast included Rajendra Kumar, who was acquiring a reputation as a 'women's star' and whose reputation was no doubt advanced by this film,[9] while Ashok Kumar appeared as a favour to promote Yash's debut:

> Ashok Kumar was a guest artist. No money was involved, he gave his blessings and his friendship, even though he defined the role of Mala in the film. I like to bless him.

At this time there was no question of using exotic locations:

> We filmed mostly indoors at Kardar Studios, near the present Raj Kamal [Studios] but also on location at the National Defence Academy in Poona. There was a lake, small dam, and in Poona University, where we shot a song at the waterfall. We also shot a song in the Aarey Milk Colony.

Yash also points out that they used synchronised sound:

> At that time we didn't dub the whole film, none of the indoors, only some scenes, where two or three of them were dubbed at once since tracking was difficult. In those days we used BNC and Mitchell cameras for indoors, which

are bulky but silent. From *Daag* onwards, I have used only the Arriflex, which is portable and easy to operate, but since it's noisy, dubbing is essential, in fact all films from *Kabhi kabhie* onwards are completely dubbed. Although a silent Arriflex is now available, it is too expensive (Rs 1 crore [10 million]) and silence is impossible.

Yash was keen to learn more about cinematography:

We made an experiment. On the way back to Bombay from Poona, it began to rain, when we had stopped for tea at Khandala Ghat. The only car was a blue and white Impala. I told Dharam to take a shot, even though we had no light and no artists. He took a long shot in the rain, and as we didn't have Mala Sinha, an assistant wore a sari.

Some of this has been remarked on:

The elaborate crane movements (especially in the scene of Mahesh's wedding procession) and the combination of high-angle 'nature' shots with tightly edited scenes were characteristic of 50s B.R. Films.[10]

Dhool ka phool was released at the Minerva cinema, Bombay in May 1959. It was a big box-office hit and its music remains popular today.[11] The film was also released in the UK, where it was shown in the Liberty cinema in Southall. This was Yash's first overseas visit:

This was my first time away. We travelled for two months by air, train, boat and cars. We stayed in Mount Royal in Marble Arch. We had breakfast in the room, we'd eat sandwiches and have a very early dinner with friends. It was hard to get exchange in those days so I had no money but we travelled as guests to the Cork Festival for a week. During the day we saw the countryside, then every night they celebrated a particular country so we had the music and food of that country. We then went to Greece, Lebanon, Switzerland, Paris, Germany, Helsinki, Sweden, Denmark, Tashkent, Moscow, Naples, Capri, and Rome. We did sightseeing, meeting people and learning about them and had great fun.

The film gave Yash little scope to develop his own style. It looks typical of its time, with none of what were later to become known as his trademark

Abdul (Manmohan Krishna) tells Roshan that he will be raised as human, neither
as Hindu nor Muslim

features, apart from good songs and fashionable clothes. Perhaps the
music's success was due in part to Yash's selection, but B.R. Chopra was
also known for producing successful music with his music directors. The
songs by N. Datta have remained popular, including Sahir's lyrics sung by
Mohammed Rafi, which are among the most famous anti-communal lyrics
of Hindi cinema, closely tied into the theme of dividing India:

> *Tu Hindu banega na Musalman banega*
> *Insaan ki aulaud hai, insaan banega*
>
> You will not be a Hindu or a Muslim
> You are the child of a human and you will be a human.

Another hit song was the romantic duet about love: '*Tera pyaar ka aasra cha-
hata hun*/I want the support of your love' (Mahendra Kapoor and Lata

Mangeshkar). This provides a moment of dramatic irony as Mahesh assures Meena that he will always love her, while she replies that he really does not understand the true meaning of love and needs to think about its social consequences, but can be recognised outside the context of the film as a woman's caution in the face of a man's romanticism.

The melodramatic story was told in realistic settings: colleges, middle-class houses, railway stations, law courts and a village, raising social issues, that were typical of B.R. Films' banner. The main issue addressed by the film is that of the fate of illegitimate children, who are made to suffer unjustly by society. The film extends the discussion to cover topics such as nature versus nurture, as it examines the role of fate and chance in upbringing and even in determining a person's religion, and of the claims of adoptive and natural parents. Although the film gives the natural mother the unquestioned right to claim her child, whom she abandoned reluctantly due to social pressures, it forbids the natural father access. The claims of blood are overwritten by those of compassion: the father is punished not for his sexual behaviour but for his failure to protect the child's mother or to provide for his child.[12] His obedience to his own father is not a virtue, as the film shows his neglect for his father as he fails to return home when his father is ill, but he is eager for a good marriage and a career. As a man, he is able to make a new life but the unmarried mother has to suffer. Ultimately, the woman finds happiness at the end in the return of her son and in the security of a loving and forgiving husband; her sacrifices are rewarded. Abdul's sacrifices for the child and his final returning of the child to its mother is the natural order of things, his only reward being his freedom to go on a Haj [pilgrimage].

The issue of illegitimacy also raises debates about premarital sex. Although Mahesh Bhatt described its lovemaking scene as typical of the representation of sex in the Indian cinema, '… the real thing is made possible by a studio downpour and the library shots of lightning and thunder',[13] he also remembers the erotic impact this film made on him, especially the song: '*Jab tum muskura do*/When you give me a smile'.[14] This is one of three scenes which Bhatt discusses as awakening his desire and pleasure, all of which present transgressive encounters, either premarital or adulterous.

Perhaps it was because in the prelude to the lovemaking, the girl is seen to be just as keen as the boy, who makes no effort to coerce her, in fact more enthusiasm is shown by her. The film makes no effort to cast blame for the sexual act on the boy or the girl, but to depict it as something natural, reinforced by the censor-avoiding scenes of images from nature. Only after the lovemaking has taken place, does the girl say that they have made a mistake, with which the boy concurs.[15] Yash says that the censors did not object to this, although they did consider cutting the scene when the couple's bicycles fell on top of each other!

It is hard to imagine the impact that the theme of the illegitimate child must have had in 1950s' India, while nowadays people would be more concerned with male responsibility rather than condemning the woman. No pretence, either of temple marriage or wartime heroics to 'excuse' the girl for her sexual activity, yet the audience is encouraged to sympathise with her and her suffering while rejecting the 'hero' who makes no attempt to fulfill any obligations he has towards her. Ashok Kumar's stardom would only have added weight to his role as Jagdish, who takes on the role of the sympathetic male, as his love for Meena is such that he is willing to forgive his wife for her 'mistake'[16] in having premarital sex. Meena suffers for her 'mistake' but is rewarded at the end of the film with a contented family life, where her husband accepts his stepson. Meena herself had been brought up in an unhappy home by people she called 'aunt' and 'uncle', who threw her out because she had 'dishonoured' them.

The film clearly condemns hostility to the child on account of its illegitimacy, making this the 'sin' rather than the act of premarital sex. This failure to stigmatise an illegitimate child is upheld in later Yash Chopra films (such as *Kabhi kabhie*), as is a lack of condemnation of premarital sex, which also criticises men who enquire into their wives' lives before marriage.[17]

Dhool ka phool is set in a very contemporary world of middle-class, urban college students, where girls and boys mix and have romances. They ride bicycles, girls wear *salwar khameez*, and live in rooms decorated with calendar art (a shot of a picture of a baby explains to us that Meena is pregnant). Social origins are no guarantee of kindness or goodness. Although the middle class is condemned for being money-grabbing – (Meena's aunt and uncle's house) or status-conscious (when Mahesh does not know who Roshan is, he forbids his son, Ramesh to play with him), the life of the educated professional lawyer is presented in a good light. Meena's servant shows her the compassion her relatives refuse, as Abdul also cares for Roshan whatever trouble it causes him. However, Abdul's village is portrayed as communal and unpleasant, willing to blame children for the acts of their parents and more interested in religious differences between Hindu and Muslim than in the welfare of the child. Education is Meena's way back into society as her degree helps her find a position as a secretary (although feminists would be disappointed that to find her ultimate happiness she marries her boss).

The law figures strongly in this film as Mahesh is a magistrate while Jagdish is a lawyer. This is one of the institutions of the state, although here the law is used as an arena for the debate between the two models of masculinity – Mahesh's irresponsibility and his desire for a 'name' in society and Jagdish's forgiving, mature love. The courtroom drama provides the setting where real justice will prevail, not just the upholding of the law, as the child's parents are revealed. The final decision about Roshan is that he must live with his mother and his new stepfather, who offers him a happy home. The natural father, who has previously abandoned his child and its mother even though he and his wife have lost their own son, has no valid claim to his son.

Dharamputra (Son of Faith, 1962)

Yash's second film, Dharamputra, is one of the few films in commercial cinema which refers directly to the Partition. Made only 15 years after the event, it raised issues which were very raw to many, namely the new hatred that arose between families who had been neighbours for centuries.

The story for this film was taken from the novel of the same name by Acharya Chatursen Shastry. The film begins in Delhi in 1925, as Hindus and Muslims are united in the freedom struggle. Nawab Saheb's daughter, Husn Bano (Mala Sinha), is pregnant, but he will not let her marry the father, Javed (Rehman), as he is her social inferior. Nawab Saheb (Ashok Kumar) seeks the advice of Dr Amrit Rai (Manmohan Krishna), who is like a son to him, as he cared for him when his friend Gulshan Rai died. Amrit Rai sees Bano as his sister, so he and his wife, Savitri (Nirupa Roy), take her to Simla for her delivery, then bring Dilip up as their own son. Nawab leaves half his property to Husn and half to Dilip. Husn Bano later marries Javed with her father's consent but they remain childless after she miscarries. Bano wants to bring Dilip home but Javed says they must leave him with their neighbours. They build a bridge (literally) between the two houses so they can become closer.

The film moves forward by 15 years. The freedom struggle continues, Nawab Saheb dies, Javed and Bano go overseas. Dilip (Shashi Kapoor) now has twin brothers and a sister. Politics and religion begin to divide the Hindu and Muslim communities and Dilip becomes anti-Muslim. India is divided and riots break out. Javed is injured and Amrit brings him into the house. Meanwhile Dilip goes to set fire to Bano's house, even though she is inside. After a dialogue about the rights and wrongs of religion, Amrit tells

Dilip (Shashi Kapoor) with his natural and adopted families

Dilip that Bano is his mother. The mob comes for Dilip but at the last minute the police arrive and after a voice-over about unity, the film ends.

B.R. Chopra was one of many who had escaped from Lahore in 1947, while Yash had seen riots in East Punjab:

> I passed through the riots, 1946 and 47. I was going around the roads seeing it with my own eyes. I portray it on screen.

Ashok Kumar and Mala Sinha starred again in *Dharamputra*, and it was the first film of many that Yash made with Shashi Kapoor, the youngest brother of Raj Kapoor. At that time the young actors hung around Gaylords restaurant in Churchgate, which is where the two met. They then met again in B.R.'s office in Kardar Studios, where Yash narrated the story of the film. Shashi says:

> He was pleasant and charming and didn't let me talk. He loves talking. I liked the role, the story which was taken from a classic Hindi novel. He had just made a film which had 25 silver jubilees. This film was very ambitious. He said I'd have to talk to B.R. about money. I came into movies as an actor for money. I liked theatre, but there was no money in it. I asked B.R. for a cheeky price, and even he was surprised, but he gave me a good signing amount.

> It's very easy to work with Yash. Stage actors are snooty about films and I was conceited but we became good friends as we both loved eating. Deven Verma played a younger brother, and even when I wasn't needed, I'd often be there for lunch.

> There was some tension between Yash and me, when I took my part too seriously. I said I wouldn't sing and Yash said I had to. One song was revolutionary and one was romantic.

Yash says they managed to add some realistic footage to the sets that they used for this sensitive topic:

> We shot the Republic Day Parade in Delhi; we used montage for mosques and filmed in Ajmer without the artistes. We shot indoors at Bombay Talkies, but mostly at Kardar Studios, and didn't have a major outdoors. We had to create the atmosphere of 1947 in a studio.

The film was released at Maratha Mandir, 26 January (Republic Day) 1962. Yash says:

> The film didn't do well, although it ran for 18 weeks and won the National Awards for the Best Hindi Film and Best Director. Dilip Kumar gave me some comments. Mehboob came in his car and took me for lunch. He gave me solace. When you're down there are only a few people that will do that.

While the major theme of this film is the communal feelings stirred up by the impending Partition, it returns to the theme of illegitimacy. Illegitimacy is a major melodramatic motif, as it may reveal that we are not who we think we are and can provide dramatic irony and a shocking dénouement to a story. It once again raises the issue of natural and adoptive parents and the role fate plays in wrenching a child from its origins. Here it also serves a political purpose in that Dilip's identity as a Hindu, oppressed by Muslims, whom he must drive from his country is one that he accepts as a birthright.

Husn Bano (Mala Sinha) and Savitri (Nirupa Roy) restrain Dilip (Shashi Kapoor)

Finding out that his natural parents are Muslims, his sectarian 'Hindu' politics become meaningless and he returns to an 'Indian' identity as espoused
by the nationalists in the freedom struggle.

Friendship is seen as binding the nation, whether in the calls of '*Hindu
Muslim bhai bhai*/Hindus and Muslims are brothers' at the beginning of the
film, or in Amrit Rai's and Husn Bano's relationship as brother and sister,
or Gulshan Rai and Nawab Saheb's relationship. Friendship is closely
equated with family ties, through the language of brotherhood, or through
the ceremony of tying '*rakhi*' (a thread a sister ties on her brother's wrist to
show he is her protector).

It seems that one of the reasons the film may have fared poorly at the
box-office is its lengthy speeches about politics and community. Lengthy
speeches in cinema tend to have either a dramatic purpose – such as in a
courtroom drama – or to create a language of love: words which are enjoyed
for their own references and poetry rather than speech which can be seen as
sermonising. The other reason is the theme of Partition itself, which was
not a subject widely or directly discussed until recently even within the family, as Urvashi Butalia has pointed out.[18]

Waqt (*Time*, 1965)

The next film B.R. directed, *Gumrah/The Errant* (1963), did well so B.R.
decided to boost Yash's spirits after the poor performance of his second film
by giving him the banner's first colour production, *Waqt*. The film was to have
starred Prithviraj Kapoor and his three sons, Raj, Shammi and Shashi but
Bimal Roy and others said that the audience would not accept them not recognising one another. (The Kapoors played their own family roles in their home
production, *Kal aaj aur kal/Yesterday, Today and Tomorrow*, Randhir
Kapoor, 1971.) The music was to be by Shanker-Jaikishen but because they
wanted their own lyricists, rather than B.R.'s choice of Sahir, B.R. chose Ravi,
who had just been the music director for *Gumrah*, after Sahir had refused to
work with S.D. Burman. Sahir was always difficult, as Yash says:

> I regret I never worked with S.D. Burman or Shankar-Jaikishen. The problem
> was that Sahir and S.D. Burman wouldn't work together. Sahir fought with

everyone, but I never met him when he was drunk. In the day he'd help anyone, but he was a different person when he'd been drinking. I was no company for drinking sessions.

The outdoor locations were in Kashmir, Simla, Nainital, Bombay and Delhi. In Delhi, the unit all stayed at the newly-built Ashoka Hotel, having fun, staying up all night, driving around. Some sequences were shot in an unorthodox manner: for the shot with Sadhana and Sunil Dutt on Dal Lake in Kashmir, there was not enough natural light so two cars trained their headlights on the artists.

Yash also used many sets:

> Although I'm not an art director, I think I formed a look then. It was colourful and glamorous. We had velvet flooring, moving lights. I read magazines about interior décor and I took my ideas from them. Vakil and I realised that it was too costly to put carpets on the floor so we got velvet, which gives a very smooth and finished look. Girl in white, boy in black. For the piano scene, we put green velvet and set it against black, turquoise and blue. B.R. copied this look for his house.

Sadhana describes her experience of working with Yash:

> He's a romantic guy at heart, his heroines look stunning. His true subject is his heroine. In the old days he was very romantic. He is very much what he is today. Same sense of humour. If you don't like your heroine, how is the audience to fall in love with her? He thinks God's gift to humankind is women.

Although Bhanu Athaiya (who later won an Oscar for her costumes for Richard Attenborough's *Gandhi*) worked on Sadhana's look, Sadhana says Yash is responsible for much of the look of his heroines, although he some-times needs persuasion to change:

> Yash knew exactly what kind of a hairstyle he wanted, exactly what kind of a dress he wanted. He made all the decisions.
>
> Soon after starting, I said Yash, 'Why don't we create a different style of dressing with *churidar* and *kurta* not *salwaar*?' He said, 'No, it's a very Muslim concept.' He refused. I had a costume designer for my personal use. She made me a white *churidar* [tight trousers with baggy ankles] and a sleeveless *kurta*

[long shirt] with gold embroidery. I wore it and he smiled, 'That looks
stunning,' he said, 'Only *churidars* in my film.' I couldn't convince him until he
saw it. He takes suggestions well, especially when he could actually see it. A
whole *churidar* trend started with *Waqt*.

Yash and Sahir were great friends by now and some suggest that the song
'*Maine dekha hai ke*/I have seen that' was a self-referential joke. Yash asked
Sahir to write a song as if it was sung by lovers over the telephone. This causes
great amusement to Yash's friends and family as Yash is known to be obsessive about the telephone, making calls constantly; it is not unusual to see him
taking three phone calls at once. His close friend Kiddy Chadha said this book
would not show the true Yash if there was nothing about his use of the phone.
He remembers long lists of numbers by heart. In the days before the mobile
phone, he would always sit near a phone or go to use the public phone when he
went out. He says he even once made a phone call which lasted all night.
He would not tell me if it was to a girlfriend but he did say that it was not to a
boy!

When the film was due for release, the Indo-Pakistan war broke out. As
Yash recalls:

> The release of the film was held up because of the war. There were blackouts all
> over for 15 or 16 days. One paper published a review of the film based on press
> releases since a print had not been screened. The unit spent time at the
> Sun'n'Sand Hotel, gossiping and swimming. On the day of release, four days
> after the end of the Pakistan war, we did a *pooja* [religious ceremony] in the
> morning in the office, then all the artists went to the press show at the Naaz. We
> all wore suits in the same colour, while the heroines wore white. We then had
> dinner at the Sun'n'Sand. We were there until four in the morning then we
> went swimming then to a *halwa* [sweet] shop. In the early morning we went
> home and slept. There was a family feeling, no-one jealous or anything. Now if
> we have a release we're tense about if the artistes will even come.
>
> The film was 18,000 feet for the first 25 weeks then was cut to three hours. We
> sold it for eight lakhs (Rs 800,000) per territory – the five domestic and the
> one overseas.

Raja (Raaj Kumar) romances Meena (Sadhana)

Yash had two major disillusioning experiences with this film. One was that
the delay of release was only known at the last minute. He says that a review
of the film was published even though there had not been a single screening, after which he has never believed what the reviewers have to say about
his films. The other was the hostility to the film industry from sections of
society:

> We went to Kenya and London with Raaj Kumar, Sunil Dutt, Sadhana and Ravi.
> In London, the Indian Film Society established by Krishna Menon. I was very
> excited because the Indian High Commissioner was coming. However, he just
> spoke against the film and the industry. I say that we have rich too, not just
> weeping and poverty. Should we publicise ourselves as a country of snake
> charmers and *Pather panchali* (*The Song of the Road*, S. Ray, 1955)? I was very,
> very upset.

However, the film was a huge success and ran for many weeks. Yash was thrilled by the public reaction after the lukewarm reception of *Dharamputra*.

A prosperous merchant, Lala Kedarnath (Balraj Sahni), believes nothing can disrupt his happy family life, but an earthquake tears his world apart and he loses everything including his loved ones. He almost finds his eldest son, but hearing he has just escaped from an orphanage where he was beaten, Kedarnath kills the warden and ends up in gaol for 20 years. The eldest boy Raja (Raaj Kumar) is raised by a criminal and becomes a professional thief, while the second son, Ravi (Sunil Dutt) is adopted by a rich couple and trains as a lawyer. They both live in Bombay while the youngest, Vijay (Shashi Kapoor) looks after their mother in Delhi. Vijay is in love with Renu (Sharmila Tagore), a rich college girl who teaches him to drive.

Raja and Ravi both love Meena (Sadhana) but Raja, finding a childhood picture of Ravi, realises that he is his long lost brother and encourages his relationship with Meena. Ravi is hired as a chauffeur by his girlfriend Renu. Ravi tells off Renu for having an affair with his driver, then Meena's parents object to Ravi marrying their daughter when they don't know who his parents are.

Raja throws a party to announce who Ravi's parents are. Other members of the family bump into one another – such as Vijay and Kedarnath – but no connections are made.

Raja is framed in a murder and hires Ravi as his lawyer. Suspense turns to courtroom drama, where Vijay appears as a witness, then his mother comes into court. Kedarnath recognises her, is reunited with Vijay then Raja tells them that he and Ravi are the other two children. They all return to open a shop with the two future daughter-in-laws settled into the family.

Although the motif of the illegitimate child is absent, the film picks up the idea of children being separated from their natural parents, being adopted, and finally reunited, what is known as the 'lost and found' theme in Hindi cinema. While it can be argued that *Kismet* (G. Mukherji, 1943) and *Awāra/ The Vagabond* (R. Kapoor, 1951) are precursors of this form, *Waqt* is the first time we see several siblings separated from one another as well as from their parents who in turn are not sure if the other spouse is alive. This form reaches its zenith with the films of Manmohan Desai, whose *Amar, Akbar, Anthony* (1977) is the most convoluted and complex version of the genre.

Waqt is also one of the earliest films that can be called a 'multi-starrer', namely one with more than one hero, more than one heroine and so on. The commercial logic is that if the star is a major attraction, then the more stars there are in a film, the greater the number of attractions. While the strategy is naturally an expensive one, the producers feel that the film is more likely to succeed. There is also scope for portraying different types of heroes and heroines to give the film a wider appeal as well as to attract fans who follow different stars. The multi-starrer became very popular throughout the 1970s, reaching its zenith with Manmohan Desai, again in *Amar, Akbar, Anthony* and his 1981 film, *Naseeb/Fate*, which had three heroes, three heroines, three villains and a whole cast of stars appearing at a party in the film.

Although *Waqt* shows the family separated by an earthquake, probably referring to the Quetta earthquake of 1935, it requires only a little imagination to see this as a Partition story, where the earthquake is a metaphor for a far greater human upheaval. The opening scenes of the film show Hindus using signs in the Urdu script, suggesting that we are in pre-Partition India, somewhere northwest of Delhi, while the family is displaced to Bombay, some via Delhi. This line of migration is the one that B.R. Chopra himself followed at this time, as did many others in the Bombay film industry.

Waqt also portrays changing gender roles, from the mother, Lakshmi, who even as a young woman blushes every time her husband mentions her to Renu and Meena. Meena (Sadhana) is a very romantic heroine, shown mostly in her own house, with its fashionable and extravagant fittings, or in romantic settings such as gardens in Kashmir, her major activities being playing the piano, having parties and singing romantic love songs. Renu (Sharmila) is a modern, college girl, who drives her own car, even teaches her boyfriend to drive, and does not care if he ends up working as a driver. (Yash assumed that Sharmila, as a modern girl, would know how to drive so planned the scenes where she teaches Shashi to drive without asking her if she knew how to drive herself. He says he is lucky they all survived.) Renu's song is a dance number, sung in a duet surrounded by college students on an outing in Nainital.

The joint family is reinstated

Sharmila and Sadhana do not share any scenes until the end. Sadhana was the greater star at this time, having joined the industry in 1958. Her hits included *Hum dono/We Two* (Amarjeet, 1961) and *Mere mehboob/My Beloved* (H.S. Rawail, 1963). Yash was (and is) very fond of her as she is a thorough professional. At this point, Sharmila was signed for only one Hindi film, 1964's *Kashmir ki kali/Blossom of Kashmir* (Shakti Samanta) although she had already worked in many 'art' films, notably with Satyajit Ray.

Waqt is justly famous for its whole new 'look', depicting a glamorous lifestyle. The women are glamorous in every respect, with highly stylish outfits, diamond jewellery, and elegant grooming. The men wear the tight suits that were fashionable at the time, while only the older generation is in 'traditional' clothes.

The film spares the viewer no detail of the lifestyle of the super-rich, who have motorboats, American cars, throw lavish parties and live in houses

adorned with fountains, circular beds and grand pianos. It is an aesthetic of
which Yash is proud:

> It's not a crime to be rich. The upper classes behave better. For romance and
> complex emotions, it's better to appear rich.

> The public liked it. People copied the clothes, hairstyles, dances. The film was a
> big hit and all these small things became the rage. We follow trends and we set
> them. We take from life and life takes from us.

> There were sensuous scenes, but we have responsibility. One should not feel
> embarrassed or ashamed.

The film also features a lengthy courtroom drama, as did *Dhool ka phool*.
This time the courtroom is the catalyst for a complex turn in the plot, to
show Ravi's brilliance as a lawyer in unravelling the truth. The language is a
more elaborate Urdu than heard elsewhere in the film which lends a formality to the whole procedure. This scene also creates tension as it looks as
though Raja's innocence will not be revealed and that it is unlikely that the
family members who are gathering will ever recognise one another. That
this recognition takes place in a courtroom lends a gravity and solemnity to
the occasion while also showing that the state is witnessing the family's
unity.

The themes of the film are fate and time; they make decisions for us and
if we think we can resist them we are fools. This theme of time was taken up
later by B.R. Chopra in his outstandingly successful television adaptation of
the *Mahabharata* (1990) where the narrator of the 92 episodes was time
personified.

The songs from *Waqt*, composed by Ravi with lyrics by Sahir, remain
popular to this day, in particular – '*Ai meri zohrajabeen*/My beauty' (Manna
Dey), which Yash's son Aditya includes in his debut film, *Dilwale dulhaniya
le jayenge/The Braveheart Will Take the Bride* (1995), as a love song for the
older generation. The other big hits were the dance number '*Din hain bahar
ke*/These are the days of spring' (Asha Bhosle and Mahendra Kapoor) and
the prophetic '*Aage bhi jaane na tu*/You don't know what's in the future'
(Asha Bhosle).

Vijay (Shashi Kapoor) as witness in the courtroom drama

Admi aur insaan (Man and Human, 1969)

Yash's next film, *Admi aur insaan/Man and Human*, was by no means such a great hit. Released in 1969 in the Naaz cinema, Bombay, it did only average business. The principal theme of this film is how corruption is destroying modern India. J.K. (Feroz Khan) and Munish (Dharmendra) are like brothers. J.K. has educated Munish, sending him overseas to study and finding him work as engineer-in-charge of a dam project. J.K.'s brother, Kuki is engaged to Munish's sister, Renu.

Munish meets Meena (Saira Banu), a social worker, and they fall in love. Meanwhile, J.K. falls in love with Meena, and, like everything else in life, he thinks he can buy her love and thinks Munish 'owes' him Meena in return for all the money and help J.K. has given him. Munish is prepared to accept that his friend may be in love with his girlfriend, but he is not prepared to accept the corruption he sees all around him. When a wall collapses because it was made with inferior material he finds J.K. was responsible for the contracts. Munish resigns in a quarrel with J.K.; J.K. orders Kuki to leave Renu, and asks people not to employ Munish.

Kuki, who is in the airforce, sees his friend, Rashid, die because of the faulty runway for which J.K. was responsible. A train plunges off a bridge and again J.K. is responsible. A committee of enquiry is set up, headed by Justice Desai, who is murdered. When Munish finds proof of J.K.'s involvement, he is abducted. Munish is framed, but when Meena lectures him about humanity, he confesses to all and is executed.

> We shot at Koti dam 45 miles beyond Dehra Dun. It was a fantastic location. A friend was an engineer there when the dam was being built. We had 250 people there, staying in rooms meant for clerks. We filmed most of the outdoors there and also in Nainital.

Mumtaz plays Rita, the vamp, whose song 'Zindagi ittefaq hai/Life is a coincidence' (sung by Asha Bhosle) was the big hit of the film, and whose performance in the film marked her ascent to stardom. She is also said to have been the great romance in Yash's life before marriage. Even Yash's family teases him about this 'romance', but he is too discreet to divulge any information. Mumtaz appears in the film as a glamorous westernised woman in contrast to Meena (Saira Banu) who always wears Indian clothes and takes life seriously, although she enjoys glamorous sports such as skiing.

The film takes up again the theme of dams, icons of modern India,[19] seen in *Mother India* and mentioned by Nargis after her maiden speech in the Rajya Sabha (upper house of Parliament), when she said that Indian filmmakers should not show poverty but positive images of things like dams.[20] Meena says in the film: 'This dam you're all working at, these dams are our modern temples.' The film suggests that even these icons of Indian modernity are ruined by endemic corruption. Yash disagrees:

> This story is not about symbols of modernity but of corruption with an unscrupulous businessman using the wrong materials. It's also the story of a powerful, emotional relationship between two friends.

Although there are romantic moments in the film, its major theme is that of male friendship, which can come under pressure from romance, as two friends fall in love with the same woman, generating a conflict of values between them. J.K. thinks that money is all important and has no shame about his dishonesty, his corrupt behaviour nor its fatal consequences. Munish puts the values of society at large before his friendship only to find that J.K. then sets out to destroy him completely.

Ittefaq (Coincidence, 1969)

When there was just a couple of weeks' work left on *Admi aur insaan*, Saira Banu fell ill and had to go to London for treatment. The film had to be put on

Ittefaq poster

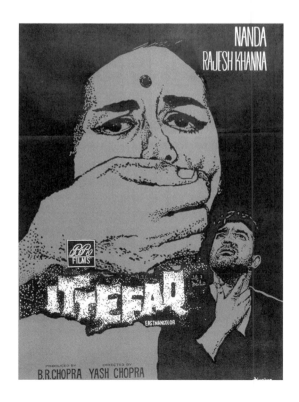

hold until she returned. Meanwhile, Mahen Vakil, a production manager who joined Yash for *Waqt* (and apart from a few years away is still with him nearly 40 years later), took Yash and B.R. to see a play inspired by 'Lamp-post to murder'. It had a profound effect on Yash:

> We saw *Dhummas*, a play in Gujarati, inspired by an English play, from a French play. We thought it was very good and let's do this without songs, without interval. We called the director of play, and the hero of the play became my assistant. We wrote the script in a week – a screenplay from the stage script. That picture we made in a month and released, so for a month we were going to be sitting idle. There would not be a staff problem. Had to wait for Sairaji who wasn't well.

Yash wanted Shashi to act in this film but he was over-committed, as he had been for *Admi aur insaan*. It was to be almost ten years until they worked together again on *Deewaar*. In the end Yash hired Rajesh Khanna, who was to become a big star with the release of two great hits *Aradhana/Prayer* (Shakti Samanta) and *Do raaste/Two Ways* (Raj Khosla), alongside others including *Bandhan/Deception* (Narendra Bedi) and *Khamoshi/Silence* (Asit Sen), all released in 1969.

> We needed a girl who would fit that role. A girl whose image should be the most innocent role on screen as that is a negative character, she is a murderer. I met Raakhee, needed girl with one month free, no strings attached, and innocent that no-one could doubt. I wanted to take her, but she was signed by Rajshri and couldn't work before the release of *Jeevanmrityu* [*Living Death*, S. Bose, 1970]. I had worked with Nanda on *Dhool ka phool*. I took Nanda, she did wonderful performance, looked very sensuous.

The script was written by Akhtar ul-Iman in eight days, the film being made in only 28 days at Rajkamal Studios. It was shot almost as it appears on screen, with Pran Mehra making the rushes the next day. It was all prepared, on time with Salil Choudhury composing background music two days after the shooting ended. *Ittefaq* was premiered in October at the Maratha Mandir, where it ran for over 15 weeks, even though it had no songs and was made on a shoestring budget.

Dilip (Rajesh Khanna) threatens Rekha (Nanda)

Dilip Rai (Khanna) is on the run after being accused of murdering his wife. Armed, he enters Rekha's (Nanda's) house as she hears on the radio that a mad murderer is on the loose. Various neighbours and police call, but she doesn't inform on him. Dilip finds Rekha's husband's body in the bathroom and she accuses Dilip of murdering him. After many twists of the story it transpires that Rekha had murdered her husband to elope with a police officer while Dilip's wife had been murdered by her sister for her fortune.

This film is quite unlike any other Yash Chopra film. It has no songs, and is filmed on a single set with only two main characters and a few brief appearances. The characters are not over-glamorised – Rajesh Khanna is unshaven and Nanda wears a simple, although revealing, blue sari. The film is a very close adaptation of the classic 'whodunnit' play, where the convoluted plot is full of twists and turns with the entire film narrative driven by the desire to find out who the murderer is.

Looking over Yash Chopra's early output, we see traces of what were to become the Yash Chopra style, in his presentation of women, music, glamorous realism, female storylines. However, it is hard to say how many of the other elements of the films are his. There are strong resonances of the B.R. film, in particular the emphasis on a social issue which leads to the audience's reconsidering its opinions by experiencing extremes of emotion.

These films not only mark Yash's years as a director with B.R., but they also bring to an end his status as a younger family member working for his older sibling. At the end of this period, Yash took a number of life-changing decisions. He got married, and in 1971, at almost 40 years' old, he resolved that he wanted to 'fly on my own wings', so left B.R. Films and the family home.

Three
The Founding of Yash Raj Films

The separation of B.R. and Yash Chopra was the object of much speculation in the film press during the 1970s. From my discussions with the family, it is clear that there is no single version of events. Misunderstandings remain and emotions run high after 30 years, so it might have been prudent to lay this to rest. However, it is important to our study for several reasons, not least because it shows how B.R. and Yash differ in their view of the family, which is the linchpin of the Hindi movie. This then brings us on to Yash's relationship with his father-figure and his relationships with his own children. It shows the family's desire and respect for privacy, rather than the need to find opportunities to settle old scores.

Yash had lived with B.R. and Prakash as a child and then from his arrival in Bombay aged 19 until his marriage nearly 20 years later. Given the fact that his father died when he was 13, and the 18-year age gap between the brothers, B.R. was clearly more of a father-figure than a brother to Yash. B.R. was not the oldest in the family as Hansraj was around ten years older than him, but the latter was always regarded as the 'black sheep'. B.R.'s educational achievements and his subsequent successful career marked him as the leader among the children and gave him an early sense of heightened responsibility. B.R. provided his younger brother, Dharam, with work as a cameraman, gave Yash the best possible start in the film industry, and shaped the career of his own son, Ravi, who was only slightly younger than Yash. As B.R. himself says, 'My word is law in the family. They do as I say.'

Dharam also lived with B.R. until his marriage, and there was no acrimony in his moving out into his own flat with his wife. Ravi and his wife, Renu, and their children still live with B.R. and Prakash. Many people speculate that B.R. was closer to Yash than he was to Ravi. The rest of the brothers lived separately and B.R. and Yash's mother, Draupadi, refused to move to Bombay, continuing to live in Jalandhar, although she would meet the family when they came to north India.

Yet although B.R. had wanted Yash to marry earlier, a marriage at the age of 37 being late by any standards, this had not happened. B.R. says, 'I wanted him to marry very early but he had some affairs which did not fructify.' As a young, successful director, Yash had been linked to many of his stars, in particular Nanda, Sadhana and Mumtaz. Although Yash is too discreet to name names or discuss any of his premarital relationships, which may have been just friendships, Bunny Reuben, B.R.'s public relations man has written about some of them.[1] Yash remained an eligible bachelor into his late 30s, driving around Bombay in a red sports car, with a circle of male friends, including Shashi Kapoor and Deven Verma, who were reputed to be ladykillers. Yash says:

> [B.R.] was always trying to find a girl when I made my first film. He must be trying. At a certain stage of your life, you don't feel like settling down. He must have arranged a lot of girls to get married. As usual, I was irresponsible. I say, 'I don't want them. I don't want a girlfriend. I don't want to get married'.

B.R. says that Yash was the only one in family who did not have an arranged marriage. Yash says he was stubborn, refusing as he felt he had not met the right person, and he also enjoyed being the baby in B.R.'s family. B.R. says, 'I was in Bombay when a friend telephoned to say that Yash had met a girl. We wanted to celebrate the engagement so we went to Delhi that day. The marriage was in Delhi, the reception in Bombay.'

Yash says that he met Pamela Singh for the first time at the music function of his nephew Ravi Chopra's wedding where she sang some songs. Her singing won him over. The next time, when he was an examiner in the Film Institute in Poona and was visiting Delhi, his distributor Mr B.M. Sharma wanted him to meet a Sikh girl for a possible arranged marriage. It was probably providence that it was the same girl he had heard singing earlier. They met one evening and although they quite liked each other, neither felt any particular wish to meet again. However, for the first time, Yash later missed his flight to Bombay. He decided to stay with the Sharmas, who called Pamela again. Yash says, 'There are moments which change life completely', and they agreed to get married: 'But even in your heart you say, *yaar*, now too much, let me settle down. So, that day I got married.'

The marriage, which took place on 20 August 1970, was announced by the press:

> [The wedding is announced of the] brilliant young director, with Pamela, daughter of retired navy captain, Mahinder Singh; August 20 with B.R. hosting a function in Bombay 22 Aug. Yash, youngest of the three film-making Chopra brothers (the other two who are in films are the famed 'B.R.' and Dharama, the noted cameraman), directed B.R. Films' *Admi aur Insaan*, a bold exposé on corruption. Recently it set a record in first week collections in a non-Hindi city like Madras.[2]

Further attention was given to coverage of the event:

> B.R. gave a reception at Taj, August 22 in the Crystal Ballroom. Guests included Chandulal Shah, A.R. Kardar, Dilip Kumar, Rajendra Kumar, Sunil Dutt, Raj Kapoor, Shammi Kapoor, Rajesh Khanna, Feroz Khan, Randhir Raj Kapoor, Balraj Sahni, Nargis, Meena Kumari, Saira Banu, Sadhana, Vimi, Simi, Kamini Kaushal ... Tarachand Barjatya ... with his sons Kamal Kumar and Raj Kumar.[3]

As he had done for other members of the family, B.R. paid for a world tour for a honeymoon, with the couple staying away until November 1970.

On his honeymoon, Yash began to think about separating from B.R. Films, but it took him some time to get around to announcing this to B.R. The problem seemed more that he wanted to set up his own company, than his desire to live separately, as B.R. must have helped him financially in the building of his house (see below), although B.R. told me that they prepared a living area within the main house for Yash and Pam. The chronology seems somewhat muddled. B.R. says: 'When he left us in 1971, after over 20 years, there was a void in the house. Now he is too busy to see too much. I don't want to interfere. If he wants me I'm there, if he doesn't, I don't. Yash and I are brothers.'

Yash says that even today, he gets very emotional at a movie in which two brothers quarrel. Yash visits B.R. on his own, while the other members of

Yash's family are not close to him, although B.R.'s grandson, Junnu trained as Aditya's assistant on *Mohabbatein* (2000). Yash says, 'I respect B.R. very much. I feel my existence is because of him. He brought me up. I behaved badly.'

People have read all sorts of meanings into the separation of the two movie banners. The two brothers have never spoken against each other; B.R. and Prakash attended the première of Yash's first production in 1973 and they come together at family weddings and Yash has interviewed B.R. for the 'special feature' section for B.R.'s films on DVD. Their silence has only encouraged further gossip. These speculations are so universal as to be banal; impossible to prove or disprove. Yet it seems that the separation was much more Yash's decision; that at 38, he wanted to be his own person, run his own concerns, change his place in society.[4] Yash was still on a salary when he left, never becoming a partner. (Yash's own children have equal rights in Yash Raj Films.) All this speculation is inconclusive, as times and people have changed. I turn instead to the creation of the identity of a separate banner, that of Yash Raj Films, founded on Yash's 39th birthday, 27 September 1971, in his office in Shantaram's studio, Raj Kamal in Parel (where he stayed until opening his own office around the time of *Silsila*, 1981), and the release of its first film on 27 April 1973.

The upheavals in his life over these three years must have been enormous for Yash. He concurs: 'These were very emotional years. My state of mind was that I was trying to prove myself to the world.' After the break, Yash and Pam moved out of B.R.'s flat in Nepean Sea Road and Pam returned to her parents in Delhi for the birth of Aditya (21 May 1971, Uday was born 9 February 1973). Meanwhile, Mr Randhawa, a friend, and brother of Dara Singh ('India's Tarzan', now a star of the television series *Hadh kar di aapne/You've Gone Too Far*), and husband of Mumtaz's sister, lent them a flat on Pali Hill. They lived there until Yash earned enough money from directing the film *Joshila/The Passionate One* (1973) for Gulshan Rai to buy Mohammed Rafi's flat on the fifth floor of the same apartment block, which he still owns.

In April 1971 work began on a separate house for Yash, on a plot of land next to Dharmendra's bungalow, B.R. having recently moved in to B.R. House in Juhu. The *bhumipuja* (ceremony before laying the foundations) took place on 14 April, conducted by B.R. and Dharam Chopra, in the presence of other members of the family and Dharmendra, Mukesh, Mahendra Kapoor, Sahir Ludhianvi, Akhtar Mirza, Manmohan Krishna, Ravi, Gulshan Nanda and Akhtar ul-Iman.[5]

Daag (The Stain or The Stigma, 1973)

Yash's immediate problem was to raise money to make his own film. This is where Gulshan Rai stepped in. Gulshan Rai (1924–), who had been a speculator in Lahore, had known B.R. for many years. Gulshan Rai's cousins ran Verma Films and after arriving in Bombay in July 1947, he began to work as a distributor, based like so many others, at the Naaz cinema, where he has his office to this day. The first film of B.R.'s he distributed was *Naya daur*. It was only in the 1970s that Gulshan Rai began production, under his Trimurti banner, taking on few films but with huge success, with nine out of the ten films he produced having silver jubilees.[6] He said he would finance Yash's first film as producer, *Daag*, offering to raise big money. He also wanted Yash to direct his own production, (*Joshila*, see below), which Yash agreed to do once he had completed *Daag*.

The story is from *Maili chandni/The Stained Moon* by Gulshan Nanda, who had already had one of his novels adapted into the hit film *Kati patang* (Shakti Samanta, 1971). Yash was to direct this for B.R. and had been working on it with Akhtar ul-Iman and others in the story department and the script was almost complete. When Yash was in London on his honeymoon, he saw *Sunflower*, starring Sophia Loren, which had a war background, where a married soldier meets another girl when posted overseas and marries her during the war.[7] Yash started rewriting the story on his return.

Many people who had worked with Yash at B.R. Films stayed with him after he set up independently. Yash's brother, Dharam, B.R.'s cameraman, did not, but his assistant, Kay Gee, worked with Yash until his death during the making of *Mashaal/The Torch* (1984), (see Chapter 7). Another key figure was the editor Pran Mehra, who had been with B.R. since *Afsana* and worked with both brothers until he died after *Kabhi kabhie*. Yash says, 'He had his first heart attack during *Waqt*. He was the best editor, a well-dressed, handsome man, with a great sense of editing.' The most important figure who collaborated with B.R. and Yash until his death in 1981 was the lyricist, Sahir Ludhianvi, who was also a great personal friend (see Chapter 6). He had no hesitation in working for Yash's own company, even waiting for his fee until after the film was released so as not to pressure Yash. These three people were particularly important to Yash (and are discussed below): 'I miss these people. I have not found a substitute for Sahir and Pran Mehra even to this day. Everything is a compromise.'

Yash felt that the film had little need of outdoor shooting and the only outdoor schedule was Simla in the snow. This was the first time that Pam helped to organise the outdoor shooting, a role which she has performed ever since. Yash says, 'She helps to organise everything, especially outdoor shootings. She knows and remembers everyone's requirements, likes and dislikes. She is the last to sleep and the first to get up.'

Yash says of Kay Gee's work on the film:

They hired a train for the children's song, of which one *antara* [verse] was in the train. They had only two sun guns, and no generator. The sun guns looked like cigarette butts. They were using a zoom, which needs more light than a trolley, we had 20–30 kids, a heroine and a star. Kay Gee shot the whole sequence with one light. He took a lot of back projection plates in case anything went wrong, but everything was wonderful.

Although the film does not have a 'rain song', thunder and rain mark erotic sequences[8] including a bedroom sequence between Sunil and Sonia which escaped much censoring. Yash, later famous for his rain songs, defends their inescapably unambiguous eroticism:

I think rain is a very sensuous thing. A woman in a sari or *churidars* who has a good body looks very sensuous in the rain. There is a thin line between vulgarity and sensuousness in films. It's a question of intentions. If one wants to excite people, you make it obscene. There's no harm in doing it but it's bad if you make it obscene and you can't see it with your friends or family. I'm not doing a *satyanarayana katha* [telling a religious story]. Raj Kapoor was never vulgar, he was only sensuous. It is how you project your image. You can tantalise, excite in showing a beautiful girl.

The newly-married Sunil (Rajesh Khanna) and Sonia (Sharmila Tagore) move
to the hills when Sunil takes up his first job. Sunil is imprisoned for killing a
man who tries to rape Sonia but manages to escape. Chandni (Raakhee), who
has helped find Sonia work as a teacher introduces her to her husband, Sudhir,
who turns out to be Sunil. Sunil explains to Sonia that he had to take on a new
identity and married Chandni to save her honour as she had become pregnant
after being raped. Sudhir is hoping to enter politics but his true identity is
revealed. He explains the situation to Chandni who testifies on his behalf as
her rapist was the man who tried to rape Sonia. The murder trial is re-opened
and Sunil's name is cleared. Sunil lives happily ever after with two wives.

Yash was very anxious about the release of his first independent film, as
he felt that if it flopped people would say that he had only ridden on B.R.'s
success. Rajesh Khanna's career seemed to be on the ebb as about eight of
his recent films had flopped and this film had a controversial storyline. The
film was censored on the day of Rajesh Khanna's surprise wedding to
Dimple Kapadia, Raj Kapoor's discovery for *Bobby* (1973), 27 March, while
Raakhee married Gulzar at the beginning of April. Gulshan Rai and the distributors praised the film, but thought it very risky. Their last sentence worried Yash: 'Although the film is very beautiful, it may not do well.'

Yash launched a publicity campaign of trailers and advertisements. One
of the display advertisements has a picture of Rajesh and Sharmila with
Raakhee in background:

> Releasing all over India on 27th April.
> Three wonderful people and three wonderful words ... 'I love you'.
> Yash Raj Films' *Daag*, a poem of love.
> In Eastman Colour.
> World rights controlled by Trimurti Films (P) Ltd.

Another proclaims

> Love is not a moment ... Love is a lifetime.
> Daag – a poem of love.

The hype paid off: when advance booking opened on the Monday before
the release, it soon became clear that the 12 prints made for Bombay were

insufficient. Every day there was an increase and six more prints were made
before release until 75 were released nationally on the Friday.[9] The film had a
great opening 27 April 1973, and was an instant hit. The première held the
night before at the Minerva cinema was very grand, with many stars attend-
ing, including Dilip Kumar and Saira Banu (who had worked with Yash at B.R.
Films), Raj and Krishna Kapoor, Raakhee and Gulzar, Rajesh and Dimple
Khanna as well as B.R. and Dharam Chopra. Yash has a full photograph album
of the event and it was also filmed for *Bombay Superstar* a BBC documentary
in the *Man Alive* series, made by Jack Pizzey.[10]

The film was appreciated by the critics, *Screen* proclaiming: '*Daag* is a
drama of good emotional conflicts, done in slick, gripping way'.[11] It was also
the first to be praised in terms which have become standard in discussions
of Yash Chopra's films today: its gloss, its drama and its depiction of complicated emotional relationships, without excessive melodrama or gratu-
itous deployment of villains and comedians. The fights were criticised, as
were some of the songs, especially the Punjabi-style dance. The excessive

Sunil (Rajesh Khanna) with his two wives, Sonia (Sharmila Tagore) and Chandni
(Raakhee)

glamour of the sets was noted, although the film was called 'tasteful' and it was said that Yash 'had an eye for the aesthetic'.

Joshila (*The Passionate One*, 1973)

Yash Chopra had clearly made his mark and proved he was more than just B.R.'s brother, but he still had his commitment to Gulshan Rai to honour. The latter had already picked his cast for *Joshila* when he asked Yash to direct it. He had signed up Hema Malini and Dev Anand and given that this was the time that time the Movie Industries Association limited actors to working on no more than six films at a time, there was no question of change.

This was the first film Yash made outside the B.R. or Yash Raj Films banners, although he knew Gulshan Rai well. Over-eager to please his producer, he added everything possible − action, rape, cabaret, music − hoping to make a commercial hit film, to follow the enormous success of Gulshan Rai's earlier *Johny mera naam*, using the same star cast. Yash says he was very nervous at this time and had 'a strange mental condition'. While many people say that he should not have made this movie, he said it represented some kind of security to him. In a piece he wrote for *Screen*, 'Making *Joshila* was a glorious adventure ',[12] he argued that *Joshila was* 'essentially an emotional motion picture':

> What a backbone is to the human body, so is the emotional thread to *Joshila* − most important. Already when I say this, I can hear dozens of my friends asking me. 'How with so many other important elements in *Joshila*, elements such as romance, crime, adventure, music, thrills, fights and an imposing procession of big stars, how have you managed to maintain the emphatic importance of the emotional thread?'

Yash says that Gulshan Rai:

> … rapidly understood what I was attempting to achieve. 'With all the glamour and bigness,' he said to me with a twinkle in his eye, 'You are not losing your grip on the emotional thread throughout the story.' Exactly, aside from not losing my grip on it, I actually worked very hard with my team of writers to make it as strong as possible.

The cast with producer Gulshan Rai (left) and Yash Chopra (second left)

Yash worked with many of his now familiar production team: Sahir wrote the
lyrics, the script was by members of the B.R. Story Department, including
C.J. Pavri, Akhtar Mirza and Akhtar ul-Iman, while Pran Mehra edited. Yash
had never worked with Fali Mistry, the cinematographer, or with the music
director, R.D. Burman. Sahir had never worked with R.D. Burman, although
he had worked with his father, S.D. Burman, so went to get his blessings
before beginning his work. The actors were also new to Yash. He enjoyed
directing Dev Anand and Hema Malini:

> Working with Dev (and having been a great admirer of his for years) I made up
> my mind about one thing: to shape the characterisation and to extract A
> PERFORMANCE within the framework of that movie thing known as the 'Dev
> Anand style'. It is a style over which girls have swooned for years. It is a style

which has kept Dev Anand an eternally youthful, heart-throb for more years that any of us can count, and it is a style which had to come across most effectively if *Joshila* had to come to life in the image of Dev Anand. When audiences see *Joshila* I think they will agree with me that in it Dev Anand has given the best performance of his career.

Hema had always told me 'I am a director's artist' and I agreed with her when I worked with her. She brings herself from home and leaves behind her private image, content to let her director shape her as he will.[13]

Yash also enjoyed working with Pran:

As for Pranjee, I have never in my life come across any actor who takes such enormous interest in his work. Once Pranjee accepts a role he throws himself body and soul into first the preparation for it, then the execution of it. In the case of *Joshila* when he first heard the story and his role he jumped with joy. He held long discussions with us about his clothes, his get-up, his 'look'.[14]

The plot is horrendously complicated, so I give the internet synopsis of the film, which is a simplified version of the original programme notes:

The path of love, they say, never runs smooth, especially a path which has its beginning in a prison.

Joshila is the saga of such a love story, which blossomed within the shadow of the prison walls, between a convict and a poetess. A love that could not reach consummation until it was tested by blood and fire and went through a series of hair-raising exciting adventures.

Amar (Dev Anand) a young man was convicted to long-term imprisonment for a murder he did not commit, but was pinned on him by the evidence of the very witness whose life and honour he had tried to save. Nobody could see his innocence, besides Shalini (Hema Malini). A beautiful young poetess, sweet and innocent as a flower, one who meets the Joshila Amar in the grim shadows of the prison-walls. Shalini is amazed to learn about Amar's past and his innocence. Fate separates Amar from Shalini when he comes out of jail. He goes straight home to his family, and is shocked to see their desperate condition, especially that of his mother who is struggling through life by taking orders of stitching clothes for people around. His sister on the other hand has taken up dancing in a night club. Amar's blood boils to see their pitiable condition and he rushes for the first job he can get. His new boss's wife turns out to be Sapna, the same girl who had loved Amar in the past. A love which was the victim of circumstances and destiny.

Seeing her, Amar goes away quietly, not willing to have his past raked up before this beautiful young woman again. Seeking solace and in an attempt to forget his past, he goes to a night club. Here Amar meets Madan Lal Dogra, an old acquaintance from his days in jail. Dogra seems obviously wealthy now and he promises to take Amar along on a strange assignment.

What is this mysterious assignment?

Impersonating Dogra, Amar reaches the huge mountain estates of Thakur Sahib, a wealthy land-owner who is confined to life in a wheelchair due to a serious accident that made him a cripple. Here Amar meets Madhu Thakur, the voluptuous and intensely attractive young wife of the crippled Thakur Sahib. Madhu casts a strange spell over Amar and draws him irresistibly into the fascinating web of her charms. Amar finds Madhu overwhelming. He also meets Kundan her paramour, who along with Madhu, has woven a plot to murder Thakur Sahib.

And, as Amar is blackmailed and dragged into a foul murder plan to kill the man who has given him a new lease of life, our Joshila gets a big shock. He comes face to face with Shalini in this huge place, and he is trapped by his love of Shalini and fear for the safety of his family. Amar has no other way out but to follow the evil plan.

Joshila takes the audience on a veritable safari of scenic beauty, a fiesta of songs and dances and a romance as fresh as a dew-kissed bud of rose.[15]

The film was released on 6 October 1973, while *Daag* was enjoying its silver jubilee week, but it did not do well (Yash says, 'It was not a feather in my cap.') This was the only film that Gulshan Rai has produced which was not a silver jubilee. However, he continued to use Yash as a director with Yash

Shalini (Hema Malini) and Amar (Dev Anand)

Dev Anand (left) with Yash Chopra and Gulshan Rai

alternating films for Gulshan Rai's Trimurti Films with those he made for his own company.

While the censorboard saw this was not going to be a hit (Mr Vyas, the chief censor, said to Yash, 'You made *Daag* with conviction. Here you've just made a film, putting things in'), the reviews were favourable. *Screen* said that although it was similar to *Johny mera naam* in its use of the stars and its slick entertainment, its new story was 'somewhat different and had the sensitive effect of serious fare'.[16] The review praised Yash for keeping the level of drama up throughout the film, supported by a good screenplay but criticised the 'ridiculous-looking fight', average songs and the poor taste of the cabaret sequences. The review uses terms which feature in subsequent reviews of Yash's films: 'It is glossy and slick; lavishly produced. The outdoors have charm but the sets are too posh.'[17]

The human emotion film

With *Daag*, Yash established his style as a romantic film-maker, regarding himself as someone whose movies deal with 'human emotions' in the style of 'glamorous realism'. It is certainly true that Yash's treatment of emotion is what makes him so popular. Every element in his films – the music, the styling, the narrative, sets and locations – is aimed towards this end.

Yash regards emotion as the linchpin of his films:

Emotion is so important. Actors are remembered only for emotion. I am emotional, I cry in movies, also in life. I cried when Pandit Nehru died. Film should produce an effect, cry for catharsis, to feel lighter, a relief. Have to fool around – if I behave seriously, then there are problems. It's good to say things, protecting myself. My wife and children want to make me happy so I don't tell them my problems. I can't tell the servants. This new generation is not emotional, very confident. Our generation, we're emotional fools. This is not a bad thing. Sad songs are not used now. We used to have better lyrics in a sad song – silent, slow things, about the moon. Now people have been to the moon and they know it's not beautiful. Today it's all about speed. No slow and sad songs, they want pep, rhythm, and dance. There is no patience, they can't make meaningful films.

My films are about human emotions. Western films are not melodramatic, but for me when I'm seeing a film, I'm moved. In real life I'm too busy. A film should do something, have some effect. The audience has to feel that they can be there. An illusion of reality is the success of a movie.

Ideas of romance are changing. If a boy sees a girl from a distance, he feels a sensation. If he touches her then it's heaven. Now they date and live together. Those days there were those mystical, magical moments. Then life was made by hands touching, now boys and girls are friends. There is not romance, but they are friends.

Indian cinema has long been castigated by critics and intellectuals as lacking in realism, while presenting an excess of spectacle and emotion. Its defenders have sometimes sought to justify these apparent aberrations by arguing that they are part of popular indigenous traditions and that to scorn them is to participate in forms of snobbery which value the foreign and the high-class. While there are clear roots of some of these features in Indian culture, notably the absence of realism, these arguments have often represented a descent into nativism. Nowhere has this been so marked than in the so-called applications of *rasa* theory to explain the excessive emotionalism of Indian cinema.

Rasa theory

While the first mention of *rasa* or 'taste' is found in a treatise primarily on dramaturgy, Bharata's *Natyashastra* (composed around the second century AD although its form was not fixed until later), it later gained a wider status as a key to Indian aesthetics in general, best known from its refinement in the work of Abhinavagupta in the eleventh century.

A summary of the concept of *rasa* is

> [A] generalized emotion, one from which all elements of particular conscious-
> ness are expunged: the time of the artistic event, the preoccupations of the
> witness (audience), the specific or individuating qualities of the play or novel
> itself, place and character, and so on.

> 'Generalization'– of character, of event, of response – is thus the key to
> understanding the continuing Indian esthetic.[18]

In summary, the transcendent *rasa*, generated by the work of art, is apprehended by the *rasika* or *sahridaya* ('man of heart, taste'), in other words, it is the effect a literary work might have on its audience. There are nine *rasas*: the romantic, comic, sorrowful, violent, heroic, terrifying, repulsive, marvellous and (a later addition) peaceful. Each *rasa* has a corresponding *bhava* ('concrete emotion or predominant state'): love, mirth, grief, fury, resoluteness, fear, revulsion, wonder and peace. The *rasa* engenders emotional pleasure in the audience by allowing it to enjoy an emotion in a pure, generalised state (*saadhikarana*), without a personal response.[19]

However, this summary ignores the fact that there is no single concept of *rasa*, as it changes during its history of several centuries. Variously described as 'bliss' or 'pleasure', in present-day colloquial use, it is used as a general term, the many meanings of which include 'pleasure; joy; elegance, charm; wit'.[20]

It is vital to remember that *rasa* forms only a part of wider theories of literature, discussed alongside concepts of rhetoric (*alankara*), (*riti*) and (*dhvani*) rather than being an exhaustive theory of literature or performance. There are strict rules governing the evocation of *rasa*, concerning character, place, time etc., and the use of a certain imagery and symbolism. It is a learned aesthetic, applied to the courtly genres, with specific origins and applications.

There remain several problems. Why are only nine *rasas* admissible and on what grounds are they selected? How does the application of *rasa* act as critical apparatus for illuminating the texts? Has a critical practice based on *rasa* theory evolved and does it actually teach us anything about modern Indian cinema? I am unable to find convincing answers to these questions.

If the use of *rasa* theory cannot be supported on critical grounds, why is it referred to in critical work?[21] If it is employed as a universal theory, as here, then it must be able to stand in comparison with other theories of the emotions. It is often invoked because of its Indianness,[22] but it usually does not actually show us any cultural specificity and fails to illuminate the texts in any new or exciting way. It seems that it is based on the fact that it is because this theory is Indian, ancient and indigenous, and so is used as a nativist concept. This is the weakest possible ground for using this theory. It

requires one to accept essentialist myths of an unchanging India and an
untenable separation of modern public culture into Indian and western.
Moreover, there is no evidence of any intellectual or other continuity
between these traditions of courtly poetry and that of the commercial Indian
cinema. The performance of Sanskrit drama ended around the beginning of
the second Christian millennium, continuing only as a written form.
Sanskrit was always a language of elites, of high-caste males, and literary
and aesthetic instruction was the privilege of a very small minority. How
could one then pose any continuity between this world and that of Indian
film-makers? It makes more sense to look at traditions that have had a more
direct impact on the cinema, many of which emerged from the hybrid world
of nineteenth-century India, such as the Parsi theatre, through which melodrama and certain forms of acting and conventions about *mise-en-scène*
entered the cinema. Such studies have been published in the last decade or
so, notably by Prasad, Rajadhyaksha and Vasudevan, who look at the complex hybridity of Indian cinema, where a mixture of forms of modern Indian
public culture, Hollywood and other conventions have merged.

Most importantly, the *rasa* theory of emotion does not answer questions
about the centrality of emotion in Hindi films, and particularly Yash
Chopra's 'human emotion films'. What are the pleasures of watching emotion for entertainment? What is the function of emotion within the film?

Hindi film, like other forms of mass art, is often accused of being over-
emotional and aimed at over-stimulating the audience's emotions and
over-exciting the passions. It seems that this dislike of excessive emotion
has its roots in western aesthetics. Although voiced long ago by Plato, it was
Kant who disparaged emotion, elevating the values of reason that had a
major impact in the late eighteenth century.[23] This dislike of emotional
excess was dragged into Indian criticism from western literary criticism
which had pervaded Indian critical idioms since the nineteenth century.
However, other interactions with the west produced a new art popularised
by Raja Ravi Varma and the western or Parsi theatre, which were seen to be
environments for kitsch or melodrama. Given that these latter forms, which
helped shape the particular form of commercial Indian cinema, were
enjoyed by the masses, their disparagement by elites was also based in

terms of class or 'taste'.[24] In other words, excessive emotion was seen as irrational as well as being a feature of mass, or common, taste.

The case for an aesthetics of mass art has been made forcefully by Noël Carroll (1998). Carroll argues that the emotions focus the audience's attention on the film so they can organise a perception of the text which makes a series of criterially prefocused propositions. In other words, the situation in the text has been structured to catch our attention by its description or depiction of the object of our attention to 'activate our subsumption of the situation or event under the categories that are relevant to certain emotional states.'[25]

Carroll, along with others,[26] argues against consequentialism, propositionalism and identification as models of the audience's emotional involvement with the text, suggesting rather that the text itself activates our emotions. That is, one can read or view the text dispassionately, but it usually gives rise to a certain concern in the reader/audience. His argument is that the narrative focuses emotion, by mechanisms of structural expectations and goals of the characters or of the narrative, leading to dysphoric and euphoric reactions, giving rise to concerns and desires about courses and events. The film shows the characters' emotions by point-of-view editing (Bordwell, eye-line matching) as a character looks out of the frame then there is a cut to another frame where we see the object the character is seeing.[27] This technique is used to fix on objects of our emotional state, highlight further features of this object that are apposite to our emotional state, making us search for more features to support and sustain this state and to anticipate further details.

Since mass art needs generic responses, its depiction of emotions tends to universal, rather than culturally specific emotions. They usually deal with love, sex, violence, mystery, heroism, wealth and belonging, especially familial belonging, giving rise to emotions including fear, anger, horror, reverence, suspense, pity, admiration, indignation, awe, repugnance, grief, compassion, infatuation and comic amusement.[28] These emotions are easily recognisable and can be read from the faces of the actors.[29] The films mobilise emotions of which we are already aware, but deepen our thoughts about these emotions. Carroll argues that if the work does not elicit the

Sonia (Sharmila
Tagore) in reflective
mood in *Daag*

appropriate emotions, then the audience cannot understand or follow the
story. It must 'attend to the story in the emotionally appropriate way.'[30]

Yash's concentration on romance and emotion was to be challenged in
the 1970s as anger came to dominate Hindi cinema. In May 1973, Prakash
Mehra's *Zanjeer/The Chain* was released, which heralded the arrival of a
new superstar, who still remains unchallenged as Bombay cinema's top
hero: Amitabh Bachchan. Yash Chopra made his next five films with this
star and I now turn to look at these movies.

Four
The Amitabh Bachchan Films

After *Joshila*, Yash decided to make another romantic film, *Kabhi kabhie*, for which he signed Amitabh Bachchan, whose performance in *Zanjeer* had impressed him. Gulshan Rai was willing to finance the project, but meanwhile Yash, excited by a script offered to him by the writers of *Zanjeer*, decided to make *Deewaar*, also with Amitabh, produced by Rai's Trimurti Films. Amitabh was to star in Yash's next five films, and to establish himself during this decade, with these and other films, as the biggest star of Indian cinema.

These five films include some of Yash's most successful productions and are also landmarks in Amitabh Bachchan's career. His image as the angry young man, or the 'industrial hero',[1] was largely created in the scripts of Salim-Javed. These films directed by Prakash Mehra (*Zanjeer*, *Muqaddar ka Sikandar*, 1978), G.P. Sippy (*Sholay/Flames*, 1975) and Yash Chopra (*Deewaar* and *Trishul/The Trident*, 1978) were great hits and remain popular today. Amitabh also took popular roles where he mixed this image with comedy in Manmohan Desai's films (*Amar, Akbar, Anthony*, 1977; *Naseeb*, 1981; *Coolie*, 1983). However, Yash was also responsible for showing Amitabh as a member of elite Delhi society whether as a poet or an industrialist. Amitabh had begun his acting career in middle-class cinema (notably in the films of Hrishikesh Mukherjee), but although the films are remembered, the image of Amitabh as a middle-class hero has been largely forgotten.

Star of India: Amitabh Bachchan

Richard Dyer argues the star is the focus of the dominant cultural and historical concerns, thus creating interest in the life of the star and his/her whole off-screen existence,[2] to produce a star text, which is an amalgam of the real person, the characters played in films and the persona created by the media,[3] which has an economic and institutional base. Christine Gledhill sums this up by saying stars 'signify as condensors of moral, social and ideological values'.[4]

Little has been written about the Hindi film star[5] which may help us to look at whether Indian stardom differs from its western equivalent.[6] The Indian star system emerged largely with the rise of the independent producer in the 1940s.[7] The star text is created within the films themselves, mostly melodramas which are vehicles for star performances. The films draw on images of the star in other films to give them roles as national icons of beauty and desire, presenting them as utopian beings. The circulation of this image in other media allows them to maintain visibility beyond the brief moment of performance and enables the creation of a star persona. Indian television is an ideal medium for this, screening the star's earlier films, video clips of film songs and interviews. The star's image is also perpetuated by the film and lifestyle magazines which tell, or claim to tell, of their off-screen exploits.[8]

Although the Hindi film star is produced in different social and historical circumstances from those of the west, it does not seem clear if there are any cultural specificities, although the practice of *darshan(a)* (a way of looking found in Hindu religious practice and also in some social and political practices[9]) has clear implications for the viewing of the star.[10] This is because the image authorises the look (rather than merely being its object), thereby benefiting the beholder. In other words, *darshana* is a two-way look, the beholder takes *darshana* (*darshan lena*) and the object gives *darshana* (*darshan dena*) in which the image rather than the person looking has power.[11]

Although there have been many stars of the Hindi cinema, the undisputed star is Amitabh Bachchan,[12] an actor who directors, including Yash cannot praise enough.

Among Amitabh's first films were those he did with Hrishikesh Mukherjee, who first hired him because of his serious and intense demeanour. Although he displays much anger in these films, it is with *Zanjeer* that he first plays the angry young man, or urban or industrial hero,

Vijay. What was it about this character played by Amitabh that led to his becoming such a star?

The angry young man roles portrayed by Amitabh were created by Salim Khan and Javed Akhtar, also stars in this firmament, as the first scriptwriters to be given top billing since well-known writers such as Pandit Mukhram Sharma and others from B.R. Films' story department. These two presented producers and directors with bound scripts, an almost unknown item in the Hindi film world.[13] Drawing on diverse sources of storytelling from Hollywood and popular American fiction to the world of Urdu literature and subtleties of language, this duo were stars during their partnership of more than a decade and have remained so, whether through their work (Javed is one of the most acclaimed songwriters today) and their family connections (Salim is the father of Salman Khan; Javed is married to Shabana Azmi). Why did they choose the angry young man?

Javed says:

> I can give long lectures about the angry young man, but we just thought of an interesting idea and story, no idea about social implications, contemporary morality, aspirations of millions. Just story and character. We were part of the times, the society developing this kind of morality. We were in synch with others.

He sees the popularity of the angry young man as a temporary digression from the main interest of Hindi cinema, namely the romance:

> Maybe the angry young man is also a kind of romanticism. Someone will make everything OK. Different way, romanticism of a bitter person. The angry young man after more than a decade and a half, has become a parody. People have crossed that stage. Now some kind of tiredness, desire to have something pleasant in life is coming back to them. On the other side they have rejected the morality of the 50s and 60s but haven't yet developed modern morality. They know that the woman played by Meena, Nanda, Waheeda is obsolete but don't understand the modern woman. How much should we compromise and how much should we stick to tradition? We don't see clearcut heroes and heroines with social values. When not confident to make comment, where do you go?

> Hide in romance. Play safe. Hollywood directors when in doubt make a
> Western. In India, love story.

Clearly the angry young man can be evaluated only in the context of India in
the 1970s. Javed says:

> Vijay, the hero of *Zanjeer*, reflected the thinking of the time. Two years later, the
> same Vijay was seen again in *Deewaar*. By then he had left the police force, he
> had crossed that final line and become a smuggler. He wages war against the
> injustice he had to endure and he emerges the winner. You can see that the
> hero who had developed between 1973–75 – the Emergency was declared in
> India in 1975 – reflected those times.[14]

Madhava Prasad connects the popularity of the angry young man with the
political violence in India at this time[15] arguing that *Deewaar* shows an
unofficial history, played out in private where the law (of the father and the
state) has broken down.[16] Yet the angry young man has not gone away,
although his struggle may have changed and his anger become more violent.
Today these roles are played by Nana Patekar, Anil Kapoor, Sunny Deol, Ajay
Devgan and Sanjay Dutt among others, while almost all male heroes are
required to have muscular heroic bodies to display in fight sequences.

Although Salim-Javed wrote for other heroes, they wrote ten scripts for
Amitabh: *Zanjeer*, *Deewaar*, *Sholay*, *Imaan dharam/Faith* (Desh Mukherjee,
1977), *Don* (Chandra Barot, 1978), *Trishul*, *Kaala patthar/Black Rock* (Yash
Chopra, 1979), *Dostana/Friendship* (Raj Khosla, 1980), *Shaan/Majesty* or
Grandeur (Ramesh Sippy, 1980) and *Shakti/Power* (Ramesh Sippy, 1982), of
which only *Imaan Dharam* was not a hit. Why was Amitabh so popular in
these roles?

Amitabh brought a new physicality into the cinema. While not a muscular action hero, he was particularly tall and long-limbed, slim and hard-
bodied and looked right for the part. Another aspect of his physicality was
his voice. Amitabh is known for his skill in reciting the Hindi poetry of his
famous father, Harivanshrai Bachchan, in his deep baritone voice. His first
film role was to give a voice-over (Mrinal Sen's *Bhuvan Shome/Mr Shome*,
1969), and he was surely miscast as a mute in *Reshma aur shera/Reshma and*

Shera (Sunil Dutt, 1971), but as the angry young man, he uses his voice as a weapon, to control, to show his temper and to mark his intelligence. Vijay is inexpressive about love, but is eloquent about the system and how it exploits people. He can deliver tongue-twisting dialogues and rapid word play in comedy scenes such as in *Amar, Akbar, Anthony*, and he can recite the language of love of Urdu poetry in his romantic roles as Amit.

Apart from other acting skills, one of Amitabh's strengths is his ability to display anger, but controlled or expressed in dialogue. As Javed says:

> People drop all their guard in a moment of anger, their real self is revealed. ... As an actor, Amitabh's anger was never ugly. Other actors mix anger with arrogance. But Amitabh's anger was mixed with hurt and tears. So you accept it, you get fascinated by it and you find justification for it.[17]

During the late 1970s and early 1980s, Amitabh's favourite director was Manmohan Desai, with whom he made hits such as *Amar, Akbar, Anthony*, *Coolie*, *Mard/Man* (1985) and *Naseeb*. In most of these he played comic roles, but incorporated elements of the Vijay persona as he did with the romantic roles he played as Amit with Yash Chopra.[18] However, there were three major directors of Salim-Javed scripts with whom Amitabh performed as the angry young man: Prakash Mehra (*Zanjeer, Muqaddar ka Sikandar*); Ramesh Sippy (*Sholay, Shakti, Shaan*) and Yash Chopra (*Deewaar, Trishul, Kaala Patthar*). How did these three directors treat the Salim-Javed scripts differently?

Javed says, when asked how the directors differed:

> We generally met directors and knew his reputation and work. We had to work with them on those. Yash Chopra had not been a maker of films like these, they were different from his sensibility, but he really did a decent job. Generally we see what type of a maker he is and what he has made and we write a good script within that genre.

Amitabh says:

> Prakash Mehra presents his subject differently. He likes to tell a story, not to disturb the frame, doesn't use too many edits, doesn't play around. He barely

uses the trolley, and very rarely the zoom. Yashji always zooms, for every shot, close-up, sequence, and song. Movement means a lot to him.

Since there was little or no scope with narration, since Salim and Javed presented the director with a bound script, the director could only add the stars, their own style of film-making, music, glamour but there were few other opportunities for improvisation.

The Angry Young Man Films with Yash Chopra

Deewaar (The Wall, 1975)

Deewaar, produced by Gulshan Rai's Trimurti Films, opened on 24 January 1975 as Manoj Kumar's *Roti, kapra aur makan/Bread, Clothes and Housing* was celebrating its golden jubilee (50 week run). It is regarded as a classic of Hindi cinema.

The film begins with Ravi Verma (Shashi Kapoor) being given a medal for his work as a policeman. He says his mother, Sumitra Devi (Nirupa Roy) was really responsible for his success and her flashback begins.

Vijay (Amitabh Bachchan) as the don

Anand Verma, a trade unionist in a coal mine, capitulates to his bosses when they kidnap his family. The unionists taunt his family so he flees. They then tattoo his older son, Vijay, 'Mera baap chor hai/My father is a thief'. Sumitra, Vijay and her younger son, Ravi, move to Bombay. She works on a building site to send Ravi to school, while Vijay polishes shoes. Sumitra prays regularly but Vijay will not join her.

Vijay (Amitabh Bachchan) becomes a dockworker where he leads a rebellion against paying protection money after another worker is killed. After a choreographed fight with stylish dialogues, Vijay emerges as the a hero but is picked out to join a band of smugglers where he makes enough money to buy his family a large house. Meanwhile, Ravi (Shashi Kapoor), encouraged by his girlfriend Veera (Neetu Singh) joins the police after finding he does not have the connections to enter other work. Vijay meets Anita (Parveen Babi) and they begin an affair which gets her pregnant.

Ravi is put on the police case against his brother. He asks to be taken off but they make him stay on it. Vijay and Ravi confront one another but neither is prepared to yield. Their father's body is found one day and they carry out the last rites.

Sumitra is ill but recovers when the priest informs her that Vijay has prayed for her life. Anita is killed going to get a sari for their wedding. Vijay goes to meet his mother in the temple. Ravi has to kill him in a shootout, and Vijay dies in his mother's arms at the front of a temple.

Yash says he was aware of the script's potential as soon as he heard it:

> Deewaar was a script which we heard. We didn't work on it. Salim-Javed brought the script to us. What you see in the script was inspired by Mother India, definitely inspired by Mother India. But even as far as I think they had written a brilliant script, and more brilliant were the dialogues. That was the one script and screenplay where you didn't have to delete anything after making, it was such ... such a perfect script. We didn't do anything. All the dialogues are wonderful. I don't think they have written a better script than Deewaar ever.

> As far as the script is concerned Deewaar's better than Sholay. Success of this magnitude you will never see. It was such a top script. And the success of Sholay

was unbelievable, but as a script *Deewaar* was even better. Dialogue-wise. Then
there was not any *dacoit* [bandit] or anything like that. It was an emotional
picture and it was not a action picture. There was only one fight. The *godown*
[warehouse] fight is famous, the *godown* fight.

Even though there was no music, the film did very great business. There was a
controversy in the music because there was no scope for music in the script.
There were only two songs.

Salim and Javed gave me a bound script, which was their best. Gulshan Rai, the
producer, wanted Rajesh Khanna as the hero but I had *Zanjeer* in mind, so
wanted Amitabh and decided on Shashi. We filmed between March and
October [1974], and released in January 1975. It was nearly all shot in Bombay
or Khandala, mostly on night shoots as Amitabh was shooting *Sholay* during the
day. Nirupaji and Shashi as his mother and brother were successful in films
and so repeated. The same with Vinod Khanna.

Amitabh recalls:

I heard the story of *Deewaar* and liked its contemporary approach. Yashji loves
beauty, nature and romance. Even when serious and dramatic he needs a
bouquet of flowers. *Deewaar* must have been painful. He took the opportunity
for romance. It has best script and screenplay, best Salim-Javed film, with
no space for music or songs. We were very happy, although Gulshan Rai was
very sceptical because of the lack of music. The *qawwali* [sufi song] was an
afterthought added at the insistence of Gulshan Rai. Yashji was not keen to
include it, but he went with the tide.

The dramatic moments were inspiring. The temple had two locations inside the
studio, one for the scene where he begs for his mother's life and another
duplicate in Chandivali studio for the sequence when they're young. The temple
sequence was very dramatic, we didn't want to dub but to do it live. The two
temple sequences were not dubbed. In the scene when he's asking for his
mother's life, you can hear the camera move on the wooden trolley. The sound
of the clock going off was an accident. We started that sequence at nine in the
morning and shot until nine at night. He is very liberal in giving actors their
lines. It's done in half an hour then left up to the actors.

Salim-Javed wrote the script but the execution is Yashji and the actor. There is little left to improvise. Salim-Javed didn't write the death scene. The gist was that his life flashes by, he thinks of tender moments, so I thought about what he would be thinking of, that he loved his mother but he hasn't received sufficient love.

Javed says about the temple scene when Vijay is angry with Shiva:

When this scene was shot, we had a discussion with Amitabh Bachchan. We felt he had too harsh a tone in this scene – a bit too defiant. But he was convinced and said, 'If I start the dialogue on a low note then somewhere in between I'll have to raise my tone. So instead I'm going to start the delivery of dialogue from a very strong stance and work my way down.' I think it did work. He was right.[19]

During the making of *Deewaar*, Pran Mehra (see Chapter 5) died. Pran was an editor with B.R. Films and when Yash was an assistant he began working with him, sitting on the floor and pasting cuttings:

Pran was very well dressed – he always wore a tie – and handsome. He was not well-educated and had not studied beyond metriculation. I used to invite him on outdoors. He had a heart attack during *Waqt* when we were shooting the car race. He had another during *Deewaar* and this time he died.

The editor is very important. Nowadays most directors are also editors. Pran taught me like a teacher. He would abuse me and would hit me but he was very important when I became a director. He was all things combined.

Deewaar ran for over a hundred weeks and was soon recognised as a classic Hindi film. Perhaps this was because it broke so many rules. It has hardly any songs, the only two being the *qawwali* number and the title song. The hero is an anti-hero. There is little scope for romance as the heroine has a very small role, and is no innocent virgin, the lost father dies before there is a family reunion, and the hero dies at the hand of his brother.

Although a critic regarded the story as a problem in that it was not new,[20] this actually turned out to be one of its strengths. The story drew in large measure on *Mother India*, even in its structure, as a flashback by the sacrificing mother as the family's sacrifice is honoured by the state. The mother,

abandoned by her husband, struggles to bring up her two sons. Her good son
conforms to the law, and her bad son takes the law into his own hands,
invoking a natural law. The mother loves the bad son more but is compelled
to choose the good son.[21] The characters have the same mythic resonance
but they are given contemporary touches, so Vijay is 'cool', handsome, and
gives stylised speeches; Ravi is a young idealistic police officer, who realises
the corruption of the system yet will not take to crime, embodying the law
directly. Nirupa Roy, although not such a great star as Nargis, plays the idealised mother, drawing on her earlier goddess roles, acting as the focus for
the film's emotion. She has to choose between the law of the state and that
of kinship, so although she loves Vijay, she has to follow the law. Vijay
rejects religion, but is superstitious about his armband which has on it the
number 786, regarded as lucky by many Muslims, which saves him from
bullets. He finally goes to pray when his mother is ill and his death takes
place in the temple where he has long refused to worship.

The two sons, Vijay (Amitabh Bachchan) and Ravi (Shashi Kapoor), fight over their
mother (Nirupa Roy)

The connection with *Mother India* draws on elements of this mythical or epic film, setting it in a modern, urban context. It also draws on other films, notably *On the Waterfront* (E. Kazan, 1954), for the dockyard confrontations and on the idiom of American urban cool that was becoming fashionable at this time. The character of Vijay clearly has the makings of a folk hero, as he supports traditional family values although he criticises the 'system' or the state, fighting for righteous causes from outside its sphere of operation. There is no doubt that he is on the side of right, as he shows in his eloquent speeches, but these values conflict with those of the state and to resolve this he has to die, adding martyrdom to his cause.

In *Mother India* the bad son, Birju, dies at the hand of his mother, who was the principal actor in this film, while here Vijay is the central figure. In *Deewaar*, the conflict between the brothers is foregrounded more than in *Mother India* and is neatly stylised in the famous dialogue between the brothers. After Sumitra has refused to take anything more from Vijay, she and Ravi move out. Vijay and Ravi meet under the bridge over the pavement where they lived when their mother used to work on a building site. The children's song, Iqbal's '*Sare jahaan se accha Hindustan hamara*/Our India is the best in the world', plays while the brothers argue. Vijay asks Ravi to change to another case as this is dangerous, saying that now there is a wall (*deewaar*) between them. Ravi says he cannot give up this case because of his principles and ideals:

Vijay *Ufh! Tumhaare usool, tumhaare aadarsh! Kis kaam ke hain tumhaare usool? Tumhaare saare usoolon ko goondh kar ek waqt ki roti banaayi jaa sakti hai, Ravi. Jin aadarshon ke liye tum apni zindagi per khelne ke liye taiyaar ho, kya diya hai tumhein un aadarshon ne? Ek chaar paanch sau rupaye ki police ki naukri. Ek kiraaye ka quarter. Ek duty ki jeep. Do jode khaaki vardi. Dekho! Dekho! Ye wo hi main hun, aur ye wo hi tum ho. Hum donon ek hi saath is footpath se uthe the. Lekin aaj tum kahan rah gaye aur main kahan aa gayaa. Aaj mere paas building hain, property hai, bank balance hai, bungla hai, gaadi hai. Kya hai tumhaare paas?*
Huh! Your principles and your ideals! What use are your principles? All your principles gathered together can't give you a square meal. These ideals for which you're prepared to risk your life – what have

these ideals given you? A job earning four or five hundred rupees. Quarters to rent. A jeep when you're on duty. A pair of khaki uniforms. Look! Look! This is what I am and this is what you are. We both grew up together on this pavement. But look where you have got to and where I am. Now I have buildings, property, money in the bank, a house, a car. What do you have?

Ravi   *Meri paas maa hai.*
       I have Mum.

Other famous speeches occur when Ravi realises the law is wrong, and visits the poor family whose child was driven to steal bread to provide food for his parents, resulting in Ravi having to shoot him. Vijay's death scene, his speeches about dignity and many other such memorable exchanges are known off by heart by many people even today.

The film has one of the best depictions of Bombay, using real locations, ranging from the docks to five-star hotels. At this time in Bombay, smuggling was a real threat and one of its most notorious practictioners, Haji Mastan Mirza, was imprisoned during the Emergency. This seamy side of Bombay is shown here in a 'realistic' manner which has been emulated in other outstanding films, notably 1998's *Satya* (Ram Gopal Verma).

Apart from music, another key ingredient of the Yash Chopra film is missing, namely romance. Ravi's girlfriend Veera (Neetu) has little to do apart from look sweet and be his boss's daughter; Vijay's girlfriend (Parveen), is a glamorous call girl. Although we see her in bed with Vijay, smoking a post-coital cigarette, we learn that she has also fallen foul of the system and nurses secret dreams of a traditional wedding, and is, at heart, similar to the ideal heroine.

Trishul (*The Trident*, 1978)

Deewaar had its golden jubilee in 1976 and at Diwali, Gulshan Rai announced that his Trimurti Films would be making *Trishul*. *Deewaar* ran for another 50 weeks, assuring its place in Hindi film history. *Trishul* was released 5 May 1978 and was also a big box-office hit.

Ravi (Sunil Dutt) romances Meena (Sadhana) in *Waqt*

Rita (Mumtaz) and Munish (Dharmendra) romance in *Admi aur Insaan*

Munish (Dharmendra) and JK (Feroz Khan) meet at the dam (*Admi aur Insaan*, 1969)

Sonia (Sharmila Tagore) and Sunil (Rajesh Khanna) in *Daag*

Vijay (Amitabh Bachchan) and Anita (Parveen Babi) in *Deewar*

The wedding night of Pooja (Raakhee) and Vijay (Shashi Kapoor) in *Kabhi kabhie*

Amit (Amitabh Bachchan) and Shoba (Jaya Bachchan) meet Chandni (Rekha) in a sari shop in *Silsila*

Rohit (Rishi Kapoor) and Chandni (Sridevi) fantasise about romance in Switzerland (*Chandni*, 1989)

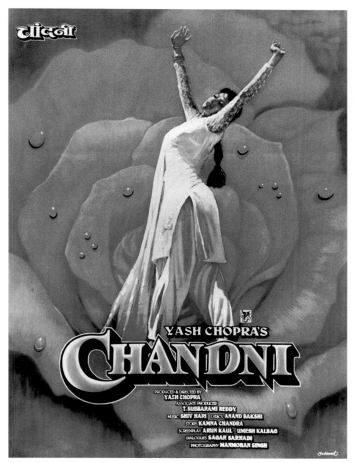

Chandni Poster

Chandni (Sridevi) works as Lalit's (Vinod Khanna) secretary (*Chandni*, 1989)

Yash Chopra directs Madhuri Dixit in *Dil to pagal hai*

DTPH lobby card

Simran (Kajol) and Raj (Shahrukh Khan) sing at the mehndi ceremony in *DDLJ*

Raj Aryan (Shahrukh Khan) and Narayan Shankar (Amitabh Bachchan) clash in
Mohabbatein

Shahrukh Khan, Karisma and Madhuri in publicity for *DTPH*

Shashi and Amitabh, who were now becoming an established pair with Yash, enjoyed socialising with him, but Yash never drinks and is always disciplined and hard-working on the sets. Yash says:

One night Amitabh and Shashi went out partying and as they came back into the hotel at 6.30 in the morning, I had the unit ready to leave for shooting. I didn't realise that they had just come in. They had no choice but to go straight to the film, snoozing in the breaks.

Raj Gupta (Sanjeev Kumar), is a young engineer, in love with a clerk, Shanti (Waheeda Rehman). They plan to marry but the owner of the company where Raj works proposes that he marries his daughter which will ensure Raj takes over the business. Raj decides to marry for money even when Shanti tells Raj she is pregnant. Shanti brings up Vijay (Amitabh Bachchan) whose driving force is revenge on his father.

Raj, now Mr R.K. Gupta, is head of a construction company in Delhi. He has two children, Shekhar (Shashi Kapoor) and Babli (Poonam Dhillon). Shekhar has studied business in London and is destined to take over the company. Babli, a student, is in love with Ravi, while Shekhar is in love with a businesswoman Miss Varma (Hema Malini). Their life of plenty is contrasted to Vijay's struggle.

Vijay comes to Delhi to destroy his father. He begins by buying land from Gupta which has illegal squatters. Vijay drives them away and begins to take contracts from Gupta. Gupta is troubled at home, his wife walking out. As Gupta's life hits rock bottom, Vijay reveals his true identity and restores his father's money but his father dies, saving Vijay, and the brothers take over the business.

The film was acclaimed by critics and fans alike. *Screen* called it a 'high voltage emotional drama':[22]

Yash's filming has the sure touch of the professional who has perfected his art in his own way. His camera moves almost effortlessly to convey the nuances and bring out the impact of every scene.[23]

The reviewer enjoyed the scenes placing characters, in particular the first shot of Vijay, 'showing him walking indifferently in a dynamited quarry, and

The first shot. The cast with Yash Chopra and Randhir and Rishi Kapoor.

The family breaks away from the father to set up their own company

lighting a cigarette from a live fuse', and 'the last party sequences, and the one showing Vijay beside the burning pyre of his mother'. All aspects of the film were critically acclaimed.

The story is very powerful, the main theme being Vijay's hatred for his father and his determination to ruin him, an Oedipal drama given justification within the film. This conflict between two of Hindi cinema's most powerful actors is a skilful blend of dialogue and silence. Javed says:

> *Trishul* was doing things that had never been seen before. When we discuss it now it seems ordinary and so unimportant, but anything that has never been tried before is regarded as dangerous and risky for an Indian film-maker. The hero of *Trishul* was the first 'real' illegitimate child on the Hindi screen. His parents ... are not seen going to some abandoned temple and exchanging *malas* to show they are married in the eyes of God, if not in the eyes of the world. Nor do they make love because it was raining. They share a mature physical relationship and that is clearly established in the film. That's how the hero's mother gets pregnant. ... When *Trishul* was released, S. Mukherjee said, 'I have seen this picture three times to try to see why it's successful, but I can tell you that if you had come to me with this script, I would not have taken it.'... Here is a hero who is knowingly out to destroy his own father ... his actions were breaking old taboos. So we had to say, 'You see, he's doing it for his mother!'[24]

> It's the first film in which the heroine sleeps with the man in her life without feeling guilty.[25]

The conversations from this film are again among some of the most celebrated in Hindi cinema and are available on disk.

Kaala patthar (*Black Rock* or *Coal*, 1979)

Kaala patthar, was released on 24 August 1979 and was the last film Yash made with Salim-Javed. Their partnership ended in 1981. It was also the last film he made with Gulshan Rai, perhaps because Yash felt able to produce all his own films after the success of Yash Raj Films' *Noorie* (Manmohan Krishna, 1979). Amitabh seemed at the peak of his career, with 1979's releases including *Suhaag/Married Happiness* (Manmohan Desai, 1979), *Mr Natwarlal* (Rakesh Kumar, 1979) and *Muqaddar ka sikandar*, all of which had jubilees.

Kaala Patthar, *Deewaar* and *Trishul* form a trilogy of sorts, focused around Amitabh Bachchan as Vijay, the industrial hero. In *Kaala patthar*, Vijay is driven by his need to atone for his own wrongdoing by righting the wrongs of the exploited coal miners.

Vijay (Amitabh Bachchan), a former ship's captain, court-martialled and rejected by his heroic father for deserting his ship in a storm, becomes a coal miner. He reveals his origins to the mine's doctor, Sudha (Raakhee Gulzar), who falls in love with this tortured hero. He becomes friendly with Ravi Malhotra (Shashi Kapoor), the sophisticated engineer and his journalist girlfriend Anita (Parveen Babi); Mangal (Shatrughan Sinha), the escaped convict, is a swaggering anti-hero, who romances the beautiful bangle-seller Channo (Neetu Singh). The evil mine owner, Dhanraj Puri (Prem Chopra), puts profits before safety. The mines are flooded, the three heroes

Vijay (Amitabh Bachchan) as a coal miner

save the day, but Mangal dies before the police can recapture him. This heroism of Vijay's allows his parents to forgive his earlier cowardice.

The three couples present three different forms of love and romance. Ravi and Anita are the ideal image of the modern, professional couple while Mangal and Channo represent the ordinary people. Vijay and Sudha are the third couple, a serious, mature pair who want to right society through their own day-to-day lives.

These three romances are set against the unlikely backdrop of a coal mine in north India. In the 1970s, mining disasters occured at Chasnala and elsewhere in Bihar, which were already infamous as sites of lawlessness and gang warfare conducted under the guise of trade union activities. Although gangs are active in the film, the villain of the piece is the mine owner, whose greed for coal at the risk of men's lives is condemned unequivocally, while Anita argues for the nationalisation of the coal mines.

Given the popularity of the Hollywood 'disaster' movies of the 1970s such as *The Towering Inferno*, one expects this film to be of the same genre, yet the final disaster forms a small, although key, part of the film, the major focus being less the spectacle of the disaster than its role in Vijay's story. The underground floods recall the storm at sea and Vijay's lack of heroism on the ship is replaced by an almost reckless heroism, leading to him saving men's lives and his *prayashchitta* (atonement) by water. His parents await him as he exits the mine, welcoming him back into the family and he is now feels worthy of accepting Sudha's love. Mangal too atones for his crimes in the floods, yet as an escaped criminal he has to die as he cannot be rehabilitated into society.

None of this sounds like a 'Yash Chopra movie', yet there are striking features in his unfolding of Salim-Javed's script. Rajesh Roshan's music provides hit songs, albeit fewer romantic numbers than one might expect, in the context of the gritty realism of the mine, these being largely confined to Ravi-Anita, the only two who appear in romantic locations, the other songs being mostly traditional wedding songs and *qawwalis* and folk-based dances. The women are presented as totally glamorous and as three very different models of femininity: from the serious, caring doctor in her white saris, to the spirited journalist in western clothes or *salwaar khameez*, to the self-possessed itinerant in her *kaccha*-style saris (when the sari is tied to give the effect of trousers dividing the skirt). Perhaps the greatest link here is to a film on which the young Yash Chopra worked as a second assistant, B.R. Chopra's *Naya Daur* (see Chapter 3), which also condemned industrial man's greed and willingness to exploit the more vulnerable members of society. This emphasis on a specific area of social concern was a hallmark of B.R.'s films and is seen occasionally in Yash's films, the last being *Mashaal* (1984, see Chapter 7), until he moves entirely to his trademark plushy romances.

Kaala patthar did good business at the box-office but was not as great a hit as the earlier films, perhaps because its emotional side was weaker. Vijay's anger lacked the epic or mythological status that it had in earlier Salim-Javed films. Yash also blames its short life at the box-office on video piracy:

> When *Kaala patthar* was released the distributors said that they were giving a high price considering the drop in the audience. This was caused by video piracy. Shashi was on holiday in the UK so Amitabh and I went there and the three of us did appearances in Leicester and Manchester. This increased the audience.

The Romantic films

Yash also made two of his big budget romances with Amitabh during this period. He produced both of these himself, with Yash Raj Films (as he had with *Kaala patthar*), but Trimurti distributed them.[26]

Kabhi kabhie (Sometimes, 1976)

Kabhi kabhie was released 27 February 1976. Yash had some problems in casting the female roles. It was unusual at the time for married women to work in films, as critics noticed when previewing the film.[27] According to Yash:

> I had never worked with Waheeda, although I was very fond of her as an artist. Although she was married, she agreed to do it. I signed Raakhee, even though she was also married. Everything was ready, then Gulzar [her husband] called me a week before saying we shouldn't take her. I said, 'I think she's the most beautiful, a poet's dream.' I was very tense. Gulzar let her go. She can't give up working in films.

Kabhi kabhie songbook

He also had trouble with the younger heroine:

> In place of Neetu, I'd signed Parveen who was in *Deewaar*, but on the day of the
> *muhurat* [auspicious moment, usually the first shot of the film] we decided she
> wouldn't look good with Chintu [Rishi Kapoor]. The next day Chintu was to go
> to Paris, so I wanted to do the *muhurat* in Raj Kamal [Studio]. I was looking for
> Parveen to tell her she was not in the film. She took it very sportingly. In the
> evening she came to my home and said, 'Yashji, don't avoid me, you must have
> thought it best.'

Rishi Kapoor was doing well at the box-office and was not keen on the idea
of a multi-starrer. Shashi narrates:

> Yash called me up to say Rishi is not doing the film. I said, let's beat him up.
> Rishi was panicky about doing it with so many stars, but eventually agreed to it.

Amitabh says:

> *Kabhi kabhie* was designed almost simultaneously with *Deewaar*. Must have been
> a huge effort. *Deewaar* began early 1975, *KK* in October 75. He filmed 80% then

came back and continued *Deewaar*. Yashji took a personal risk casting me in *Kabhi kabhie*. Yashji's great theme is romance, but the actors don't have to be young and romantic. Waheedaji was my favourite leading lady with Dilip Sahib, so playing opposite her was unbelievable.

Amitabh's parents play Raakhee's parents in the *kanyadaan* (the giving of the girl in marriage).

The film was shot mostly on several locations, Kashmir, Delhi, Goa and Bombay as Yash explains:

The only set was for the rain song – *'Pyar kar liya to kya'* ['What does it matter if I've fallen in love'], which we shot in Mehboob Studios. The rest was shot on real location, including some bungalows in Bombay. We did a lot of shooting in Delhi because I like Delhi. There we had the house of Shashi, the TV centre, and we used the Qutb Hotel. Our financier was V.V. Puri, who owns *India Today*. His house, in the diplomatic enclave, was empty as he'd just sold it, so we decorated it for our purposes and did a lot of shooting there.

The film took several risks that worried some, including Gulshan Rai, as Yash recalls:

When I showed it to Gulshan, he felt it may not work, since Amitabh was playing an older person, and he felt the music may not work. We did some reshooting – I spoke to Amit, 'Let's leave the first of January.' There was no time to go by road, so we flew to Kashmir. Shot recitation and some indoors which made the film look good.

The film was released 27 February 76 at the Metro. It ran for 37 weeks. It was an instant hit, but in Bombay didn't look too good although it picked up after three or four days.

Amit Malhotra (Amitabh Bachchan) woos Pooja (Raakhee) with his poetry. Although they fall in love they agree that they should not transgress their parents' wishes so she marries an architect Vijay Khanna (Shashi Kapoor) and he abandons poetry to take over the family business, a quarry. Amit's parting gift is a book of his poetry, which she has inspired: *Kabhi kabhie*. Vijay, while no poet, loves poetry and presents her with this book on their wedding night. Pooja sings the poem to her husband as he undresses her. She falls in love with him and they form a happy family with their son, Vicki (Rishi Kapoor), sharing close and loving relationships. Vicki becomes a jockey, falls in love with Pinky (Neetu Singh), the daughter of Dr and Mrs Kapoor (Simi Garewal and Parikshit Sahni). Kapoor is the Khannas' doctor and both families readily agree to the marriage when the children tell them of their love. Meanwhile Amit is interviewed on television by Pooja; he recites a revised version of *Kabhi kabhie* where hope has been replaced by loss and misery. On visiting the Khannas, he leaves abruptly. The Kapoors and the Khannas discuss the dilemma they face in telling Pinky she is adopted. Although the Khannas advise against it, they decide to do so and give her the name of her natural mother. Vicki tries to dissuade Pinky, but when she goes to find her mother, Vicki follows her on his father's advice. Pinky's mother, Anjali (Waheeda Rehman), invites her to stay, pretending to her husband, Amit, and her daughter, Sweetie (Naseem), that she is her niece. Her excessive affection is noted with anger by Amit, whose love is entirely centred on Sweetie. Vicki arrives but hides his connection with Pinky; Sweetie falls in love with him and persuades Amit to employ him in the quarry. Vijay brings Pooja with him on a business trip to build a hotel. When Amit comes to collect them for dinner, Vijay overhears him and Pooja talking of their previous affair, and, although he realises the awful irony of his giving Pooja the book on their wedding night, he bears no grudge against either of them for their past affair. In contrast, when Amit finds out that Pinky is the illegitimate child of Anjali and an airforce pilot who died before their marriage, he rejects Anjali, branding her a sinner. Events come to a head when Sweetie, on discovering that Vicki and Pinky are lovers, tries to commit suicide by heading for the part of the quarry where blasting is to occur. She is saved by the concerted efforts of all. Amit suddenly remembers Anjali and rushes back to the house to find her about to leave. He expresses his regret for his lack of understanding. The film ends with the marriage of Vicki and Pinky; the three sets of parents performing the rites, with Sweetie as the bridesmaid.

Kabhi kabhie is not only one of Yash Chopra's personal favourites, but also one of his most popular and critically-acclaimed films. It weaves together two different stories, contrasting romantic love in two generations in the context of love in the nuclear family unit. The first story, the Romantic poet who cannot free himself from the past, was inspired by the life of the film's lyricist, Sahir Ludhianvi, and by a visual image Yash Chopra has long cherished: a long shot with a man in the foreground whose beloved is marrying another man. Yash says:

> The idea was that a girl was getting married, while a man under a tree was remembering sweet moments with the girl. He's a poet. But the film needs a next generation – if she gets married we need romance in the next generation.

This second story was developed from a feature his wife, Pamela Chopra, read in *Woman and Home* magazine about a woman meeting the daughter she had given up for adoption. The presentation of the erotic is minimal; the film is almost exclusively concerned with romantic and familial love.

Amitabh Bachchan plays the role of Amit, who courts Pooja by reciting poetry in romantic landscapes.[28] Their love is depicted as being remarkably passionless, the only hint of eroticism occurring when she loosens her hair over him. Unwilling even to consider raising the matter of marriage with the girl's parents, Amit almost encourages her to leave him when they arrange her marriage. He abandons poetry, only reworking his great romantic poem, *Kabhi kabhie*,[29] into a poem of misery and loss,[30] and one he composes for his young daughter.[31] He marries, becomes an ordinary business-man, seemingly resolved to live his life uncreatively, full of anger and misery, unbearable in his behaviour to others. His love is focused on his daughter, Sweetie, perhaps as a way of avoiding his wife, Anjali, who seems insecure even after 20 years of marriage. Even though Amit does not love Anjali, he cannot bear the revelation of her former love affair, the fact that she has loved another, taking a harsh unforgiving attitude, calling it a sin. He refuses to see this as paralleling his own college romance and is unrepentant about his inability to forget it even after 20 years.

The other two couples of his generation are happy because they can live in the present, without dwelling on their pasts. Pooja weeps for her lost love on her wedding night, singing their love song at the request of her new husband, but as he discreetly and erotically undresses her, images of the two

men merge in her song, and the sexual love between Vijay and Pooja is made
clear by scenes of the couple in bed and her giggling in the shower on their
honeymoon. Pooja asks Vijay to compose poetry for her. He says he cannot,
but his whole persona is full of life and love, contrasting sharply with the
brooding, silent Amit. When he learns of Pooja and Amit's college affair and
the awful irony of his asking her to sing *Kabhi kabhie* on their wedding night,
he shrugs it off within a matter of hours, saying any sensible young man
would have been in love with her.

The three members of the younger generation (Vicki, Pinky and Sweetie)
confide in their parents about their love affairs, the parents accept their
choices and are willing to arrange their marriages. They encourage their
children to fight for their loved ones. Vicki and his mother tease each other
about courtship. She says: 'We were not like you: say "Hi", in the morning,
drink tea in the afternoon, get engaged by the evening.' Vicki retorts: 'For
six months you caught glimpses of each other through a window; after a year,
"Hello, how are you? Good weather we're having!" and making a plan to look

The young couple romance in Kashmir: Vicki (Rishi Kapoor) and Pinky (Neetu Singh)

in each other's eyes. Then when you were ready to talk about love you found out that the girl's parents had fixed her marriage to someone else and the poor loverboy was left in the lurch!'

Vicki is like his father, Shekhar,[32] happy and fulfilled in love, he tells the world about it. Soon after his first appearance, he bursts into song: 'So what if I've fallen in love? Love is not a crime.' This music is in a different style from the slow love songs of the older generation, no longer a slow langorous lyric but a happy, upbeat song.[33] Nor are their love songs necessarily depicted with romantic and erotic imagery, instead they partake in modern urban life: they go swimming, ride motorbikes, go dancing and eat in restaurants.

The theme of family love is very strongly developed in this film and is used to establish a generational contrast. Amit does not struggle against the wishes of Pooja's parents but gives in without a fight, although Pooja makes it clear that she is still keen to marry him, arguing that they do not have the right to destroy their dreams, while the love affairs of the younger genera-tion are positively encouraged by the parents. The happy families are those who place emphasis on trust and love (the ones who learn to trust their chil-dren). The norm is the nuclear family, with great love between husbands and wives, parents and children, whether natural or adopted, the joking relationships of in-laws and the love of friends for each other. The final scene allows Pinky's adopted parents, her natural mother and her new hus-band to take an equal part in the *kanyadaan*.

The reviewers picked up on the film's unusual characteristics. One reports that the film treats love:

> ... not in one narrow sense but in several of its stages and shades. This is what makes the film off-beat, while being lavish and star-packed and puts it on a level higher than many of the love stories done before by other film-makers in the same genre.

> It does require some courage and conviction to make an expensive film entirely round the emotional interplay of characters in different age groups. This is especially so when the prevailing box-office trend is for films with a lot of action, violence, sex-appeal, comedy and other loud gimmicks.[34]

The film's strengths are also seen to be those now closely associated with Yash Chopra, saying that like his:

> Daag, [it] provides another warm human drama, posh in visuals, rich in emotional conflicts.[35]

The script was criticised for its illogicality, but was praised for its visuals and in particular for showing love at all difference stages of life, noting in particular:

> The film-maker shows a rare spirit in not using the stars in their popular images but rather as artistes etching realistic characters. The players, also deserve a lot of kudos for this, like Shashi Kapoor and Amitabh Bachchan playing superbly in most parts as greying old men, with grown-up children. The same applies to Waheeda, Raakhee, Simi as graceful mothers. The young ones, on the contrary, cut a rather sorry figure near them.[36]

Silsila (The Affair, 1981)

Silsila, which came out in 1981, was controversial from its beginning. Even before it was released there was gossip about the casting, due to persistent rumours that it depicted a real life love triangle between Amitabh and his wife, Jaya, and Rekha:

> At the Delhi film fete inaugural, everyone was surprised when Amitabh Bachchan, Jaya and Rekha walked in together. And then the seating arrangement staggered them some more: Pam Chopra, Jaya, Yash Chopra, Amitabh, Shashi Kapoor, Rekha. Everyone, it seems has come to terms with everyone else or is it musical chairs?[37]

In an interview with K.N. Subramaniam, before the release Yash said:

> 'Everyone I meet keeps asking me to tell them the story of the making of Silsila. But there is no story to tell,' Yash Chopra says wryly. 'There were no daggers drawn, no bitching, no cattiness,' he reports – 'if these were what people expected.'[38]

The history of the film-casting was more complicated. Yash had originally wanted to cast Padmini Kolhapure, but she could not give dates so he

Silsila poster

took Parveen Babi and Smita Patil. He felt that they were not suitable and so dropped them from the film. He said Parveen took it really well; he got Shashi to talk to Smita, which was her major complaint.

Amitabh says about this *Silsila:*

The gossip about the casting of *Silsila* was quite unwarranted. We were on location with Parveen Babi and Smita Patel. Yashji came to me, saying he would prefer Jaya and Rekha to do it. I spoke to the ladies. *Silsila* was made 15 years ahead of its time. B.R. and Yashji were bold in their films, especially B.R.'s extra-marital themes.

Although Yash argues, in his usual words, 'There are no fights, no smugglers, no gimmicks at all,'[39] the magazines focused on this issue of off-screen romance with *Filmfare* using a cover of the famous back-to-back shot of Rekha and Jaya.[40] The adverts proclaimed: 'Love is faith and faith is forever'.[41] However, the recently released DVD version (2000) refers to 'the casting coup of the century', which suggests the controversy is far from over.

Yash said to me in a different context about gossip, which exasperates him:

> I don't understand. My actors should only have professional dealings with me. I have no business with their private life. It's not my concern who's sleeping with who, who's gay. It's their private life. Their sexual behaviour doesn't make a difference to me, it's only their work. A friend of mine is a friend of mine. There are so many rumours. If I stop every time a dog barks, I'll never reach the end of the road.

Silsila was shot between November 1980 and 14 May 1981 in Yash's house, in Kashmir, Delhi and Amsterdam. Some of the shots in Delhi were at dawn, at 5.30, when it was really cold. Rekha says:

> I hate cold and Yashji wanted so many shots in the snow and cold. I wouldn't do this for anyone else.

Yash paid great attention to the costumes and the look of this film which is one of the features for which it is well-remembered:

> Jaya's saris were bought by Pam and Jaya. What colours! Rekha worked very hard on her dresses, personal jewellery. This was all her own design, although we discussed everything. She's very particular. As for the men's clothes – Amitabh had looked fantastic in *Trishul*, where all his clothes were made by Mr Akbar, now of 'Gabbana'. In *Kabhi kabhie* and *Silsila*, his costume was his own clothes.

Yash Chopra had always used lyrics by Sahir Ludhianvi and had not found a replacement since his death. For *Silsila* he took a team of lyricists, including Harivanshrai Bachchan, Amitabh's father, who gave him '*Rang barse*/Colours rain' and the first lyrics of Javed Akhtar, who was to become one of the most

Amit (Amitabh Bachchan) and (Chandni) Rekha romance in the snow in Kashmir

celebrated lyricists. Javed wrote his first song, *'Dekha ek khwab to/*I saw in a dream' for a tune of Shiv-Hari, and also wrote *'Yeh kahaan aa gaye hum?* /Where have we come to?'* and *'Neela asmaan/*The blue sky'.

Amitabh recited the lyrics to the *'Yeh kahaan aa gaye hum?/*Where have we come to?'* and sang two songs: *'Rang barse/*Colours rain' and *'Neela asmaan/* The blue sky'. The former was very popular and has become a classic song to be sung at Holi, but the distributors deleted the latter as they claimed that the audience was booing and jeering it.

Yash Chopra's films are said to have one Punjabi folk song, one triangle song with either two men and a woman or two women and a man, one very, very romantic song and often a sad, despondent song of rejection and pain. In *Silsila*, Yash introduced Shiv-Hari as music directors. They were both famous as classical musicians, Shiv Kumar Sharma as a santoor player, and Hariprasad Chaurasia as a flautist. They had played in the orchestra for Yash's films, and he had thought of taking them as composers some time before this film. They worked with him in many of his films until *Darr*, 1993.

Shekhar (Shashi Kapoor), an airforce pilot, and Shobha (Jaya Bachchan) are lovers who are about to be married. Shekhar invites his younger brother Amit (Amitabh Bachchan) to meet his fiancée and they discuss the marriage with her mother. Amit meets Chandni (Rekha) at a wedding and falls in love. An aspiring playwright, he invites her to a performance, after which romance follows. He tells his brother he intends to marry her but when Shekhar is killed in the (1971?) war, leaving Shobha pregnant, Amit agrees to marry her to save everyone's honour. Amit is involved in a car accident in which Shobha loses the baby. Her physician, Dr Anand (Sanjeev Kumar), turns out to be Chandni's husband. Chandni and Amit subsequently meet and he explains why he had to leave her and their affair recommences. Shobha meanwhile begins to fall in love with Amit. His friend, Vidyarthi, and Shobha become suspicious of his relationship with Chandni but nothing is said. Chandni knocks a boy down when she is out with Amit at night. They go to the police station and narrowly avoid meeting Dr Anand. However, the policeman turns out to be Shobha's cousin, and, recognising Amit, reproaches him. At Dr Anand's Holi party, Amit consumes too much *bhaang* (marijuana paste), and sings a traditional song about a cuckold. As he sings, his relationship with Chandni becomes clear to the other spouses, who later discuss this in parables. A scene (possibly a dream sequence?) is shown where Shobha and Jaya agree to fight for Amit. Meanwhile Amit and Chandni decide to set up a new life together. Chandni leaves while her husband is out of town and Amit tells Shobha he is leaving her. Shobha declares her resolve to win him back. Amit and Chandni meet Amit's friend and go to his parents' golden wedding celebration. The ceremony reminds them of the sanctity of marriage. Suddenly the phone rings: Shobha tells Amit Dr Anand has been in a plane crash. Amit and Chandni rush to the site: as Amit rushes to help Dr Anand, Shobha reveals she is pregnant. Amit promises to return to her. Amit saves Dr Anand who leaves on a stretcher, accompanied by Chandni. Shobha and Amit are reunited.

Amit, although under no real pressure, marries Shobha, thus abandoning his lover, Chandni. Previously there had been no opposition to Amit and Chandni's marriage from either family: Chandni's parents were even prepared to cancel arrangements with someone they had found for her.

When Amit and Chandni meet again after Shobha's miscarriage, Amit woos Chandni again with words drawn from his play[42] and the affair recommences. While many Indian movies have dealt with extra-marital love,[43] this was the first one to show the consummation of adultery. While some justification for it is given by the couple having been lovers before Amit sacrificed their love, the film raises the question: can adultery be romantic? The film portrays the quick decline of the relationship which collapses when they realise their loyalties lie with their partners: Chandni because Dr Anand's life is at risk; Amit because he finds his wife is pregnant. The innocent lovers become a sleazy couple, notably in the eyes of the state, embodied in the policeman who also turns out to be Amit's brother-in-law; in front of Amit's friends (Vidyarthi, Gurdip); and in front of older people who should be respected (Gurdip's parents). The sadness and silent suffering of the partners, who discuss the affair in riddles in the context of a medical examination, also make the lovers look shabby. Particularly reproachful and symbolic is Shobha's role as the archetypal Hindu wife, invoking absolute devotion to her husband through using Meera's discourse of her devotion to Krishna. Perhaps this creates grounds for the forgiveness for Amit's philandering by linking it to Krishna's dalliance with the Gopis. We later come to realise that she is pregnant in this scene[44] but she does not reveal this until she fears he will risk his life and she will lose her second lover.

Yash Chopra's heroes and, more unusually, his heroines can fall in love more than once and even have sexual relations with more than one partner. However, one must make one's commitment to the bourgeois nuclear family, one must come to love one's spouse in whatever way one can and one needs to let go of the past, live in the present. Everyone needs understanding and forgiveness, and the bestowal of these virtues is always praised.

Silsila was released when the big hits were action-oriented, namely Sanjay Dutt's debut *Rocky* (1981), and Amitabh was playing the angry young man in *Laawaris/Orphan* (Prakash Mehra, 1981), which has been famous partly because he also sang a song in drag. Amitabh was enjoying success with Manmohan Desai and *Naseeb* was also released this year, and he was working on *Coolie*. Nevertheless, romantic films were also popular, as

Amit (Amitabh Bachchan) plans to leave Shobha (Jaya Bachchan)

Kumar Gaurav's one hit, *Love Story*, was proving. *Silsila* was released on 14 August. A week later, a gala performance of *Silsila* was held at the Metro in aid of the Nargis Dutt Cancer Unit, which collected the sum of Rs 10 lakhs and a further Rs 5 lakhs from the Chief Minister's fund, although none of the stars were present. It was already clear that the film was not a success:

> When *Silsila* didn't do well, I was very upset. It ran only 16 weeks and I didn't go out. There was an HMV party to honour Nazia Hussain. I went only to show my face, but inside I was very depressed. Raj Kapoor saw me from a distance. He said, 'I saw your film in Loni. You don't make a run of the mill film. I saw you'd gone to Amsterdam, where you'd captured the poetry of flowers.' I felt happy and I felt upset. Then Bhabhiji [Krishna Kapoor] spoke and I was very moved. His wife giving a compliment goes a long way.

Some even felt the film had failed because Amitabh was popular as the Angry Young Man and the audience wouldn't accept him as a lover, Javed Akhtar argued against this:

Given the role of an obsessed lover, I am sure, Amitabh will excel himself in a romantic film too … he can convey intense passion. But they will not accept him in a romantic role which evokes pity. *Silsila* didn't flop because Amitabh played a romantic role. It failed because it had a weak script. After picking a bold theme on extra-marital relationships, Yash Chopra develops cold feet, and the film becomes apologetic … probably because he wasn't convinced of the moral stand he himself had taken.[45]

A stand which Javed repeats over a decade later:

We know the old morality is obsolete, but we're unclear what the new one is. Sometimes a film like *Silsila* appears – which again is made by people who aren't very clear about this new morality. They try to be brave and then they withdraw. Two steps forward and three steps back. You see confusion.[46]

Nevertheless, *Silsila* has now become something of a film classic, and is much loved for its music and its performances, and, of course, because the so-called 'real life' triangle is still discussed 20 years later.

Silsila marked the beginning of the downward curve in Yash Chopra's career, which was to reach its nadir in the mid-1980s. There are no clear reasons for this but there are several factors which need to be considered. One was a change in film viewing as action and violent movies became more popular, perhaps due to a change in audience with the greater availability of the VCR. I return to this in the next chapter, but there were several points of closure for Yash after *Silsila*.

One was the split of Salim and Javed as writers, so Yash was no longer able to find such consistently good scripts. This was also a turning point in Amitabh's career – the well-documented accident on the sets of *Coolie* in 1982 and the brief entry into politics. Yash worked with Anil Kapoor and Rishi Kapoor over the next decade but it was not until he hired Shahrukh Khan in the 1990s (see Chapter 8) that he found another male star with whom he had such an instinctive working relationship.

One major loss which Yash suffered at this time was the death of Sahir. Sahir was a close friend of Yash's and was able to provide the lyrics Yash wanted in his films.

Yash is a great fan of Urdu poetry, which he recites by heart. The late Iqbal Masud, one of the few film critics who had a background in Urdu literature and pre- and post-Partition Indian Muslim culture explains:

> There were three key elements to the Urdu poetry in film lyrics: lost love, lost wealth and liquor. This was seen in Guru Dutt's films, where they were the only way of surviving. Hindi poetry is now substantial while Urdu is living on its past. Urdu poetry had a great influence on men of Yash Chopra's age group, who love the mystique of this poetry. It is only his age group that remains secular, although religion was important in the Punjab before the Partition.

Yash was a great fan of Sahir's even in his college days, carrying a copy of Sahir's collected poems, *Talkhayain/Bitterness*, around with him. When Yash

Sahir Ludhianvi

came to Bombay to see B.R. in his college vacations, when B.R. was making *Afsana*, the only person he wanted to meet from the industry was Sahir:

> When Chopra Sahib was making *Shole*, Sahir was ghost-writing, which he did for *Chandni Chowk*. We used to meet every day. I introduced him to B.R. for *Naya Daur*, after which he wrote all his films. He also died of a heart attack. He wrote for me as long as he lived. Before marriage we lived opposite each other, Sahir in Four Bungalows while we lived in Seven Bungalows. He called me 'Naujawan' or 'Virji'. Sahir was scared of flying and went by car or train, even to Delhi. His poetry was very romantic. I had the distinction of becoming his friend.

> I told Sahir a story, he would suggest situations for a song, or sometimes I would tell him the situation. He would then shut himself in his room, no air-conditioning, only a fan, and drink only water. Then he would start writing. He would write and then keep it in his pocket, but in his mind he would still try to improve. He wouldn't want anyone to request changes.

> Sahir came to Bombay after working as an editor. He had no job but he made money copying scripts and ghost-writing. He wrote for *Baazi/The wager* (Guru Dutt, 1951) and when S.D. Burman won the *Filmfare* award for the music, he complained about the lyrics being ignored and it was only after that they brought in an award for the lyricist. His *Pyaasa* was hugely popular, as was *Naya Daur*. He became very popular and had a great ego. He was not greedy for money, but he did have a great ego. He wanted artists to be respected. He insisted on having his name mentioned on the radio, on posters, and he would only work if the music director was paid less than him. That's why he didn't work with the most popular music directors. Nowadays often the music director gives a tune and the songwriter provides the lyrics. The previous way was that the writer knew the situation, he writes and then the music director composes. This is correct. His best poetry was for *KK*, the story of a poet. Really great poetic works. In *KK*, Sahir was very unhappy with Amitabh's character. He felt that a poet was always a poet and it was not possible that Amitabh could become a construction man. He felt that Guru Dutt in *Pyaasa* was closer to him, 'Yeh duniya/This world' and *Chakle/Brothels*. Sahir's forcefulness and bitterness and anguish.

He was very political and preferred to talk about politics than poetry. When Lumumba died in Africa,[47] he wrote '*Khoon pe khoon*/Blood on Blood' his poem in *Dharamputra* about mutiny.

He quarreled with many people, from Lataji to most music directors. He never married, but he lived with his mother and was very lonely after she died. He was always bitter about his father. When his father died he was called from Pakistan about this property but he didn't want it. He died of loneliness. I was in Kashmir, shooting for *Silsila* when we heard from Amitabh Bachchan's father that Sahir had died.

I still miss him today.

Five
The Lean Years

The early to mid-1980s saw an unsuccessful period at the box-office for Yash Chopra, and it seemed that after 25 years, his career was almost over. Following the failure of the romantic film *Silsila* (1981), Yash made two more action-oriented films which although they won critical acclaim fared only respectably at the box-office: *Mashaal/The Torch* (1984) and *Vijay* (1988), the latter often seen as a remake of *Trishul*. He also made the only film that has ever lost him money, the romantic *Faasle/Distances* (1985), unkindly dubbed *'Kabhi kabhie Part II'*. This chapter looks at these relatively unimportant films, examining the reasons for the dip in Yash's career in the context of 1980s' cinema and how he reacted to these setbacks, which would have driven many directors and producers out of business.

The 1980s were turbulent times in Indian society and in the film industry. The beginning of the decade saw the so-called restoration of Mrs Gandhi following her electoral defeat after the Emergency. The state faced one of its biggest crises, as the troubles in the Punjab resulted in the assassination of Mrs Gandhi and the ensuing massacre of thousands of Sikhs. Often forgotten, is the Indian involvement in Sri Lanka, which affected the army not only in terms of losses but also raised questions of Tamil identity and relations between Indian and Sri Lankan Tamils.[1] India also saw radical economic changes as Rajiv Gandhi introduced economic liberalisation, which led to the emergence of new consumerist classes,[2] and increasingly vociferous support for Hindu nationalism.

During this decade, the 'middle' cinema flourished,[3] and mainstream cinema was still making some hit films about social issues.[4] Sub-genres emerged: split heroes and heroines, in 'double roles', depicting a kind of cultural schizophrenia,[5] Muslim socials,[6] pure fantasy films, such as Shekhar Kapur's 1987 hit, *Mr India*, and several films where the heroine is a secret

snake-goddess, but the trend remained for violence in film. This was typified
by movies like *Qurbani/Sacrifice* (Feroz Khan, 1980), *Naseeb/Fate*
(Manmohan Desai, 1981), fast-paced, full of high spirits, brutal machismo,
bogus idealism, male bonding and comedy.[7] Later examples include
Tezaab/Acid (N. Chandra 1988), *Ram Lakhan* (Subhash Ghai, 1989), Tridev
(Rajiv Rai, 1989) and *Parinda/Bird* (Vidhu Vinod Chopra, 1989).

Despite the success of several films, Hindi cinema perceived itself to be in
crisis, as in 1985 there were estimated losses of Rs 1,200 million.[8] Of the 132
films made in Hindi in 1983 only 17 recovered their cost.[9] This was blamed
variously on the excess of black money that was flooding film production and
also on higher star salaries. The personnel was changing at many levels of the
industry. With Amitabh out of action after his accident and his move into politics, the biggest stars were Dharmendra and Rishi Kapoor along with the
dancing stars, Jeetendra and Mithun Chakraborty, while emerging stars
included Anil Kapoor and Sanjay Datt. Rekha and Hema Malini were still very
popular, with Sridevi becoming a major star. New directors established
themselves, notably Subhash Ghai, while Laxmikant-Pyarelal were still the
top music directors and Bappi Lahiri and Anu Malik were beginning to make
an impact. New playback singers, such as Kumar Sanu, Alka Yagnik and Kavita
Krishnamurthy were gaining in popularity.

Whatever the merits of the films, it seems that the most important threat
to the film industry was the rise of television and the VCR.[10] In 1980, Indian
television was controlled by the state network, Doordarshan, which reached
only 15.2% of the population. Colour television was introduced to India in
1982 in time for the Asiad Games which took place in Delhi. There was a
large (although proportionally small) market for colour television, whose
ownership shot up rapidly to five million by the early 1980s. By 1984, 50%
of the population had access to television, after a huge investment made
largely because Mrs Gandhi saw it as a political tool. Under Rajiv Gandhi,
the reach was extended to around 70% by 1986. This public service television ran for just a few hours a day, and gave little space to entertainment,
apart from a weekly screening of a Hindi film and a regional film, plus two
30-minute programmes of clips from films, *Chitrahar/Necklace of Pictures*
and *Chaya Geet/Shades of Songs*.

In the late 1980s television began to allow advertising. The advertisers, largely detergent companies, began to sponsor serials of which the most popular was Ramesh Sippy's (the director of *Sholay*) *Buniyaad/Foundations*. Film personnel began working in TV: scriptwriter Manohar Shyam Joshi wrote *Hum log/We People* and *Buniyaad*, while B.R. Chopra's *Mahabharata* had the highest audience reach of any television programme ever. Personnel from the middle and art cinemas directed for television, including Satyajit Ray, Mrinal Sen, Gulzar and Hrishikesh Mukherjee.

Video was an even greater rival. Ownership of VCRs soon reached around 1.5 million. Given the many viewers per television, this largely meant that the middle classes (including even some of the lower middle classes) stopped going to the cinema,[11] preferring to hire videos from the video libraries which sprang up on every corner, with the *videowala* visiting houses every day. (This period also saw the dreaded video bus becoming a staple of long distance travel.) Thus the cinemas were largely frequented by the urban poor (of course a large segment of the population) and cinemas fell into disrepair and disrepute. Other public screenings were offered by the video parlour or video teashop, a hall that could seat 30 to 100 people, where films were shown from 9 in the morning to 2 the next. These had different identities as the cafés could cater to local and specific demands, for different language films or different genres, including pornography.

The film industry was slow to realise the threat the video cassette posed. Unlike the west, where films are routinely released on video around six months after their cinema release, the Hindi film industry made no provision to sell video rights, with the main producers' association, IMPPA, disputing video rights, actually preventing people from selling them, such as Ramesh Sippy who tried to sell *Sagar/The Ocean* (1985). The video rights were sold overseas only, but video piracy became rampant as these tapes were brought back into India and sold alongside screen prints (made when a hidden camera films the movie during an actual screening) so the industry made no money at all from video and lost much of its theatre audience. Yash says that even at the time of the release of *Kaala patthar*, the problem of video piracy was becoming apparent and it became much worse during the 1980s.

The action films that were doing well at the box-office were not suited to the kind of cinema Yash Chopra preferred to make. He had not made a real action or violent movie although he had shot fight sequences in Amitabh's 'Angry Young Man' films, which were part of the Salim-Javed, Amitabh Bachchan corpus and mostly Gulshan Rai productions. Perhaps the popularity of action/violence in contemporary films was the major reason he faced a reversal of fortune in this decade, in that he tried to follow this trend. Or perhaps he lost his way after the limited success of *Silsila*, and failed to make films with conviction drawing on his particular talents. He tried his hand at two action-oriented films, *Mashaal* and *Vijay*, but even his attempt at a romantic movie, was not successful, *Faasle* being cinematically his worst movie to date. Yash admits he made the mistake of trying to please an imaginary audience rather than himself, but sees this time as a fatalistic down-turn in his career graph, shrugging it off with the Sanskrit proverb: *vinaashkaale vipariita-buddhi* ('In bad times, the intellect is contrary'):

> Film depends on state of mind. Not doing well. I believe in destiny, awkward time. Time is very important. Man remains same. All my qualities are the same. At that time I got desperate to make a commercially-successful film.

At the time *Filmfare* said:

> To Yash Chopra it seems this is why he can't sell his: 'soft romantic' variety, compelling him to resort to a film like *Vijay*, an 'action-oriented multi-starrer'.

> 'There was a time', elaborates Chopra, 'when social films were the mainstay of the industry, followed by musical-romance, action-thrillers and the Dara Singh brand of films which specialised in *dishoom-dishoom* [onomatopoeic term for fight sequence]. Today thanks to a change in the audience profile, the situation has been reversed. The 'in' film is the violent, action-thriller, which is only a sophisticated but more exploitative version of the old Dara Singh starrer, followed by the sex-oriented film.'[12]

Yash faced further problems during this decade with the loss of two of his closest associates, his lyricist, Sahir Ludhianvi,[13] and his cameraman, Kay Gee.[14] Yash has always preferred to work with people he knows well. This is most clearly demonstrated in his decision to work mostly with a major star and it is striking that after he no longer made films with Amitabh Bachchan, it was only when he worked with other major stars, notably Sridevi (*Chandni*, 1989; *Lamhe/Moments*, 1991) and Shahrukh Khan (*Darr/Fear*, 1993; *Dil to pagal hai/The Heart is Crazy*, 1997), that he made his most successful or critically-acclaimed films.

Mashaal (*The Torch*, 1984)

Mashaal was released on 9 February 1984. Yash had missed Salim-Javed's scripts, but had used Javed as a lyricist for some of the songs in *Silsila*. Here he gave Javed the opportunity to write the screenplay, dialogue and lyrics for the whole film. He took Lata's brother, Hridaynath Mangeshkar, as music

Mashaal songbook

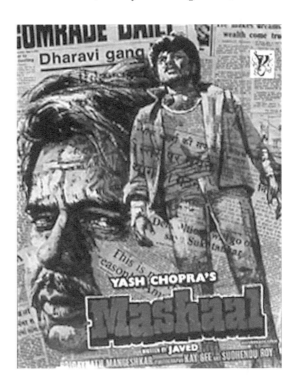

director. Yash still regrets that one of his favourite songs composed for the film 'Om namah Shivay/Hail to Lord Shiva' did not fit in, as there was little scope for music, but has included it on some anthologies of his film music.

Yash was keen to work with Dilip Kumar, whom he had yet to direct, although he had been an assistant when Dilip was starring in B.R. Chopra's Naya daur. He says that Dilip is like an older brother to him and they are still great friends. Yash had not worked with Waheeda since Trishul and this was one of several films in which he worked with her subsequently. Yash presented a host of newcomers, some of whom went on to be big stars such as Anil Kapoor, Amrish Puri and Gulshan Grover. He included other acclaimed actors such as Saeed Jaffrey and Mohan Agashe. He planned Kamalhasan for the role taken by Anil Kapoor. When Javed Akhtar was in Hyderabad he narrated the story[15] to Kamalhasan who was hesitant as he thought Dilip Kumar had a bigger role and he wanted an equal role. At this point Javed suggested Anil to Yash and they went on to work in several more films together.

This film is quite unlike all Yash's others in that it is about real life, about a journalist dismissed for trying to expose crime, and life in a slum. Robert Wise, director of The Sound of Music (1965), visited the sets when they were shooting the Holi song. He thrilled Yash by saying that he thought it was a very authentic set, as near to reality as could be.

Vinod Kumar (Dilip Kumar) is a newspaper journalist crusading against organised crime in Bombay. His newspaper editor is in the pay of S.K. Vardhan (Amrish Puri) so sacks Vinod when he writes an article exposing Vardhan. On losing his position, Vinod and his wife Sudha (Waheeda Rehman) are evicted from their house and forced to move to a slum. He sets up a new press with another journalist, Geeta (Rati Agnihotri). Vinod meets the leader of a gang, Raja (Anil Kapoor), who is won over by Vinod and Sudha's kindess, and encouraged by them goes to Bangalore to study to be a journalist, after falling in love with Geeta. Vinod's press is burnt to the ground then he is evicted by a court order. Sudha is ill and Vinod cannot get anyone to take her to hospital so she dies on the pavement. Vinod decides to beat Vardhan at his own game by taking to crime himself. Raja returns to write for a communist newspaper where he is reunited with Geeta. Shocked to find Vinod has become a criminal he continues to respect him but sets out

Raja (Anil Kapoor) finds new parents in Vinod (Dilip Kumar) and Sudha (Waheeda Rehman)

Raja (Anil Kapoor) sets out on a new adventure in Bombay

to expose his crime connections. Vinod saves Raja from Vardhan's gang and
in the end Raja and Geeta make a new beginning under the gaze of memorial photographs of Vinod and Sudha.

The film had good reviews,[16] but did not make much money, doing only
average business. The family theme is strong, with Raja the hoodlum being
tamed by parental love and guidance, and fulfilling the role of a son to the
childless couple. However, the romantic elements are limited, with the only
romantic song being shot on the railway tracks. The most striking difference between this and a typical 'Angry Young Man' film, is that Vinod is
clearly not young and only takes to crime in his middle age. Meanwhile the
young man has learnt to channel his anger to fight the system from within by
adopting communist beliefs.

Almost 20 years on, the film has become a landmark, in particular the
scene in which Vinod tries to flag down a car as his wife is dying. This has
helped the film to achieve something of a cult status. I think this film is one

Yash Chopra with Dilip Kumar and Waheeda Rehman

of Dilip Kumar's later fine performances as he is totally convincing as both Vinod the journalist and Vinod the gangster, while Anil Kapoor brings a new sense of the man on the street to the cinema.

Faasle (Distances, 1985)

Yash's next release was *Faasle* on 27 September 1985. The adverts ran: 'A simple love story simply told' and 'Love is music',[17] while a preview story went as follows:

> Let's discover love. Love means many things to many people. Love has been the language, the subject of any number of films down the years. Love in Hindi films and Yash Chopra are almost synonymous. Yash looks at young love this time, young love today. The film – 'Faasle'. Rohan Kapoor (son of Mahendra Kapoor) and Farah, two newcomers, give love a new meaning in the film. Yash has a galaxy of other stars – all of them in love.[18]

Yash says:

> *Faasle* was the first film I shot in Switzerland. It's now the area everyone goes to. I know that area more even than the locals. I tried to accommodate the dates in Switzerland then go to Kashmir with Sunil Dutt. I don't know how it came to my head to have these two dates. Sometimes one's foolishness ...
>
> Rekha was very correct for the role. Sunil Dutt's wife had died a long time back. I called her. She said, 'Whatever you think proper, you pay me.' She came for two days as a guest artiste. She said, 'Whenever you have a role, I am a good friend.' I even forgot to bill Rekha as a guest artiste, but she has forgiven me.

Faasle is the story of family and love across the generations. Vikram (Sunil Dutt), a widower, is having an affair with Maya (Rekha) but feels he cannot marry her. His son Sanjay (Farooque Sheikh) is an exuberant, flirtatious man who falls in love with his foster sister Sheetal (Deepti Naval). Chandni (Farah) and Vijay (Rohan Kapoor) fall in love and spend time horse-riding together. Without knowing about this romance, Vijay becomes friends with Sanjay and later with Maya. However, Vikram wants to buy a horse from Vijay but feels he is insulted when Vijay tells him that not everything is for

Chandni (Farah) as a typical Yash Chopra heroine

sale. Vikram forbids Chandni to see Vijay, and marries her off to the wealthy
Shivraj (Raj Kiran). Vijay hangs around Chandni's house in which she has
become a virtual prisoner, enduring beatings by her husband. When she
returns home for Sanjay and Sheetal's wedding, a fight ensues when Shivraj
tries to drag Chandni away. Maya, who has just moved into the house, pro-
tects Chandni, claiming she is her mother but Shivraj taunts her that she is
just a mistress. Chandni is made to return home, but Vikram realises his
mistake and when Shivraj threatens to shoot Vijay, her sister-in-law helps
her to escape. Chandni, Vijay and the whole family are reunited.

Yash says:

> The day it released it was a flop. I checked accounts, saw I still owed a lot of
> money to Rekha and Sunil Dutt. I said, 'I will pay you, but may not be able to
> now.' Today when I make film no-one asks. Both said, 'Don't give me, we're
> friends. If the film's not done well ...' I just needed some time. I paid every
> penny to them.

Faasle was a disaster. It was controversial and lost money. The problem
was I shouldn't have had the father-in-law going against the son-in-law, but
once I started getting it wrong, it kept going wrong. The young boy was a big
mistake.

The film clearly had many faults, the most glaring of which was the casting.
The young hero, and, to a lesser extent, the heroine, were not up to their
roles. Rohan Kapoor, son of singer Mahendra Kapoor, had no screen presence or conviction in the role. The romantic scenes between the couples
were staged like others – hillsides with trailing scarves, window panes with
rain pouring, a lengthy sequence of their (imagined) *suhaag raat* (wedding
night), extreme close-ups and so on – but the acting did not gel.

Rekha had a wonderful role, similar to that that the popular gossip
magazines attribute to her even today of 'Maya Memsahib', the mysterious,
wise, passionate beauty. Yet the film failed to explain why she was unable to
marry Sunil Dutt and had to continue their sexual relationship outside

Maya (Rekha) and Vikram (Sunil Dutt) romance

marriage. More seriously, Hindi film tradition would require Vikram to see Vijay's merits just before Chandni's marriage to Shivraj, but instead the film allows the relationship to continue after marriage, trying to justify her leaving her husband to return to her lover. The Hindi film never questions marriage, and as in traditional orthodox practice, a married woman can never remarry. Here the situation is exacerbated by the fact that Vijay and Chandni meet outside her house as soon as she married, her note saying she does not want to see him again being unconvincing. Nevertheless the film contains some good songs which are still remembered including '*Hum chup hain*/We are quiet' and '*Janam janam mere sanam*/From birth to birth, my beloved'.

Apart from beginning a succession of film shoots in Switzerland, this film also proved important for Yash in that he found the cameraman, Manmohan Singh who he was to continue to work with until the present day. Yash says:

> The cameraman is very important. He gives a visual translation of my concep-tion. Dharam, K.G. and Manji, they all did this.

When Yash left B.R. Films, he had hoped that his brother, Dharam, would work with him but Dharam stayed with B.R., so Yash hired Kay Gee, Dharam's assistant instead. Kay Gee stayed with Yash until he died during the making of *Mashaal*, which his assistants completed (Kay Gee's son, Raju made *Yeh Dillagi/This Attachment* (Naresh Malhotra, 1994) for Yash Raj films):

> He was a revolutionary cameraman. He never needed so many lights. Everything was wonderful and he'd do anything. He left other films to work with me. He was not interested in money. He was a nice person. He had many friends, he was a gem of a person.

> When Kay Gee died, I had seen *Souten* [*Co-wife*, Sawan Kumar, 1981] and *Betaab* [*Untamed*, Rahul Rawail, 1983] [filmed by Manmohan Singh] and I liked them. Manji was an assistant to Radhu Karmakar, Raj Kapoor's camera-man on *Satyam, Shivam, Sunderam* [*Truth, Auspiciousness, Beauty*, 1978]. I wanted a cameraman, so I approached him and I liked him. He said some

good things about Kay Gee and we agreed to work together. In the quality of his work, as a person, he is a poet, a cameraman, a saint. I have never seen him shout, be angry, lose his cool. He's a freelancer, but his first preference is for me.

I explain to him all the scenes, discuss and sit down. We decide. As the set progresses we visit and discuss. He is ready. Trolley or crane, the first shot of the first day takes time, then he's very quick. He does lighting. Whatever you want. I may look at a shot or two but I have so much confidence in him, I may look only to assure myself not to check his work. I don't have to tell him anything. We have a good rapport.

Manmohan Singh took a diploma in cinematography from the Poona Film Institute in 1975:

I am a big fan of Freddie Young, all his films and his works. He's one with great visuals, big camera, realistic subject, but never loses glamour (*Lawrence of*

Yash Chopra and Manmohan Singh on location for *Chandni*

Arabia [D. Lean, 1962], *Dr Zhivago* [D. Lean, 1965]). In India, I like Fali Mistry, Jai Mistry, and V.K. Murthy's black and white.

I was an assistant to Radhu Karmakar. I was a fan of R.K.'s style, the showman. I had worked on Punjabi films, worked with Rahul Rawail on Sunny Deol's first film, *Betaab*, and worked on another film, *Souten*, at the same time. Mangesh Desai was mixing these at Rajkamal Studios, where he was also mixing Yashji's film. Kay Gee died. Some people in the industry didn't think Kay Gee was such a great cameraman, that he didn't operate the camera himself and he kept experimenting. His shots were often careless, badly-composed, not balanced, especially for panning and trolley. I liked *Silsila* very much. Before that, I didn't like Kay Gee's frames, his jerky movements. But I say that we can't compare work now to work then. It's not of the calibre we're doing today.

Faasle was very disappointing. It was a bad script which he knew when he was making it. The film was made in two schedules, Switzerland and Kashmir and he couldn't resurrect it. He says it's his own mistake.

He has great charm, but he's a great task-master, a very demanding director, no nonsense. Great visuals, nature and romance. Others stick to formulas, but he makes films ahead of his time. Very bold. Yashji constantly innovates, changes, adapts. He makes films because he has something to say.

The team is very touchy. He doesn't like anyone on set he doesn't know. Just click. He gives a hint and it's done. He never looks. He plans shots, gives a breakdown. He's thoroughly prepared, then he gives full liberty. I have so much confidence in him. He's very cautious when he's working.

Yashji edits while shooting, takes very few extra shots and is absolutely clear that this is the subject. It has to be very visually-stylised or it will be boring. Has to be slick, fast-paced with short scenes. It shouldn't look normal, it mustn't lose glamour. He does not like normal lighting, but plays with lights. It is through lighting and the frame he achieves glamour. Yashji lives, eats and breathes films. No-one else in the industry has survived so long because they lose interest.

Vijay (1988)

Yash decided to make a 'commercial calculation' after his last films had fared poorly at the box-office, opting for a film with story, action, dances and a multi-star cast. His trailer promised, 'A violent story of powerful emotions', but he says, 'It was not a film from my heart.'

The casting kept changing. Yash thought of Sanjeev Kumar then Dilip Kumar for the role eventually taken by Anupam Kher. For Sonam's role he had wanted Madhuri Dixit but she was unable to give him the dates he wanted, while he had intended Jaya Prada to play Meenaskhi's role but her price was too high. Yash said that Sonam's role was simply to look beautiful. Yash wanted Naseeruddin Shah to play the role of Ajit but took Rajesh Khanna with whom he had had a misunderstanding after *Daag*.

Yash planned to shoot outdoors in Hyderabad and Switzerland:

> All the bags were lost on the flight to Switzerland apart from Meenakshi's. She was the only one who wore Indian clothes so we could manage with the rest, buying them there. Hyderabad was good as we managed to shoot in the Krishna Oberoi before it was open to the public. However, we could not stay there and at the last moment I had to ask my friends to help accommodate the stars and the crew. Another time Sonam almost drowned and my son had to save her.

Lala Yodhraj (Anupam Kher), a wealthy businessman has two children, Suman (Hema Malini) and Shashi (Raj Babbar). Suman marries Ajit (Rajesh Khanna), with whom she has a son, Vicky (Rishi Kapoor). Lala refuses Shashi permission to marry his girlfriend, Rita, even when she is pregnant. Lala leaves her with a blank cheque, her son Arjun (Anil Kapoor) being brought up by Gujral (Saeed Jaffrey) as his own son after Shashi is killed in an air crash. Meanwhile Lala makes Suman managing director of the company leading to Ajit leaving her as he feels she is more Lala's daughter than his wife. Vicky and Arjun and their girlfriends Nisha (Sonam) and Sapna (Meenakshi Sheshadri) become close friends although they later quarrel. Friends of Vicky are out to kill Arjun who has come into conflict with Lala over a plot of land which Lala wants but on which Arjun has vowed to build a hotel. Lala destroys Gujral who commits suicide, and a campaign to smear Lala's electoral campaign with the slogan 'Who killed Gujral?' is successful. Ajit, Suman and Vicky are reunited;

Arjun meets his dying mother obtaining the blank cheque with which he bankrupts Lala. Lala finds Arjun is his grandson but meanwhile his henchmen have set out to plant a bomb in Arjun's new hotel. Vicky and Arjun defuse the bomb and the family is reunited.

This picture did very good opening business and covered its costs with some profits but after four weeks had no staying power.

Vijay was a hit for four weeks, it was not a drowning man's effort. It didn't lose: it brought the chicken home.

But *Vijay* didn't have glamour, I missed something. Perhaps I was experimenting, perhaps too realistic after *Faasle*. *Vijay* had romance, visuals and good songs, but it needed a good script. After Salim-Javed I was looking for someone with whom I could work properly. The film was made in two schedules, in Switzerland and Kashmir. We couldn't resurrect it.

The grandfather, Lal Yodhraj (Anupam Kher), and his grandsons, Arjun (Anil Kapoor) and Vicky (Rishi Kapoor)

Sonam's bikini was a mistake, while Meenakshi's Indian clothes were fine. I was confused. Found Sonam by accident. Her aunt, Sabina is a dress designer and she's a niece of Raza Muraad. She was sixteen when she joined, she signed 57 films before release, married an eligible bachelor, Rajiv Rai (Gulshan Rai's son). When we went to Switzerland, we lost the costumes apart from Meenakshi's, so some wore their own clothes, others bought some there. If the costumes are bad, it's my fault. I can visualise Indian but I'm not so good with western clothes. But the girls are not really part of this story. It's really Anil-Anupam-Chintu-Rajesh, and the girls are decoration.

Anil Kapoor comments:

He made *Vijay* after he'd just given the audience one of the biggest disappointments of his career. I'd established myself quite a bit. The film was a complete disaster. He narrated the script. My first reaction was not very positive. I felt he was trying again so I said, 'Yashji it looks like a rehash of an old film'. He's a very nice person, he said, 'I'll work on the script again.' It was not of his standard. The films he had made from the heart were not clicking. He made *Vijay* which was average. Not a flop, not a hit, not one of his good films. During the making of *Vijay*, he launched *Chandni*. He asked me to do this too, in Rishi Kapoor's role and I turned it down. Felt too weak, too women-oriented at this stage of my career – didn't want to sit in a wheelchair. I worked with him again in *Lamhe*.

Rishi:

At this time Yash Chopra was at rock bottom. He was never comfortable, it was not his style, nor his way of thinking. I worked in the film *Vijay*, which is best forgotten.

The film has many overt references to the battle of Kurukshetra, the location for the telling of the *Bhagavad Gita* within the *Mahabharata*, in which two families of cousins engage in deadly warfare. These are seen in the title song that is repeated later in the film. Nevertheless, the similarities are fairly loose. Arjun, to whom Krishna told the *Gita*, is the name of the role of the wronged cousin, who seems to have closer parallels to the character Karan, the wrongly excluded brother of the Pandavas. In the film the family is reconciled rather than almost wiped out as in the *Mahabharata*.

Although Yash thinks the story was the film's main failure, I think the story has great melodramatic potential, much of which it exploits, while the real problem is the film's lack of romance. All three couples were given little space, with Suman (Hema Malini) being the only female character with any, although little, depth. The other two girls Nisha (Sonam) and Sapna (Meenakshi) were there only for decoration, notably in Sonam's skimpy, spangled red bikini with waist chain.

There are a couple of appearances to amuse those in the know: the speech at the college function which opens the film is read by the cameraman, Manmohan Singh, whereas Yash himself hijacks the role of cameraman to take the family photograph at the end.

While only *Faasle* was an outright flop, the average business of the other two films meant that Yash had not had a major hit since *Trishul*. How did he deal with failure?

> When there's a failure, I feel bad. I make a film from the heart, it doesn't run, I feel bad. Time is a great healer. I collect my things and start again. To feel bad, to weep is human emotion. I am not alone.

> There are two reasons to be upset when your film doesn't do well. One is that we have failed in our judgment of the audience; the other is that we worry about what we should do next. If we're wrong now, will our next decision be right? The field is very narrow.

Shashi Kapoor says:

> When his films were not doing well in the 1980s we met at an airport. He was going on a shoot. He's very stubborn, he doesn't accept failure nor does he take major success seriously.

Yash did not admit defeat, and was already planning a new film, *Chandni*. The late 1980s, however saw a reversal in the fortune of romance, as the romantic film returned to top the box-office with *Qayamat se qayamat tak/From Apocalypse to Apocalypse* (Mansoor Khan, 1988). This revival was helped in part by a revolution in the music industry caused by the enormous popularity and availability of the audio cassette.[19] Gulshan Kumar and his T-series Super cassettes broke the monopoly HMV had on the music industry and for the first time music began to make a significant contribution to a film's financial success. Yash stuck with HMV, but he too began to make more money from his music. With this change in mood, Yash was set to return to the genre he loved best with a romantic film, replete with gloss, high-production values and hit music – *Chandni*.

Six
Romantic Films

1988 marked a turning point in the history of Hindi films, as the release of Masoor Khan's *Qayamat se qayamat tak (QSQT)* began the revival of the romantic musical film which had been under such pressure from the violent movies of the 1980s. Perhaps this division is overstated, since the romance had always been popular, but the focus certainly shifted from the male urban underdog struggling against society to the stories of romance that had been popular in the 1960s and early 1970s, exemplified by narratives of poor girl–rich boy, love triangles and so on. Far more important was the rise of the theme of love as friendship, in which the boy and the girl become friends, falling in love only as their friendship deepens. Although this relationship was seen in Raj Kapoor's *Bobby* (1973), it became widespread only in the late 1980s, as films saw friendship replacing the theme of love as passion, an aesthetic found in the formerly dominant Urdu love lyric (*ghazal*). The couple were no longer elite or feudal, nor innocent rustics, but urban college kids, where the sexes mixed freely and as equals. Reconciliation of the lovers to their families remained an important theme, but now the young couple won the family over by persuading the parents that they were truly observing family values, which, paradoxically their parents may have somehow forgotten.

These new narratives required new stars. As the industrial hero, typified by Amitabh Bachchan, had supplanted the earlier elite heroes, so he was replaced by a new generation of leading male actors, the so-called Khan brothers (who are not related). The first to emerge were Aamir Khan (*QSQT*) and Salman Khan (*Maine pyar kiya* [*MPK*]/ *I Have Fallen in Love* [Sooraj Barjatya, 1989]), followed in 1993 by Shahrukh Khan, an established television actor. They were not only younger than the existing heroes, such as Anil Kapoor (who moved away from hero roles only in the late 1990s), but were

baby-faced and clean-shaven, more in tune with the norms of a middle or
upper middle-class look, with their toned bodies and light skins. Heroines
largely remained secondary to the heroes, although there were some big
stars in the new generation: while Sridevi was an established star, new faces
included the classically beautiful Madhuri Dixit, who dominated the box-
office in the 1990s, and the vivacious Juhi Chawla; with the innocent
Bhagyashree and the young and tragic Divya Bharati having shorter careers.
The return of the romance introduced many other new people into the
industry, from new music directors, the most successful of whom were
Nadeem-Shravan, to dance directors such as Farah Khan.

Chandni [1989]

The huge box-office success of *Chandni* in 1989 marked an upturn in Yash's
fortunes. At the age of 56, he was clearly much older than the new generation of directors, despite his much-touted youthfulness of spirit, but his
resurgence was perhaps also influenced by the contribution of his new
assistant, his teenage son, Aditya, whose 1995 film *Dilwale dulhaniya le
jayenge* (see Chapter 10) was to become a landmark in Indian film history.
Yash's return to form was overdue, given that many features of the new
romantic films were also part of his established repertoire, such as melodic
music, an elite context, the feeling for the contemporary – manifested in
attitudes, behaviour and the film's 'look' – yet they were handled in a different, more subtle form in Yash's romantic style which he had established
a decade earlier.

Yet when Yash decided to make *Chandni*, he felt it was something of a
'suicide attempt' as he had tired of action films:

> We began with a different treatment of the same film, more like an art film. We
> had a *muhurrat* in November with Sridevi, Vinod Khanna and Chintu [Rishi
> Kapoor]. It was a romantic shot, with fantastic, beautiful people. In the first
> version, Sridevi marries Chintu, has a son. In the second half of January we went
> to Delhi. We started a two-day shoot. When mixing I thought it was wrong and
> decided to change. The next morning I sat day and night changing the script to the
> interval. Sridevi said she had full faith in me. Chintu asked me to tell him the

scenes. Vinod was an action-oriented hero, so there was to be a scene where he
saves Sridevi from a fire. I cut it and rang up Sridevi and said I was going to
repicturise it. The distributors were worried. How can you have Vinod Khanna
and no action? One distributor even left the picture because I was taking Vinod
Khanna in a non-action role. I wanted him because he was a mature person and
would suit Sridevi. I gave them discount so the terms were in my favour. I wanted a
romantic film with beautiful music. I was sick of violence.

Chandni changed considerably as the production unfolded. Yash liked Raj
Kapoor's 1982 hit, *Prem rog*, and hired its writer, Kamna Chandra, for
Chandni. Vikram Chandra recounts how his mother first got into screen-
writing:

Chandni poster

My mother wrote for All India Radio way back when, and then for Delhi
Doordarshan in the old black-and-white days. Mostly plays. She used to act
too, in radio and television. She wrote some fiction as well. We shifted to
Bombay in the late seventies, and she had a story that she was working on which
she insisted could only be done by Raj Kapoor. So she just called his studio and
spoke to his secretary and got an appointment. Went off the next week, and the
short story conference turned into a long one. She's a great storyteller. Raj
Kapoor called her shortly after and told her he wanted to make the film. They
had someone else work up the screenplay, and this writer was supposed to
direct it. But after a few days of shooting, R.K. took over, and the film became
much bigger. This was *Prem rog*.[1]

Kamna Chandra says:

We had just returned from Hong Kong, where we had been living. *Prem rog* had
already released. I suppose they had seen it. I got a call from Pam Chopra,
asking if I had any stories. So I went for a meeting with Yash Chopra, and I
narrated a story, a love story. And he said, 'Yes, start writing this today.' So I
wrote quite a long treatment, a prose novella really, maybe a bit more than fifty
pages. Then he got in two screenwriters – I can't remember their names – and
they wrote the screenplay, and somebody else did the dialogue. They deviated
quite a bit in the second half from my story; I thought a lot of these changes
were quite *filmi* [belonging to the film world, tinselly]. I told them so, but then
they were out to make a commercial film. And the people liked the film, and
Yashji had a hit on his hands after a long time.[2]

Chandni (Sridevi) meets Rohit (Rishi Kapoor) at a wedding in Delhi and
they fall in love instantly. They romance during her stay in Delhi and corre-
spond after her return to Uttar Pradesh. Rohit's family disapproves of
Chandni as she is not from a wealthy background but Rohit is adamant he
loves her, covering his wall with her photographs. While Rohit showers
roses from a helicopter onto Chandni's roof terrace, he falls from the helicopter and is paralysed. Although Chandni is keen to continue her relationship with him as before, he tells her he no longer loves her and his family
abuses her.

Chandni stays with friends in Bombay where she works as a secretary to Lalit (Vinod Khanna). Lalit lives alone with his mother (Waheeda Rehman) since his partner (Juhi Chawla) died. With his mother's encouragement Lalit proposes marriage to Chandni before going on a business trip to Switzerland.

Rohit has been cured in a a Swiss sanatorium and meets Lalit. He tells him that he is going to try to marry his former lover. Lalit tells him about his life; they do not realise they are talking about the same woman. Although Rohit tells Chandni he wants to marry her, she agrees to marry Lalit. At their

Chandni (Sridevi) performs a fantasy dance

wedding, Rohit arrives drunk and falls down the stairs. Lalit realises that Chandni loves Rohit and he helps them to get married.

The film première was at Metro cinema, September 1989, one of Bombay's premier theatres, where the film ran for 15 weeks, until Yash had to give it over for the release of *Maine pyar kiya*. The film was a huge success.

Chandni was unusual for its time in that it was heroine-centred. Yash feels that this was helped by taking a big female star. When he first thought of the film, he had originally planned to cast Rekha but took Sridevi instead:

> I like working with Sridevi. She says, 'You do what you want.' We gave her a totally new look, jewellery, hairdo and costume. Bhanu Athaiya, who won an Oscar [for *Gandhi*], did all the dresses for the first schedule in Delhi but we had ego clashes and took Leena Daru. We had a lot of white, very simple clothes. We designed her saris and colours, middle-class *salwars* and *churidars* which changed when she was working but she could wear different clothes in the dream sequences, such as modern dresses.
>
> She's a damn good actress. She puts something extra in her work. I could notice this the first day I started working with her in *Chandni*. She comes a step further. Never knew what she was doing. She didn't know language, assistants told her dialogues. But she contributes so much to each dance, scene, emotion. All have something extra.

Manmohan Singh confirms:

> For *Chandni* we knew from the title and the idea of a beautiful girl that we wanted to give the effect of a moonlit night and her beauty. It's much easier with a good actress like Sridevi.

Sridevi was proud to be cast by Yash and of her role in the film:

> I liked the role of Chandni. It was a different role, where any other girl, very ordinary girl can identify with that character, she can imagine herself as a Chandni, a very simple and very down-to-earth character. I liked it, because always I played larger than life, snakes this and that. This was the first film where I played a very simple girl. It was Mr Yash Chopra's idea to give me light colours, pastels, very simple, I used to feel as if I wasn't shooting. People

started calling them Chandni dresses, even today, people call me Chandni.
They really see me in that character. It's very difficult to get that kind of
popularity. Credit goes to Yashji for portraying that kind of a character.

Rishi Kapoor says that he was worried about it being a heroine-centred film
but he liked the story:

During *Vijay*, he offered me a role in *Chandni*. While shooting in Bangalore I
asked him, 'Chandni wears white, she is shimmering moonlight. Very poetic,
but what's the story?' He said, 'It's Chandni.' 'What am I in there? Am I a star,
am I the darkness? There has to be a story.' Then he gave me a line about a guy
who jilts her then changes his mind. If you incorporate a film I've seen, *Whose
life is it anyway?* [J. Badham, 1981], which had Richard Dreyfuss in it, the
character like that, paralysed for life, in love with the girl, the girl with him, he
feels why should I spoil her life because I'm going to be an invalid. She should
have a life of her own. So he starts making the girl hate him. Supreme sacrifice.
Humiliates her and she walks out. Mission accomplished. Meet later.

Vinod Khanna and Waheeda Rehman on set with Yash Chopra and Manmohan Singh

The narrative of *Chandni* was typical of a Yash Raj Films' love triangle (or quadrangle), in which A loves B loves C and so on. This plot device is common to many of Yash's films, since although subject to various variations and permutations, it expounds the idea that love is not always reciprocated and that human relationships have foundations other than those of romantic or sexual love. For example, the parents' wish that their child should marry a person of their choice may prevent lovers marrying, but they may find love with their new spouses (*Kabhi kabhie*). A brother preserves his family's honour by marrying his brother's pregnant girlfriend when his brother dies, and eventually gives up his former lover and later his mistress for his wife (*Silsila*). The plot of the love triangle in *Chandni*, while following this well-known device, contains unexpected twists. Chandni loves Rohit all along but is very fond of Lalit and his mother and agrees to marry him out of a sense of duty.

The film has many typical features of a Yash Chopra romance. It is once again set among the super-rich, some of whom are shown to be obsessed with status, regarding financial gain as the major purpose of marriage (Rohit's family), while others are comfortable with their situation (Lalit's family). Although it seems that Lalit was not married to his former lover, the domestic space is the arena in which romantic love occurs, with love contained, prevented, and encouraged by the family. *Chandni* has similar depictions of intimacy and private space as his other films, with voyeurism to the fore, not only in the heroine's depiction (see below), but also in shots through glass roofs, often through rain, into bedrooms and other private spaces.

The film also has two very different heroes, one the romantic, the other the silent, supportive type, while the heroine is an independent working woman, another familiar Chopra element. Switzerland once again represents healing (a high-tech cure combined with a miracle) and the location for romantic songs as well as a fantasy holiday destination (the theme of travel is reinforced by Lalit's travel agency). There are wedding songs, a rain song as well as other romantic songs, all of which were very popular, but the portrayal of Chandni makes this film special.

Chandni is an ideal woman, seen through the eyes of her two lovers. Rohit photographs her from the moment they meet, and decorates his room with these pictures, which he whitewashes when he claims the relationship is over. He remembers her through her bangles, also a reference to the song she sings when they first meet: 'Mere haathon mein nau nau churiyaan hain/I have many bangles on my wrists'. Lalit has a screen at work on which he watches her (similar to one Yash has in his office for monitoring his reception area). Many scenes show still images, or fragmented sequences of her as she is imagined by the men; similarly, Lalit's former partner is also shown only through his imagination. Chandni is unable to return the man's look, but remains its object to an almost obsessive degree. Yash tends to keep the same names for his heroines, with Chandni being the name given to his heroines in *Silsila* and *Faasle*. In this film, she is shown as a figure of idealised beauty, dressed in white outfits, occasionally in yellow, in a style which created a whole new fashion craze across India – 'Chandni-look'.

Lamhe (Moments, 1991)

Lamhe was a controversial film largely because of its supposed incest theme. It is one of Yash's favourites, and has found many fans. Yash says:

> I had the idea of *Lamhe* for seven or eight years. Once I'd made a successful film, I thought that I should make the film I wanted to make. People kept telling me the end was wrong, but I felt that if I changed that and both of them died there was no point. People liked the film very much. Even the distributors, who didn't say to end the film early.

Anil Kapoor says:

> I was in a phase in my career when I was trying to run against time, doing many films. Everything was going right for me. Whatever I did, I felt now, it's time I forget I'm a star and concentrate on acting. Something different, something which will be remembered for many years. The script and the role were very exciting. Showed feelings. I loved the script and my role. Commercially, I wasn't very sure. My brother told me that and a few friends, but I'd made up my mind. Really enjoyed that. Had to finish. Shaved off moustache, cut hair short. Second shoot in Rajasthan, you have a star persona – it was as if I destroyed it, changing the look. Persona remains the same, they don't change, but I was on that trip.

Yash has enjoyed working with Waheeda:

> Waheeda is the most hassle-free actress ever. We had gone to London for
> shooting *Lamhe*. Sridevi's father died, so she had to go back to India. Waheeda
> said, 'I'll go to stay with a friend of mine in London. When she comes, I'll
> come.' She knew those scenes were indoors. We had 18 days waiting. She made
> no complaints, no hassles.

Yash was glad to have Sridevi in his film again:

> Once the film started in July in Nunsmere, I took the place here Nunsmere Hall,
> near Cheshire, I did 37 days shooting there. During that period only I think we
> didn't enjoy any pressures so it was wonderful we enjoyed day, night shooting,
> staying there, going around. We've never seen such a happy Sridevi ever. As God
> would have it, when her father died she had to come back to India. I didn't tell her
> that her father was dead. Her mother told me not to tell her. Tell her he's very
> serious, all this journey she'll be upset. But I think she smelled, she had some
> fear. I say, 'Sridevi, I am waiting for you here. I can't match this thing anywhere.
> Don't worry about the money because it's all in the game. But I'll be waiting.' Anil
> Kapoor and everyone waited, we didn't want to go anywhere. She came back after
> 16/17 days for shooting. And the next schedule, I shot in Rajasthan, then when we
> came back I shot indoors, one or two sets. I made the whole film in two schedules.
> I was very happy, I was very thrilled, I was excited.

Viren, aka Kunwarji Birendra Singh (Anil Kapoor) comes to Rajasthan for
the first time aged 18 in order to sign some papers. His foster-mother, Daija
(Waheeda Rehman), begins his introduction to the land and its customs,
which is continued by Pallavi (Sridevi), through music and a visit to the
desert where she makes him wear traditional clothes. Daija realises that he
has fallen in love with Pallavi even though she is older than him, while
Pallavi is oblivious to his feelings, shocking Viren when he finds she is in
love with Siddharth Bhatnagar (Deepak Malhotra). Although encouraged by
his friend Prem (Anupam Kher) to reveal his love to Pallavi, he helps to
arrange her marriage to Siddharth, and returns to London.

Siddharth is killed outright in a car crash, while Pallavi dies soon after,
giving birth to Pooja who is raised by Daija. Viren comes to Rajasthan

annually for Pallavi's memorial ceremony (*shraddh*), leaving a present for Pooja's birthday which falls on the same day, but he never meets the child. He decides to marry his girlfriend Anita Malhotra (Dippy Sagoo), but is thrown into confusion when he meets Pooja (again, Sridevi) for the first time when she is 18, an exact replica of her mother.

Daija and Pooja join Viren and Prem in London. Prem and Pooja become great friends, and he soon realises she is in love with Viren. Anita tries to confront Pooja who declares her love for Viren to her and then to him. Viren rejects her so Pooja decides to return to India, but when she is about to leave she finds his drawings of her mother, which she takes to be of herself. She confronts him with these and he tells her of his love for her mother. Pooja and Daija return to Rajasthan.

Pooja agrees to accept an arranged marriage only if Viren gets married first. After receiving his wedding invitation, she decides to break her side of the bargain. Daija is unwilling to leave her alone, so Viren and Prem come

Romantic moments between Pooja (Sridevi) and Viren (Anil Kapoor)

to Rajasthan. Viren and Pooja revealing they have both broken their word to get married. They declare their love for each other.

The film did not do well at the box-office in India, although it did well overseas. Yash says:

> It was a much anticipated picture, but didn't do well. It's strange *Lamhe*, I still don't know. This road on which we're going,[3] it's called Aurobindo Road, I'm telling you, on this side it's Bombay called West, this called Bombay East. The picture did very well on the West side, not on the East side. I said same city, same people, same sensibilities, same exposure of the people towards the world. It did very well, it did very, very good overseas, I think outstanding business overseas, the audience is only Indian, there not different audiences, here it did very well at the Metro, but not on this side of the city. Doing very well in Bangalore, doing well in Delhi, but not in Uttar Pradesh.

Many people regard it as one of their favourite Hindi films. Sridevi confirms, saying 'Every family, they say they have got the cassette of *Lamhe*, but it was too westernised for the Indian audience.'

Yash says:

> I don't make films for the magazines or the critics, for the reviews. I believe if I release a film and my distributor's happy, my audience is happy, I'm happy. I'm not making a picture for one person or what that person is going to write. There are reasons people write against people so, but, still I think, when you start a subject like *Silsila* or *Lamhe*, what went wrong? Somebody should tell you there's something wrong, understand what went wrong. I still don't know what went wrong. It was a very entertaining film, *matlab* [I mean], forgetting what the subject matter or anything, it was an entertaining film, very good music, very good dances, very good comedy, so I don't know what went wrong. People say it's not done. I say what's not done? It's not his daughter that he's marrying. But anyhow, it does everything. These ups and downs make your life. *Lamhe* [is my favourite.] The maker has likes or favourites which don't do well. Which films don't do well, the director or the maker is more fond of them. My case not that. I'm not fond of *Faasle*, I'm not fond of *Joshila*, I'm not fond of *Parampara*. They've not done well. I'm really very fond of *Silsila* and *Lamhe*. I say these

three films I feel in every way, mentally I know what was wrong with me while making those films. I've no excuse for those films. I know I've made a bad film. And I'm not really fond of these films. Emotionally I was upset when making *Joshila*. That was the first film in my life I was doing for outside. I was trying to please a distributor and the producer who was financing me. I was a producer for *Daag*, his [Gulshan Rai's] film had become very big hit, *Johny mera naam*. I say maybe that's what makes him happy, I put everything that's called 'box-office' in the film, that's where I went wrong. I mean to say, *Lamhe* or *Silsila*, I don't equate those, I'm very, very fond of these two films. Every film doesn't do well, you're not fond of it. Certain films, you are fond of. So, it happens in life. Now I have a company, you should go on trying to make films, you should make good films, because, the result is not in your hands, is not in your hands at all. Is in somebody else's hand, is called God Almighty. But you should always try to make a good film, because when people will say this is a good film, it is obviously a good film. They do different things, a good film and a successful film. I try my level best to make good, nice, decent aesthetic films.

I made a very good film in *Lamhe*, I'm very happy about that film, and people tell me that because of the controversy, it didn't do well. And then the controversy, because Sridevi was the daughter of Anil Kapoor. I think in my own way I tried to tell the film in one or two very obvious scenes between Anupam Kher and Anil Kapoor: She's not your daughter, you didn't have the guts even to say the name of your beloved, who's dead. She's the daughter of Pallavi and Siddharth. She's in love with you. I tried my level best. Even after that how can people think she's his daughter? He's performing the ceremony. It's not performed by husband, no relation, she has no relation in the world. The very fact that Waheeda is bringing up the daughter in his house, she's his daughter. I don't agree. Of course people did tell me that this is a risky thing. So what's the use of making this film if both die or one dies or they don't meet and go different ways? I think, I may be wrong, people will turn around and say I am wrong but I definitely feel that I thought of my subject I wanted to make. It doesn't dishearten me so that I won't make any more controversial films. Every film is a controversy. In our country only 5% of films are successful, only 5%, and some bad films, some meaningless films also don't run. At least every film is a different film, controversial, basically a film is controversial because we depend on millions of people and their taste. Would they like it or not? We do our best. I was very, very upset, very hurt and depressed, after the release of *Lamhe*, because I had seen that film with the audience in Delhi and I felt that up to a certain point, it was doing brilliantly as people were carried away with emotions but the last 500 feet they didn't accept it. I thought how can the last five minutes make the whole difference to a film which is more than three hours long? I was really upset. When I get upset I can't function properly.

Dilip Kumar was admitted to hospital around the time of *Lamhe*'s release. It was critically-acclaimed, but it didn't do well. I went to see Dilip Kumar. He couldn't talk much so I sat on his bed. He said, 'We are known by our films, not by our success.' He gave me a lecture of encouragement. These things you remember.

The film has a great number of fans. Many people, from stars to fans, told me that this is their favourite Yash Chopra film, as they love the comedy, the

Pallavi (Sridevi) performs a Rajasthani dance

dialogues, the songs, the performances and so on. Although not a personal favourite of mine, it is a landmark film for Yash and for Hindi cinema.

In *Lamhe*, women represent the NRI's[4] links with India, in particular his nostalgia for beautiful women. India belongs to the women he has lost, his mother, and his first love, Pallavi. These figures find substitutes in the film in his foster-mother, Daija, and Pallavi's daughter and double, Pooja. Daija is the archetypal maternal figure of Hindi movies: kind, gentle, selfless, nourishing. She is a nostalgic figure to the diasporic audience, almost a representative of India itself. Since she is played by Waheeda Rehman, a screen idol of the 1950s and 1960s, she provides further nostalgic connotations for the older diaspora, who remember her from their youth. The lively Pallavi represents a certain ethnic mode of the 'Indian woman', which her daughter Pooja has inherited, despite her western gloss, through her knowledge of folksongs and folktales. This is typified at the moment Pooja thinks Viren is in love with her, when she promptly changes from her western fashions to an elaborate form of Indian clothing, and sings a song, '*meri bindiya/My bindi*', celebrating traditional decoration (*solah singar*, the 16 ornaments) and clothing. This, along with the use of the double, provides the audience with a reassurance that however much a woman may change on the surface, she is still the same, the guardian of traditions and family values. At the end of the film, Viren ultimately has to return to Rajasthan, to Pooja, the ideal 'modern yet traditional Indian woman'.

Lamhe showed that the Hindi movie had already created its own globalised market, among the Indian overseas (diasporic) or NRI audience. This was one of the first of a number of 'diasporic' films which subsequently became very popular. The pleasures for this community[5] of this romantic film lie in its depiction of the diasporic male, which provides a ground for character engagement[6] for the diasporic audience, and a nostalgic view of his relationship with 'home' not found in British culture.

The diasporic male has been a stock character in Indian movies from the earliest days, such as *Bilat pherat/The England Returned* (N.C. Laharry, 1921), right to the present. The character has usually returned from abroad and their overseas visit is seen as more of a humorous device than a social marker. For example, the publicity for *Bilat pherat*, declares it is about 'a young Indian [who] returns to his native land after a long absence and is so mightily impressed with his foreign training, that, at his parental home, he startles everybody with his quixotic notions of love and matrimony' (*Bombay Chronicle*, 20 August 1921).[7]

When shooting overseas became popular after Raj Kapoor's *Sangam/Union* (1964), it was often justified in the plot through the device of a holiday or a medical visit, although not necessarily referred to at all within the film. Usually it is an excuse to show spectacular scenery in tourist destinations or rich and exotic consumer lifestyles, in the perennial favourites, London and Switzerland. Yash Chopra has been a key figure in this trend: his first overseas locations were for *Silsila*, 1981, where he went to the tulip fields of Holland. Switzerland subsequently became his hallmark, after he first shot there for *Faasle*, 1985, replacing his earlier locations, which were often popular Indian tourist resorts like Kashmir, Nainital and Simla. Once others followed this trend, Yash sought new locations (eventually choosing Baden Baden in Germany for *Dil to pagal hai*), while making his indoor sets ever more international or even transnational. The film-makers argue they also include foreign locations for commercial reasons, namely that the audiences enjoy seeing exotic locations, they get more value for money from their stars who are less able to cancel shoots, and who regard the travel, on which they usually bring an entourage, as something of a perk. Yet overseas locations also perform a wide range of functions and meanings within the text, including the visual pleasure of spectacular, exotic locations or ideas of places suitable for romance, mainly parks and gardens. They also suggest that the moment of love is not bound by the chronotopes of the mundane, the place of everyday life, the moment of leisure, but can move effortlessly in time and place.[8] The songs also often involve numerous costume changes by the heroine, thus reinforcing the possibility of an excessive consumerist lifestyle, already invoked by the travel, an emblem of the cosmopolitan Indian.

There have, however, been far fewer films set genuinely in the diaspora. One of the few early examples is *An Evening in Paris* (Shakti Samanta, 1967), where the entire film is shot overseas, the characters being Indians who live in Paris, speaking Hindi while pretending to be Europeans. The 1990s have

Prem (Anupam Kher) and Pooja (Sridevi) try to amuse Viren (Anil Kapoor)

seen a huge explosion in this trend, after the success of two major diasporic
films, *Dilwale dulhanya le jayenge* (Aditya Chopra, produced by Yash Chopra,
1995) and subsequently *Pardes/Overseas* (Subhash Ghai, 1997).[9] The former,
one of India's all time box-office hits, concerned Punjabis settled in London,
travelling in Europe and returning to the Punjab; the latter featured people
from Uttar Pradesh, living in the US. *Lamhe* may have started the trend for
this recent wave of diaspora films to include the depiction of the NRI hero,
whose values remain Indian in spite of his foreign gloss, and who is uncor-
rupted by the temptations of the west.

   Viren, who has been brought up in the UK, does not live like an
Englishman,[10] but like a rich Indian in the UK and so may serve as an aspirational model of the successful NRI businessman in terms of his lifestyle, in
particular in the international 'five-star' look of his homes.[11] To a western
audience, or perhaps to a specifically English one, this house has resonances
of the English upper-class country house, a true class marker, yet Viren does

not use this space in the way that the English aristocracy or upper middle class would: there are no country activities, antique furniture or country clothes in evidence, but instead televisions, fully-equipped kitchens, luxury cars, city clothes and plastic garden furniture. The 'family' eschews long country walks, but goes for outings, mostly to London, to classless public spaces, such as Whiteley's shopping mall, London Airport, Trafalgar Square and Regent's Park, although the heroine's imagined romantic song sequence is set in the Lake District. The English countryside is meaningless for these characters, who even indulge in such non-English country activities as grape-pressing and lighting log fires in the open. Prem, Pooja and Daija are untouched by the UK, which for them is a place of consumerist lifestyles, mostly shopping, and theme parks. The physical surroundings may change as they all move easily around the world, but they see no need to change lifestyle, food, clothing and so on, for they can live their five-star hotel lifestyle anywhere in the world, the major difference being that the west is a place where they can indulge in infinite consumption.[12] These seem to be aspirational views of the wealthy section of the British Asian community, which is forming its own separate transnational class.

Although Viren's lifestyle and mannerisms are not recognisable as English to the English, the film makes fun of this over-Anglicised NRI. He has taken on some of the old-fashioned concepts of English ethnicity which are still recognised in India, such as introversion, self-restraint, formality and a dislike of gaudy clothes, a contrast to Blairite attempts to create an image of Cool Britannia. This gentle mocking of the westernised Indian is one which some British Asians like to project about themselves, which is supported in the film, where there are no negative images of westernisation, although opportunities for this abound in the text. For example, Anita could have been a vamp, contrasted with the 'Indian' women, but instead only a slight coldness is suggested. This may be a utopian rendering of a non-racist Britain, but also reflects the view of the elite British Asians who argue that their wealth, social status and independent business enterprises have largely protected them from at least overt racism.

The choice of Rajasthan as the home of this 'family' is initially surprising. This is one of the few films Yash Chopra has made which is located

outside of a north Indian world, focused on Delhi and the Punjab not necessarily in terms of locations, which may be global, but in terms of the characters who are usually upper-caste Punjabis. He could easily have used these
familiar areas as the place of origin for his diasporic hero, since most of the
UK's Asian population is from localised areas of the Punjab, Gujarat and
Bangladesh; the only Rajasthanis settled in the UK are the Marwari business
community, who are not referred to in this film at all.

It seems that Rajasthan has been chosen as the premier tourist destination of India. Yash Chopra shows specifically tourist images of Rajasthan, its
exotica including the palaces, the camel ride, the folksong, all of which have
been used to market the area overseas in a depiction of its five-star hotel
culture alongside a happy folk culture. This would have probably appealed
most to the Euro-American audience, whereas *Indian Summer* (English
dubbed version of *Lamhe*) has cut many of the images of Rajasthan in *Lamhe*,
which also appeal to the diasporic audience, who enjoy seeing the 'heritage'
depiction of India as a change from the hackneyed images shown in the
west, with their twin themes of poverty and exotica.

Viren has a complicated relationship to Rajasthan and to India.
Although very wealthy, he does not want to visit Rajasthan, even to see his
foster-mother, unless he has to go for specific duties. When asked to
worship the ground, he is more concerned about the heat as he steps out of
his air-conditioned Rolls-Royce. This relationship to the earth is
contrasted to that of the women, such as in the sequences where he and
Pallavi listen to the folksong about Rajasthan (*Mhare Rajasthan ma/My
Rajasthan*). Her close relationship with the earth is finally signified by the
scattering of her ashes on the sand.

On the surface, Viren's relationship to India is one of cultural nostalgia,
typified in his only form of relaxation, that of watching old Hindi movies.
This creates a position of empathy, for this is a practice common among the
South Asian diaspora who regard watching Hindi movies as an important
part of their culture. The first South Asian migrants, Indian and Pakistani,
to the UK watched Hindi films at weekends in their local cinemas,[13] then on
videos and DVDs at home, now supplemented by the return to cinema-
going and the arrival of Indian satellite and cable television channels. They

encouraged their children to watch these movies to learn about India and Indian culture, and now the younger generations of British Asians have become Hindi movie fans. Most of the British Asians' domestic languages are not Hindi or Urdu,[14] so watching movies is the main way in which they acquire at least a passive knowledge of the national language of their family's country of origin. Even if this generation is more comfortable in English, they often enjoy the Hindi of the movies, as this language of emotion and intimacy evokes a certain nostalgia. They are particularly fond of film songs, and those in *Lamhe* are particularly evocative of such emotions, such as the lullaby, the *bhajan* (Hindu devotional song), and the love songs, which mention the rainy season as the ideal time for romance. This use of language, in particular the language of love, is an important component of British Asian identity. It seems that this audience for the Hindi movies already exists and, although the bulk of its movie-viewing may be Hollywood, the cultural, linguistic and emotional referents of the Hindi movie guarantee their popularity.

While the major audience for the Hindi movie outside of India is the Indian diaspora, it is also consumed by the Pakistani and Bangladeshi diaspora and by many other audiences throughout the world. Although Hindi cinema is most often discussed as a national cinema, it is clear that it is also a transnational or even postnational product.[15] The collective viewing, criticism and pleasure of the Hindi cinema provides the diaspora with a group identity, a transnational 'community of sentiment',[16] rather than a national 'imagined community'.[17] This study of the diasporic popularity of the Hindi movie supports Arjun Appadurai's argument that globalisation is often a vernacular or local process which does not necessarily imply Americanisation.[18] Thus Hindi cinema is important for the younger generation as a linguistic and emotional resource. (For more on the diaspora and Hindi movies, see Chapter 9.)

Parampara (Tradition, 1992)

During a hiatus in the making of *Lamhe*, Yash signed as director for *Parampara* for another production team, this time the Nadiadwalas. Yash explains:

Parampara did not do well. It was not a good film also. Nadiadwala is a friend of mine, he must have said, let's do a film. That period I was working on my own script maybe *Darr*. It does take time to make a script, about six to seven months. So, the previous times when I made a film, sometimes I'm very impulsive. Because of the problems, because Sridevi's father died and Mr Boney Kapoor's handling her dates, after August I finished shooting in London, next dates I got in February. I was feeling irritated. What's the use of sitting here idle? I'm sitting idle because somebody doesn't have the dates. My time is also money. I'm not working because if I don't have dates I can't shoot, and he gave me dates in February. I went to Rajasthan to complete the film. In that state of irritation, you'll finish in six months.

Although Thakur Bhavani Singh (Sunil Dutt), a landlord, killed Raja Bahadur, leader of the gypsies, in a duel over disputed land, their sons, Prithvi (Vinod Khanna) and Gora Shankar (Anupam Kher) become friends. Prithvi falls in love with Shankar's sister, Tara (Ramaiya), but his father makes him marry Rageshwari (Ashwini Bhave). When Thakur Bhavani Singh learns that Tara is about to give birth to Prithvi's child, he attacks the gypsy camp and kills Tara but Rageshwari saves the child, Ranbir, whom she raises with her son, Pratap. Prithvi is killed in a duel with Shankar, who then reclaims Ranbir. Grown up, Ranbir (Aamir Khan) and Pratap (Saif Ali Khan) become friends, and date Vijaya (Raveena Tandon) and Sapna (Neelam) in a foursome, but they eventually decide to sort out the dispute between their families with another duel. Thakur Bhavani Singh is killed as he tries to stop the fight and pleads to the boys to end the dispute. The family is reunited.

The film was released in 1992 and flopped immediately. Yash explains:

I think these kind of things don't work these days. The whole atmosphere of *thakor* [landlord] and *banjaras* [gypsies] and this and that. Today's audience feels this is an old film, old-fashioned film, not old film. This whole thing didn't work, only we were lucky in this respect, I shouldn't say this, that when this picture was to be released, there was some problem in Bombay, the bomb blasts and all that, after all these political problems. I had fixed up the shooting of *Darr* abroad so I couldn't attend the release of the film. I was not in India, and when I was there it was released so I didn't face the music. I came back after three weeks and at that time the story was written off. I was feeling very bad about this film but the producer didn't lose money. He was a good producer, he paid me everything, but he was to pay to me what was our understanding but he lost money, not because it didn't do well but because he kept a lot of territories himself to be distributed. Sometimes some pictures do make a bad start, but for that film we had taken Anil Kapoor instead of Vinod Khanna, so I think we had to do some juggling of script age-wise. The moment Anil Kapoor went out of the picture, the whole thing became unbalanced. The whole romance at the centre of the film went bad, I feel. And he went out of the film what only three/four days before we went first outdoor shooting to Jaipur. At that time either we had to cancel the whole outdoor shoot or take somebody else. I think the start was not good but in short the film was not good at all.

A very close associate of Yash's says:

Lamhe had been released 22 November 1991 and flopped immediately. In the first week of December the song recording began, then they went off on the shoot. He was very depressed about Lamhe. He had made a good film and was proud of it. He wanted to give up this film, but couldn't back out. He was not involved with the music and there is no passion in it. He really didn't believe in it. It only ran a week. He took good money for it as he was taking risks himself. The film made no profit.

Although the plot of the film is clichéd, the movie loses sight of the characters as it focuses on parampara or 'tradition'. Thakor Bhavani Singh personifies this tradition, inflexible in the face of the demands his family makes on him. Rageshwari personifies virtue, as she accepts instantly the gypsy woman as the elder co-wife and Ranbir as her husband's older son, rather than being seen to struggle to come to terms with his other romance. Prithvi dies halfway through the film after his romantic scenes with Tara and his masculine activities with Shankar while the two young heroes appear only in the latter half of the film. The young romances are very sketchy, the girls having merely an ornamental function. The contrast between the college kids and the older generation makes it hard to believe they exist in the same film. Some of the music is very good, but many of the songs were filmed in the early 1990s' style that Yash Chopra himself hates but must have decided to shoot as a commercial decision, where the romantic couple(s) find themselves amidst troupes of colour coordinated dancers for their most romantic moments.

Darr (Fear, 1993)

A big box-office success, *Darr*, contrasts mutual love with one-sided, obsessive passion. It is one of several hit films in Hindi cinema in the early 1990s which had the central character played by an anti-hero (a so-called 'negative role'). Shahrukh Khan played this role in two other films: *Baazigar/The*

Darr songbook

Gambler (Abbas-Mastan, 1993), where he kills his girlfriend as part of his revenge on her family, and *Anjaam/The conclusion* (Rahul Rawail, 1994). *Darr* established Shahrukh Khan as a major Yash Raj hero, as he acted in all his films subsequent to it. As Yash says:

Shahrukh is very good. He can act with no words. He wants to do action films, but the immortal actors are those who do emotional roles. Action is physical aspect, emotion is what counts.

Darr underwent many changes before it was even begun. Yash says:

Darr was to be made by my assistant Naresh Malhotra. He was not successful in getting stars. Rishi Kapoor told me, 'Make this film, it's a very good subject. I'll be in it if you make it.'

Rishi Kapoor recalls:

He came to me for Shahrukh's role in *Darr*. I said, 'Yashji, do you think I can create terror? I am a romanticist, I have a romantic image, I have a film behind me. I played a negative role which did not do well. It bombed at the box-office. Do you think I can do justice to the role?' He said, 'You're a good actor, you'll carry it off.' I said, 'Carry it off is one thing, but image is a very important thing for a film.' He said, 'Do the other role.' I said, 'There's nothing to do in the other role. After working with you in *Chandni*, do you want me to do a subordinate role again? If you give me a good role, it need not be a big role, but there must be some meat in it.' He probably understood I was not very comfortable and thereafter we never met.

Yash then signed Sunny Deol and Aamir Khan. Aamir agreed to do the negative role but then withdrew from the film so Yash cast Shahrukh. Casting the heroine also proved difficult as Yash explains:

The girl has to be so sensuous to him that he becomes obsessed with her. It's not as if it needs a star. I first took Raveena, then she had problems with the dates. I wanted a girl who was decorative. I wanted Madhuri but she wouldn't give dates for a year so I signed Juhi, who had a small role in *Chandni* then had acted in our production, *Aaina/The Mirror* [Deepak Sarin, 1993]. I told her, 'If you have any reservations tell me now.' She did it very well.

As well as being a big hit, *Darr*'s music did very well. Rahul (Shahrukh Khan), son of an admiral, is in love with Kiran (Juhi Chawla), who is engaged to one of his father's officers, Sunil (Sunny Deol). Rahul's room is decorated with photographs of Kiran and he talks about her on the telephone to his mother. However, we know that Rahul's mother is dead and this is one sign of his madness, along with his refusal to acknowledge that Kiran wants to marry Sunil. Kiran does not know it is Rahul who is the stalker who telephones the house she lives in with her brother (Anupam Kher) and his wife (Tanvi Azmi). In the end, she becomes so disturbed that Sunil takes her on holiday to Switzerland. They meet Rahul there and socialise with him. Rahul stabs Sunil severely in a fight, then takes Kiran to a boat on which he has the paraphernalia for their marriage. She rejects him but just when he is about to force her into the wedding, Sunil reappears to save her.

Shahrukh was delighted with his experience of working with Yash:

> Yashji gives me a lot of passion. He doesn't tell me how to do a scene. He's never told me, he's never told any actor. He's an eccentric and instinctive filmmaker. He's eccentric, 100%. I have worked with him and just one shot, he came and he said, 'You're a good actor.' This was for the shot at the train station in *Dilwale* when Kajol asks me, 'Will you come for my wedding?' He's very nice to me, but this is only time he said this. When I remember, it would be that one, the other one on the boat in *Darr*. If I had to pick out two shots from my career, it would be these.

Rahul's obsessive nature and deranged state of mind is made clear in the sequences of looks in the film. Rahul decorates his bedroom with pictures of Kiran, as he imagines that she reciprocates his feelings. Again he fantasises sequences of romance with her, in which his magic casts a spell on her. Rahul is able to escape Kiran's look, but the camera suggests it is he who sees her removing her wet clothes after a storm. In the song sequence which follows ('*Jaadoo teri nazar*/Your look is bewitching'), she runs around the college looking for her lover, and it is only later we realise that it is not her lover but her stalker who is serenading her. Rahul is also able to enter the private space of the family unobserved, whether in disguise as a musician at Holi or

Rahul (Shahrukh Khan) fantasises about dancing in Switzerland with Kiran (Juhi Chawla)

as himself, in Switzerland, where the couple are unaware that Rahul is the stalker.[19]

These instances show the film's dangerous attractions. The performance by Shahrukh Khan was so disturbing because, although he is a psychotic stalker, the audience sides with him at the time of his confrontation with the hero. Yash says:

> There is no vamp or villain. The villain is your weakness. Love may be the weakness and the villain. The hero is one who does something right. *Darr* has no villain. [Rahul is a] positive character, he's a man who is obsessed with a girl. He doesn't rape, he doesn't kill. His only crime is that he loved someone who doesn't belong to him. The villain harms people, morally or emotionally. He, poor fellow, died. Every sympathy was with him.

Rahul in many ways comes across as the star of the film. It is rumoured that Sunny Deol was furious when he saw the film and realised that this was the case. There is no doubt that the audience preferred the deranged obsession of Rahul to the alternative masculinity offered by Sunil. It is also hard to draw the line between the pursuit of women depicted in many other Hindi films from that in *Darr*, although the anonymous phone calls and the phone calls to the dead mother are much more disturbing than almost anything seen in older films.

   Darr was the last picture that Yash released on video at the time of release. All subsequent Yash Raj films were on 'video hold-back', that is the video came out some time after the theatre release of the film. This practice was begun in India in 1994 by Sooraj Barjatya for his film *Hum aapke hain kaun...!/What Am I to You?*, which broke all box-office records and saw a return of the middle classes to the cinema hall. At the same time the threat of VHS film piracy was largely supplanted by that of cable television, which expanded rapidly with the advent of satellite television into India from 1991, allowing unscrupulous local cable operators to obtain pirated prints that they screen illegally. While television may have created new audiences for its soaps, quiz shows and so on, it has also transformed the marketing of films. Teasers, trailers and songs from films are screened on the new channels in the weeks before a film's release alongside a 'documentary' called *The making of...*, about how a film was produced. The cable and satellite channels also offer many other programmes, the content of which is film-based, such as (film) music chart shows, star interviews as well as the screening of classic old films which show stars in their early careers, many of which attract young audiences who missed them the first time around. It was thought that television would draw the audiences away from the cinema halls but hit films still can sell out theatres for several weeks, although the days of the 'B' movie may be numbered. Yash Chopra was quick to respond to these new threats and possibilities as we shall see below.

Dil to pagal hai (*The Heart is Crazy*, 1997)

Yash Raj Films was transformed by Aditya Chopra's directorial debut, *Dilwale dulhaniya le jayenge* (*DDLJ*, 1995), one of the highest-grossing Hindi films of all time. Although Yash Raj Films financed this film itself, its returns enabled the company to expand further throughout the 1990s. (For more on the film see Chapter 7.)

After the success of *DDLJ*, Yash decided to direct another film himself, one that underwent several changes of story, cast and personnel. Yash says:

> We were going to call it 'Maine mohabbat kar li' ['I fell in love'], but *Dil to pagal hai* is more of a young title. This film went through about five or six versions, the only consistency being that 'someone, somewhere is made for you'. Some thought it was too serious. Finally Adi gave a narration. The unit liked it, they thought it was young, of today and happening but there wasn't a story. I thought it just needed outstanding music. Adi said that he would never make this film but I wanted to do it. My stories were *Daag, Kabhi kabhie, Silsila, Lamhe*, but Adi feels words and dialogues, he knows how people speak.
>
> Script is seen as being all important. The film has to be good. If your product is good it's going to work. The artists are not necessarily key. Here they take a mechanical attitude. Waste time, energy, effort. They are often stars, not actors. When we write a script, we fix on two or three characters. We needed dances in *Dil to pagal hai* to convey chemistry, passion. We needed good actresses so had a very limited choice. Many of them are beautiful, but I'm not so sure about talented.
>
> I want people involved in their work. The actor must be involved. Has to grasp my conception, can't be mentally somewhere else. Should do like Hollywood, one film at a time, not so many. This is a problem here.
>
> I wanted Madhuri from the beginning, but for the other role we tried Urmila at first, taking Karisma later.

Shahrukh says of his role:

> I'm not a lover, I hate love stories, I always complain, 'Yashji, I used to fight, kill women, throw them off buildings and you've made me a lover. I hate you for that. Completely a lover. Look I want to work with you to make *Deewaar*.' Yashji's fantastic, he will be remembered for love stories. He thinks I'm wasting my time on action films.

The film was held up when Yash fell seriously ill in late August 1996. He was in hospital for over a week, his stroke leaving him unable even to sign a cheque, so he decided to bring in the sons as equal partners in the company with himself and Pamela:

> I was in the Hinduja hospital for eight days. I couldn't sleep so Adi brought me a TV and films. While I was ill, all my hate was washed away. I may not want to meet people, but I have nothing against them. I take some medicine now. I am scared that this could happen again, so every day I should do everything.

Soon after his recovery, on 19 November 1996, he started work on the film.

Yash took a gamble on a new music director, Uttam Singh, a violinist, trained in western and Indian music. He had arranged music for Sooraj Barjatya's *Maine pyar kiya* and *Hum aapke hain kaun...!* and composed background music for several films. He brought a hundred tunes to the Chopra family, who, as is their custom, sit together to hear the music directors' offerings, out of which they took seven or eight. Several playback singers sang the songs including Lata Mangeshkar and Asha Bhosle who have been working with Yash for nearly 50 years:

> Lataji – Didi – sang in songs way back but I was very much in awe of her. I came closer to her when I became a producer. Over the last 15 years, she has been very kind to me. If I request anything from her, she won't say no. She loves music. Music is good for everyone and not controversial. She sang before independence, she has sung in so many languages. She has a gift from God. No-one else has achieved what she has. I'm very lucky to know her and to work with her. No-one can sing as well as her, with such sweetness and purity.

Yash was keen to modernise his unique visual aesthetic. Instantly recognisable, his cinematic style has been frequently imitated, notably through duplication of his trademark shots of misty valleys, snow-capped mountains, lakes and rivers, women in chiffon, and fields of flowers. This is what Yash calls 'glamorous realism', in which he depicts the dilemmas of the super-rich in extreme emotional situations, often featuring love and sex outside marriage.

> The audience enjoys identifying with the hero: she's our girlfriend, we can be here, roaming around – the illusion of reality is the success of the movie. The

ads are a different psychology. People want to own all these things, need quick money, fall into crime, corrupting poor people. Suggestive ads.

Yash hired Sharmishta Roy, who had worked as an assistant to her father Sudhendu Roy, on many of Yash's films and had designed the sets for *DDLJ*:

> We introduced Sharmishta here, the daughter of our art director. We gave her a chance in *Aaina* and she did a brilliant job. She's talented, hard-working and costly, she doesn't know how to save money.

> I take charge of money. I don't want to waste money. If I make films I have no right to luxuries.

Yash also hired the designer Manish Malhotra, who was famous for his makeovers of actresses, notably Karisma Kapoor in *Raja Hindustani/King of India* (Dharmesh Darshan, 1996), for the women's costumes. Manish says:

> Yash Chopra is very exciting to work with. He wants something new: no saris. New colours, *ghaghras* [traditional skirts] in plain chiffons. I provided Madhuri with 50 costumes in *DTPH*, with a budget of up to Rs 25,000 per costume.

Yash himself is interested in costumes although he does not design them:

> I give girls a very north Indian style of dressing, making a special effort to make them look beautiful. Most film clothes are bad and now the term *filmi* is derogatory. I like them to wear clothes that a girl can wear normally. They can look bloody fools with all that make-up and jewellery. They don't need elaborate jewellery and hairstyles, but dresses. I've not evolved a style. I choose north Indian style and I hate jewellery. It may not be totally real, but I don't want to show ugly things.

> In different films, we've used clothing in many ways. In *Admi aur insaan*, Mumtaz wore western clothes while Saira wore saris. In *Dhool ka phool*, we were using contemporary fashion. In *Waqt* the clothes were more westernised.

> We copy fashions from English magazines or the designers go to London to look at fabric, design and cut. Previously only bad girls wore western clothes, now they all can. It's part of our life. What's the harm in western clothes? We have to show what's happening.

We also have to think about the girls' figures. Some have bad legs, some shouldn't show their midriffs and even the best designer can't change that. We used to like big girls, now it's changed and everyone's very figure-conscious. The fashion for faces has changed too, so have hairdos and makeup. If we give an Indian hairdo, they'll say the girl looks 'verny' (vernacular), so we can't do that. Some of the girls may not look beautiful in private life but look good on screen.

Many of our dress designers and hairdressers are unqualified and need training. We have a real problem with professionalism.

However, this is a male-oriented industry and the men are more important. The heroes of today need something that appeals to the audience, but I like to make a women-oriented film, not one which is about men and action. Women are more emotional, more delicate and more beautiful. Men should be dressed in a more manly way. Amitabh wore very good clothes, so does Shahrukh. He lets Karan (Johar) choose some because they have to be in keeping with his character as a theatre director.

Micky Contracter, the top make-up artist in Bombay, was hired to work on the look:

Simplicity and natural beauty is Yash Chopra's style. He underplays. Plain chiffons, open hair, minimal jewellery, very upper-class.

Manmohan Singh elaborates on Yash's working style:

He narrates his subject, which he likes to be very visually stylised or he thinks it will become boring. This has to be slick, fast-paced with short scenes. It shouldn't look normal and mustn't lose glamour. We haven't lit it normally, we've been playing with lights because of the theatre background which allows us to take liberties. As usual, we use the lighting and the frame for glamour.

Shot division is planned there and then. Yashji is not communicative, which can be difficult for the actors, so he prefers to work with people he knows. Shahrukh works well. Yashji is very impatient, wants to get on. Knows instinctively when to move or when to steady the camera.

Yash Chopra with Karisma Kapoor and Shahrukh Khan

Goes for overall feel. Yashji is very classical – he has an eye for modern things, but never MTV, no flashy cuts. His is old-fashioned film-making but his tastes are modern. He shoots simply, in a style that is modern and beautiful.

Yash hired Farah Khan as dance director (choreographer) for several songs, but also Shiamak Davar, great nephew of Homi Wadia and 'Fearless' Nadia, who were key figures in the Indian film industry in the 1930s. Shiamak performs in musicals, stage shows, adfilms and the national games and is famous for his summer dance schools in Bombay. Gauri Khan, Shahrukh's wife, is a student of his and had recommended him to the Chopras. Aditya wanted him to work on *DDLJ* but Shiamak was not sure he wanted to work in films. However, he has since contributed to other films after *DTPH*, as he very much enjoyed that experience. He contrasts Yash and Aditya:

I find Adi more practical, Yash Uncle is romantic, goes with his feeling. Adi, it's technique and feeling. They are both professionals.

Yash was very tense before the movie was released. When I interviewed him on 3 May 1997, he said:

Now they all expect a *DDLJ* miracle. How can it go near that? It wasn't a hit, it was a blockbuster. I'm sure this won't be as good as *Dilwale*. I know the lines they'll write. I know I'm not going to make a bad film, but it won't be as good as *Dilwale*. This is a simple, pure, romantic film. I've made a very hip, very young film, which a teenager should make. It is a picture with complete emotions. Only the songs, the embellishments, are left. I'm very scared; only God can help me.

Lolo [Karisma] has role, one of the best in her life. She is very emotional. She is a dancer in the film, but there's more to it than that: there's depth, meat. The role you don't get every day.

There are just moments. Karisma and Shahrukh could be friends for ever. If Akshay Kumar hadn't heard the tape, then Shahrukh would have gone out of Madhuri's life. Karisma knows she should be happy but admits she is jealous. In the climax, Shahrukh is in the wings watching, he says *DTPH*. He brings head to the shoulder, not stopping but there are tears in Karisma's eyes. These make ordinary moments great. In the first half, the characters are established, then when the heart is full, we make the dramatic scenes.

The film's music broke the record of all previous releases and when it was about to release, on 31 October 1997, it was sold out for the first week. Despite negative reviews, the film was a great hit, albeit not on the scale of *DDLJ*. I quote my own review:[20]

The rightly named 'teaser' showed only the three stars and told us the film would be 'A Yash Chopra musical'. The name 'musical' was intriguing. Hindi films are often dismissed contemptuously as being 'formulaic' and lacking in generic specificities. This is simply untrue, there being a range of genres from the mythological to the Muslim social, but there is no musical genre, since music is a key component of all Hindi films; indeed the removal of the music is often regarded as a way of making a film 'international'. The musical is largely associated with the Hollywood musical, which in its classic form was a backstage drama where a love story unfolded as the actors were involved in staging a musical show. This allows the music to be incorporated in a realistic way, as staged performances within the movie, and to be staged in a spectacular way with dances, elaborate costumes and sets. This is true of *Dil to pagal hai*, which concerns a group of stage performers, but it also has a number of songs shown in the usual Hindi movie way as expressing inner thoughts, tying the emotions of the singers together even if they have never met (notably *Pyaar kar!*/Fall in love!), and for dream sequences (*Dholna*, a term that baffled all but the Punjabis; it means 'sweetheart').

Uttam Singh's music had outstanding sales before the movie's release and the tantalising clips used for the songs that were released for TV led to record advance bookings. But the film critics hated it (with the sole exception of Maithili Rao in *Screen*) and audience reports were mixed. Where were the features one expected of a Hindi movie? Where was the plot? Who were these people and where were their families? Had Manhattan come to Bombay, with its loft-living, designer clothes and jazz dancing? Where were the Yash Chopra hallmarks of romance, drama, love songs and a saturation of beauty? Had *dostana* ('friendship') become an episode of *Friends*? I too was baffled, even though I'd seen much of the filming. Had Yash Chopra gone too far in challenging his audience? The industry thought its top banner had made a mistake and muttered, *Yash Chopra to pagal hai* ('Yash Chopra is crazy').

I attended the London preview but something made me want to see it again quickly. The opening sequences were fast, setting the film's dilemma – love is predestined: someone, somewhere is made for you – then cutting quickly to happy couples (including Yash and Pam Chopra), then straight into Karisma's big number *Le gai/Took away*, where she revels in her role as the 'top performer'. The narrative was there, but it was so seamless and smooth, not the story of the play itself, but the story that the Indian guy may live like a westerner, love his buddies, both male and female, but will fall in love with a traditional Indian girl and the traditional Indian girl must reconcile her family duties with her own desires. You could just sit back and enjoy the glamour, the froth, the romantic intensity, the jokes, the strong performances from all the actors and, of course, the songs and dances.

Shahrukh was not criticised by the audience, but, although he gave a great performance, it was not his film. As Yash Chopra's alter ego, he is in charge, but mostly from a distance. Karisma's performance was acclaimed, but her costumes were thought too skimpy. They were cool, they were appropriate and we looked at her from the audience, closing in only on her face. Madhuri was said to be old and not as slim as usual, but she looked like a woman, not a girl; her acting and dancing was excellent. Some said it wasn't Indian. I thought it was Indian to the core: it's over 40 years since Raj Kapoor told us it's not what you wear, but your heart that makes you Indian. The *dil* of this film was certainly Hindustani.

This film, which fans may not love as much as some of Yash Chopra's other films, will be seen in future as a landmark film, with its depictions of love, friendship, its whole look, its music and its rapid editing. After almost 50 years in the industry, Yash Chopra has set the pace for a younger generation of film-makers who have to run to keep up with him. The industry's wags were almost right: *Yash Chopra ka dil to pagal hai* ('Yash Chopra's heart is crazy').

The new cinema audiences

A major component of this new audience for films and film music was formed by the new middle classes, who emerged with economic liberalisation in the early 1990s.[21] They enjoyed different patterns of leisure, consumption and spending power, and were soon targeted by astute film producers, usually quick to seize on indicators of social change. They were among the audiences who returned to the cinema when the VHS rental market was killed in the 1990s by cable and satellite Asian TV channels and the practice of video hold-back. There was also a return to cinema in the west at this time, so other considerations, such as technical advances, modernised cinemas and so on may also have been instrumental in the revitalisation of cinema-going.

The rich metropolitan audience in India now pays up to Rs 100 for a cinema ticket, thus making the lower-class cinema halls, which charge much less, of little interest to producers such as Yash Raj Films. The elite producers also want their expensive productions to be shown in the up-market cinema halls which do justice to the Dolby digital soundtrack, and which are associated with a more affluent and aspirant audience (referred to as 'classes' rather than 'masses').

Although the family audience remains the major target for the producers, the 1990s saw the college crowd, a new, young audience flocking to the cinema halls. Hindi film became cool, even among the most Anglophile students at the elite colleges. They were mainly attracted by the music, which was no longer regarded as 'naff' but as hip, and enjoyed alongside western popular music. Gradually the films became fashionable among the middle classes and the elite. The other attraction was the rise of new stars who became the pin-ups and heroes of the younger generation. Among the male stars, Shahrukh Khan was particularly popular in the 1990s, being perceived as cool and sporty, while the female stars began to approach the status of models in the west. The top star at the end of the 1990s was Aishwarya Rai, the former Miss World. The clothing and lifestyles of the film stars also became increasingly admired, counting as a major attraction in film-viewing.[22]

The diasporic audience

During the 1960s and 1970s, Hindi films were screened in the UK in cinema halls, mostly on Sunday mornings and other off-peak times.[23] This ended in the 1980s, largely due to the advent of the VCR. This market in turn was killed in the 1990s by cable and satellite Asian TV channels such as Zee TV. However, with the practice of video hold-back in the UK (see above), cinema halls once again began to screen Hindi films, and again, Bombay's producers and directors were quick to pick up on social trends in the UK.

It was an awareness of this market as a major source of revenue which led to Yash setting up distribution offices in London in 1997 and New York in 1998, after opening a Bombay distribution company a few years earlier. He is keenly aware of the importance of certain audiences to the success of his productions, notably those of Bombay and the UK, the US and Canada, which are almost exclusively of South Asian origin. There is a non-South Asian audience for these films elsewhere in the world, but in Europe and America, Hindi cinema is viewed almost exclusively by people of South Asian descent. Nevertheless, even this limited audience has managed to push several films into the Top 10 box-office rankings in the UK, and into the Top 30 in the US. In some countries, such as Egypt, there was a strong market for Indian films until the 1980s, but this seems to have declined.

However, Hindi films are finding new markets: a similar situation prevails in Israel, where *DTPH* is a huge hit (dubbed as *Halev Mistagya* in Hebrew), its soundtrack ubiquitous, even turning up in a television advertisement for noodles.

The overseas market is of crucial importance to the top-ranking producers, since ticket prices are higher (*DTPH* tickets were initially £15 in London, or Rs 1000, ten times the top Indian ticket price), and earn the producers hard currency, making it easier for them to fund future overseas productions. For Yash Raj Films, the UK and US markets have proved outstandingly profitable, with *DTPH* earning £900,000 and *KKHH* (*Kuch kuch hota hai/Something Happens*, Karan Johar, 1998) £1.7 million in the UK and around the dollar equivalent in the US.

Perhaps the most surprising element in this return to cinema was that the audience was no longer the older generation, one often supposed to consist of bored housewives and the elderly, who watched Hindi films to while away the time and because their English was too poor for them to enjoy British television. Instead, a new generation of Hindi film-goers has emerged from the South Asian diaspora. This younger audience is educated in English and brought up in a western cultural environment, at least at school and often in its patterns of media consumption. Few of them know Hindi well, for the British South Asian diaspora is largely Punjabi- or Gujarati-speaking, with a significant number of Sylheti speakers from Bangladesh. There are very few mother-tongue Hindi speakers in this diaspora, although many people of Pakistani origin learn Urdu, the national language of Pakistan, which in its colloquial spoken form is largely identical to Hindi, the national language of India.[24] This younger generation of people of Indian origin knows Hindi almost exclusively through watching Hindi cinema, and young people are often encouraged by their parents to watch movies in order to improve their language skills.[25]

Going to the cinema is only a part of the whole experience of the Hindi movie in India, where movie viewing is supplemented by other media, including music (see above), star magazines[26] and television programmes. These are all widely available within South Asian community shops, but perhaps more important is the access to the numerous websites on the internet, which provide links to discussions about movies, stars, song lyrics, samples of music and excerpts from films.

Given the long association of the two countries – pre-colonial, colonial, and post-colonial – it is hardly surprising that Indian culture has pervaded British culture for several centuries at many levels, such as language, food and fashion. The 1980s saw an outbreak of Raj nostalgia[27] alongside the emerging importance of English literature from India that was to gather impetus in the 1990s (in particular Rushdie, Seth, Roy and Chandra). This was followed by a particular fashion in the UK for Asian cool,[28] ranging from clothing, music and the club scene to television programmes. Asian musicians, such as Talvin Singh, won national awards; television shows such as *Goodness Gracious Me!* were aired at prime time; and films such as *East is East* (D. O'Donnell, 1999) were internationally successful. While the popularity of Asian culture was largely driven by the British South Asian community, it was also imitated by others, most notably the international icon Madonna who wore a *bindi* and henna on her hands.

Yet while Hindi film is often referred to in music remixes and in fashion, very few non-South Asians go to see Hindi movies. Hindi film producers are keen to reach this wider audience, but it remains to be seen if that audience will be attracted to this very different form of cinema. Although most DVDs of Hindi movies are subtitled in English, the films shown in the cinema halls are rarely subtitled, although Yash and others are now releasing subtitled prints of their films.

The 'Yash Chopra' woman

Yash is celebrated for his depiction of women, and many female actors are appreciative of the way he has worked on their image in his films or say they would welcome the opportunity to work with him. In the film industry and among film fans, the 'Yash Chopra woman' is common parlance, but what exactly does this term mean? Many regard the Yash Chopra woman as the ideal Indian woman. Yash usually casts established actresses who are recognised beauties. Then, in consultation with top stylists such as Manish Malhotra, he works on their clothing, hair, make-up and jewellery to present a simple, natural and romantic image.

In *Dil to pagal hai*, we see two heroines presented as two models of femininity, one the friend and one the beloved. The difference between the two is sharply drawn. The friend, Nisha, sees herself as no different from the men, and despite her revealing clothes, Rahul thinks of her in this way too. When she declares her love for him, he is non-plussed as he has only ever considered her to be a friend. Pooja, the beloved, appears in his dreams before he meets her, running through green fields, trailing a chiffon scarf. They keep passing each other, but the first time they meet, he sees her dancing without her knowing he is watching her. This is enough to make him fall in love with her.

It is clear that one of the pleasures of Yash's films is the presentation of the idealised woman as an object of visual desire. This pleasure is not only for the heterosexual male viewer but also for those who enjoy looking at the

Sadhana in *Waqt*

stylised depiction of the ideal woman, and relate to her in a variety of complex ways. One of these is undoubtedly the consumerist and associated pleasures offered by the glamorous realism of Yash Chopra's films.

The lifestyle of the super-rich depicted in these films is increasingly
modern or western. Yash first depicted modern, lavish interiors in *Waqt* and
set the model which others have followed. (This lifestyle is emulated by the
movie Mughals themselves, some of whom model their houses on film sets.)
The theatre group in *DTPH* lives in a Manhattan-style loft apartment, complete with a Pepsi machine, a fireman's pole, and a cityscape of skyscrapers
visible through the windows. The gender rules are relaxed: women have
their own apartments; men and women go to bars together to drink tequila
slammers; boys and girls go clothes shopping together; and girls get drunk
with no condemnation of their behaviour. The young crowd has birthday
celebrations and goes to Valentine's parties, festivities recently condemned
by the Hindu right as Christian imports.

Clothing codes have shifted in this decade as well.[29] While men have
worn western clothing throughout the history of Indian cinema, western
clothes for women were associated with western values and often suggested
a certain moral laxity, to say the least. From the late 1980s, western clothing
is worn as fashion: in *Vijay* Nisha wears miniskirts and western clothes,
while in *DTPH* the dancers are clad in minimal Lycra, and American and
British designer sportswear. Yet it is striking that in *DTPH*, the hotpants-
wearing Nisha is seen as barely feminine by Rahul, whereas his beloved
Pooja wears floating chiffon saris or Punjabi suits. Certain stars, such as
Karisma Kapoor, are known to wear the most fashionable clothes and many
women go to her films just to see her latest outfits. Copying stars' clothes is
a universal phenomenon,[30] and feeds into the consumerist pleasures of the
film, as plans are made for shopping expeditions in order to emulate the
movie's glamour.

Consumerist pleasures: romance and travel

Romance is part of the consumerist lifestyle portrayed in Hindi films, as it
becomes associated with activities such as travel, going out, and giving presents, essential components of courtship. Moreover, travel is one of many

ways in which Hindi films depict space and place, in particular places suitable for love and romance, and the idea of the transnational Indian.

In addition to movement of media (mediascapes[31]) and other such flows, we also see the actual movement of people. To be part of a transnational family is almost a hallmark of being middle class in India, since nearly every middle-class South Asian has at least one family member living in the diaspora. In recent years an ever increasing number of Indians travels overseas as this is no longer the preserve of the super-rich, but a real possibility for the middle classes, with their increased consumerist activities and leisure time.

Travel and romance have been linked in western culture[32] as consumerist activities. This is also seen in Hindi films, where travel is associated with consumerism, ranging from shopping in duty-free shops, eating and drinking out, and medical treatment in Swiss clinics, to expensive sports such as sailing and skiing. The films also allow for a new range of costumes, cars and specific references to travel that associate it with romance. For example, in *Chandni*, Rohit promises Chandni a honeymoon in Switzerland, although only the two men go to Switzerland in the actual diegesis of the film. In the fantasies of the characters, we also see an almost unconscious reference to travel.

Space is not only connected with consumerist pleasures, then, but also with romance. India's great lyric traditions have associated romance with nature; the Sanskrit traditions with the rainy season, gardens, cuckoos and lotuses; the Urdu with spring, gardens, nightingales, tulips and roses. Western romanticism, which pervaded Indian literature from the nineteenth century onwards, had its own specific romantic associations with nature.[33] The early Hindi films showed Kashmir as the ideal location for romance, and it was only in the 1970s that this site came to be displaced by Europe – above all Switzerland, with Scotland gaining popularity in recent years, along with Germany, North America and New Zealand. These places also constitute some sort of privacy for the romantic couple, a private space in the public domain, where they can escape from the surveillance of the family which prevents, encourages and controls romance, love and marriage.

The attraction of these locations may not be so important to the diasporic audience, but the films also give meaning to places in India. Chandni
is from a small town in north India, presumably the Punjab, while her
romance with Rohit shows the sights of Delhi as a backdrop. Delhi is
referred to specifically in a song ('*Mehbooba*/Beloved'), while Chandni's
career and relationship with Lalit develop in Bombay. *Lamhe* shows
Rajasthan as a place for love and romance for the NRI, while the younger
girl falls in love in England. *Darr* uses little outdoor space in India, except
as a place of fear, as the fiancé and the girl's family are unable to protect
their own privacy and private space whether at home, in their garden, or in
Switzerland. In *DTPH*, overseas space is not only a holiday destination, but
also an economic space, somewhere one travels to find work and money, in
Germany or Japan. India is portrayed as a Manhattan cityscape or as a
country resort for a dance school. The film could almost be set in any
metropolitan city in the world. However, the characters speak Hindi and
shop in Indian markets and at well-known Mumbai stores (The Bombay

Interior design in scene from *Dil to pagal hai*

Store, Shoppers' Stop and Rhythm House). The shots of the Leelavati Hospital indicate we are in Mumbai. The only Indian 'outdoor' location is named as Khandala, where the use of several specifically Maharashtrian elements confirms that this metropolitan city is Mumbai. However, the characters are all Punjabi, as is indicated by their names (e.g. Pooja Malhotra) or other cultural features (e.g. Jimmy's wedding is Punjabi, Nisha's aunt is Punjabi).

It also seems that the important thing about these spaces is that the Indian can wander anywhere in the world, being at home wherever she or he desires. He or she can pick up and put down the west, because what really matters is a sense of home, somewhere to belong, a *watan* or *desh* ('homeland'), sanitised and acceptable, with no trace of it being in any way inferior to, or more 'backward' than, the west.

These films thus promote the idea of the transnational Indian, who may enjoy foreign travel but whose heart lies in India. Although some of the audiences I have seen these films with in the UK applaud as the tourist sights of London are shown on screen, the interaction with the film is far more complicated than simply the pleasure of seeing something with which they can identify.[34]

Indian values and the diaspora

When I discuss Hindi films with people in the industry, the recurring theme is one addressed directly by the films themselves, namely Indian values. In *DDLJ*, the hero teases the heroine after she gets drunk and blacks out, by telling her that they have had sex. When she starts crying, he reassures by saying: 'I know you are an Indian girl, and I know what her honour means to her.' In a film recently distributed internationally by Yash Raj Films, David Dhawan's *Dulhan Hum le jayenge/I Shall Carry Off the Bride* (2000), whenever the heroine behaves in a way unacceptable to the hero, he asks her: 'Are you English? Are you American? Are you? No, you are Indian.'

But what are these Indian values, and why do they mean so much to the younger generation in India and to the diaspora? The key features are not those of the modern or post-modern world, but those of a world that is almost feudal: family (*khaandaan*), honour (*izzat*), modesty (*laaj*), and increasingly, religion (*dharam*), as opposed to work, companionate marriage, self-knowledge, or the pursuit of happiness.

The treatment of the nation (*desh, watan*) has also changed in recent years. The early movies also discussed Indianness, but in a very different way. Then the emphasis was on national values, and the relationship between the state and the citizen, whereas in recent years, with almost every movie paying lip service to being 'Hindustani', 'Bharatiy' or 'Indian', the notion of what 'Indian' means seems to be negotiable. Yash Chopra's films of the 1990s were among the first to portray Indianness as something inherent, not a relationship to the state nor a question of domicile; one can be Indian whether one is a citizen of India or whether one lives in the diaspora.[35] His films show that being Indian has to do with a survival of values, a certain emotional structure, with the mother tongue used for intimacy, although English is spoken in many other contexts, including the formulaic expression 'I love you'.[36] Being Indian is cool, and pretending to be western has lost its appeal. Even the half-Italian Indian returning home to his roots, as Sameer Rossellini in *Hum dil de chuke sanam/My Heart's Already Given* (Sanjay Leela Bhansali, 1999) comes to India to learn classical music.

The younger generation of British Asians has grown up watching Hollywood films and British television, in which South Asians were rarely visible before the late 1990s. They say they prefer Hollywood films for action, but they much prefer their romantic films to come from Bombay, finding Hollywood and British romance unappealing. Their private sphere remains Indian, and here romance and love need to be negotiated through ties of family, religion and honour. Other relations of the diaspora to the Hindi film remain to be explored, and are likely to pose interesting issues around emotional structures, but we may begin to ask questions such as: Does 'Indian' mean something other for this diaspora than the nation in which one lives? Are these people bound by ties other than those of the modern? Is this a post-colonial, transnational, global community, linked through media, transnational class, and language? Is Hindi cinema one of the world's major globalising cultural forms which is not American and is not in English?[37]

However we may try to answer these questions, it is clear that the glamorous realism of Yash Chopra and his production house remains a principal means of seeing Indianness for these new middle classes in India and in the South Asian diaspora. Chopra's films challenge the boundaries of the nation while complicating ideas of authenticity and tradition.

Seven
Production

My focus in this book has been on the films that Yash Chopra directed but I must mention the films which Yash Raj Films produced because of the impact at least one of them had on the company and hence on his creative freedom.

Yash Raj Films produced several films by other directors, most of whom were former assistants of Yash's. These films included: *Doosra aadmi/The Other Man* (Ramesh Talwar, 1977), *Noorie* (Manmohan Krishna, 1979), *Nakhuda/The Saviour* (Dilip Naik, 1981), *Sawaal/The Question* (Ramesh Talwar, 1989), *Aaina* and *Yeh dillagi*.

Yash says:

> *Doosra aadmi* and *Noorie* were films of my sensibility. The former was about a young boy, and an older woman. It did well and had good music. Poonam was a newcomer in *Noorie*. *Nakhuda* was a very emotional film with newcomers. It was low-cost but was a failure. *Sawaal* was not my type of film. It was made by Ramesh Talwar, and was action-oriented.

On 20 October 1995, Yash released one of the all time blockbusters of Indian cinema, *Dilwale dulhaniya le jayenge*, directed by his older son, Aditya Chopra. Yash says:

> Previously boy and girl fall in love and elope. Adi took another stance. He values traditions. All customs and traditions of marriage are there. Atmosphere can't be anywhere but India. He wanted consent of parents. He won the whole family though they hated him at the beginning. The parents' acceptance is very important for a happily married life, or bitterness is there.

A close associate of Yash Chopra's says:

> Films need pace. Aditya moves the camera much more than Yash. Aditya trolleys, Yash prefers zooms. Yash differs from Aditya in his choice of costume.

For the songs, Aditya wanted Simran to look simple, so no silk suits, whereas Yashji wanted them. Aditya goes in for fine detail, Yash for the wider canvas.

For the song '*Zara se jhoom loom*/Everything is spinning', Aditya wanted no romance, whereas Yash suggested that there should be sensuality, romance, feeling. Yash would sacrifice anything for beauty. That's why he goes to Switzerland and other places abroad. He has a small town mentality and wants to show the world. Aditya wanted *DDLJ* to show interaction, a different lifestyle, a meeting on the train, where the landscape wasn't just for beauty.

The Yash Chopra banner and the youth of the media-shy director misled many into expecting a Yash Chopra romance. All the hallmarks were there but the young couple does not challenge society's prohibitions and taboos as their passion unfolds nor do they resolve to live unhappily as Yash's lovers would. Instead they persuade the harsh but well-meaning patriarchy to accept their love. Yash Chopra's cities are friendly homes for urban elites while here we have cold and anonymous London, an inappropriate location for romance, which flourishes in Swiss idylls but reaches a state of passion only in the rural Punjab. The nuclear family is the norm in London while the Punjab has the extended family and traditional hospitality, its fields full of yellow mustard, a place appropriate for religious occasions and romance.

The film is also more focused than many of Yash Chopra's as the hero's love for his heroine transforms him from a brat to a responsible adult, driving the story forward. A critical factor is the dynamic pairing of Shahrukh and Kajol, who have since become one of the most popular screen couples in India. Aditya Chopra's assistant on this film, Karan Johar, has developed its magic in his *Kuch kuch hota hai* (1998), itself a tribute to the Chopra family.

The film is also interesting as it works as Prasad's 'feudal family romance', in which desire is subordinated to familial authority, addressing tensions as it deploys the rhetoric of family duty to sanction the romance by using rituals and norms.

Aditya released his second film, *Mohabbatein/Loves*, in 2000. It was a big hit although not as great a success as *DDLJ*. Yash has since decided that the company should produce at least four films a year and is currently working on *Mujh se dosti karoge?/Will You Be My Friend?* (Kunal Kohli, 2002).

Several other companies work alongside Yash Raj Films, including Yash's television company, Metavision, which produces programmes including a song competition *Meri awaaz suno*/Hear my voice', winners of which sang in *Mohabbatein*. Yash says:

> I've never wanted to make anything for television myself. I have a TV company, but I think that visually the small screen is like a close-up and I prefer bigger canvases. I make a movie every two or three years.

'The economics of ideology: popular film form and mode of production', in Madhava Prasad's ground-breaking book[1] presents the only non-economic analysis of production in the Hindi film industry. He discusses 'the nature of the nexus between economic, ideological and political forces that shape the conditions of possibility of cultural production in India',[2] and goes on to conclude, firstly:

> As regards the production sector, I will argue that the mode of production in the Hindi film industry is characterized by fragmentation of the production apparatus, subordination of the production process to a moment of the self-valorization of merchant capital, the consequent externality of capital to the production process, the resistance of the rentier class of exhibitors to the expansionist drive of the logic of the market, and the functional centrality of the distributor–financier to the entire process of film-making.[3]

Secondly, Prasad argues, the Hindi film is produced by a heterogeneous form of manufacture, rather than the serial or organic form seen in Hollywood. In other words, the various elements of the film are produced by specialists then assembled rather than focusing on the development of a central material, which he argues affects the status of the 'story' in the Hindi film. Thirdly, he identifies a struggle in the industry between India's state-controlled capitalist development which aims at producing a national culture and pre-capitalist ideologies. He argues this tension has led to a demand for certain types of state-intervention, 'a campaign for realism and melodrama' and attempts to set up an independent production sector.[4]

I am not taking issue with the validity of Prasad's argument but my research into the work of Yash Chopra and his production house, Yash Raj

Films Pvt Ltd, presents a very different scenario. I draw here on my observations of Yash Chopra's recent productions, *Dil to pagal hai* (*DTPH*, 1997)
and *Mohabbatein*, showing how he deploys a very different system of production from that described by Prasad.

When I began this book on Yash Chopra, I had only considered the films
which he directed, but the more I saw of the production processes and
appreciated the economic and creative freedom of self-production, the
more I realised that this was the key to his work. In the first place, the form
and content of his films differed according to the producer with whom
he was working, so I look at how he masterminds the team that is Yash
Raj Films for his own movies and that of others, referring to the only two
films of which I have detailed knowledge of production: *DTPH* and
Mohabbatein.

In *DTPH* (see also Chapter 9) the central idea was Pamela Chopra's: a
story of predestined love and wrongly-paired couples. The family (Yash and
Pamela, along with their sons, Aditya and Uday) elaborated the story,
notably by introducing the hero's group of friends, in a manner somewhat
reminiscent of the American comedy, *Friends*. Yash Chopra decided to
direct the film and began the mechanisms of production, with Pamela,
Aditya and Uday as co-producers.

Aditya, Pamela and Tanuja Chandra began writing a screenplay. Aditya
wrote the dialogues in English, which he then translated into Hindi, while
Yash Chopra dealt with the question of finance.

Film finance

Most producers have to approach financiers for funding and they can put
certain restrictions on the film. While many of the financiers are
respectable figures, there is a long-acknowledged relationship between
film-financing and the laundering of black money. Since the average ratio
of a movie's success to failure is very poor, financing a film is a high-risk
business, unlikely to appeal to the cautious investor, but the opportunity of
laundering money and associating with such a glamorous industry prove an
irresistible combination to some of Bombay's richest inhabitants. The
implications of this association with the underworld are unclear, but there

has been talk of several unpleasant incidents in the industry being linked to the mafia underworld of Bombay and the Gulf States. In addition to these risks for the producer, the financiers charge a very high rate of interest, said to reach as much as 60% by the time the film is finally made.

The producer often uses distributors as a major source of funding. In brief, India is divided into five major territories for the purposes of film distribution. These territories are sold by the producer to the distributor at different rates according to the film's predicted market value (based on a conjunction of the choice of director, stars, and so on), with the most expensive being Bombay for some genres or stars and Delhi/Uttar Pradesh for others. In recent years, the overseas market has become more important than any of the Indian territories, with the UK being the most profitable, followed by the US. These two markets have come to form independent territories while the other overseas circuit is usually not subdivided. Distribution rights are sold in three major ways in the Hindi film industry, according to the status of the producer and various predictions about the box-office success of the movie. The producer may sell the film on a profit-only basis, where the distributor pays an advance to the producer, paying a pre-arranged percentage of profits once this money and extra fees for the cost of prints (Rs 80,000 per print) and publicity have been covered. The producer has the advantage of advance funding for his film and a low risk if the film fails, for the distributor bears the loss. The second is a percentage-only sale, when the distributor and producer agree in advance the percentage share of box-office receipts. The third is an outright sale, where the distributor buys the film at a fixed price and keeps the profits for himself, although he also may have to shoulder the losses. The distributor in turn sells the film to exhibitors, and he may similarly spread his risks. The distributor and producer negotiate the number of prints to be released. Rajshri (the Barjatyas' company) is the only distributor to have a national network, the others all being local concerns.

Yash Raj Films had profited from its big hits *Chandni* and *Darr*, and when Aditya Chopra decided to direct *Dilwale dulhaniya le jayenge*, Yash Chopra acted as producer, deciding to finance the film himself. The resounding box-office success of this film has allowed Yash Raj Films to finance all their own films subsequently without recourse to taking money from financiers or distributors. Yash Chopra decided that since Bombay was his most profitable territory as well as being the closest to home, Yash Raj Films opened their first distributors' office there in 1995. For the release of *DTPH*, it opened a UK office, Yash Raj Films International Limited, and in 1998 to distribute *Kuch kuch hota hai*, a film produced and directed by their close friends, the Johars, it opened an office in the US. These are fairly small offices, largely for distributing the new Yash Raj Films, but also for films of some of the other top directors and producers and for marketing DVDs and videos of films whose rights have reverted from other distributors to Yash Raj Films and for some other top production houses (B.R. Films and R.K. Films among others). These films are all the works of other major producers and directors, and while not all are in the style of the Yash Raj banner, they share at least the commitment to high production values. The income from these offices has been substantial and, since it is in hard currency, allows Yash Raj Films to receive certain benefits as a foreign-currency earner, given India's shortage of hard currency.

Yash Raj Films is not a production banner which comes together as a package for making films, but consists of two major parts. One consists of the people who work for the unit regularly but who are hired only for the films, and hence also work for other banners. These include the cameraman, Manmohan Singh, who has worked on all Yash Raj Films since 1986; while the music directors have often remained the same, Yash Chopra using Shiv-Hari (Shiv Kumar Sharma and Hariprasad Chaurasia) on most of his films since 1981, while Aditya Chopra uses Jatin-Lalit; Yash Chopra used the same lyricist as B.R. Chopra, Sahir Ludhianvi, after whose death, he has used Anand Bakshi for all his films apart from *Silsila* where he used a number of lyricists; Lata Mangeshkar has sung on nearly every film so far. It is largely this staff who are hired on a daily rate or on a fixed contract for the making of the film whose costs have risen so highly. While the rates for the spotboys [runners] remain fixed at Rs 350 per shift, the other costs have risen enormously: the dance composer charges up to Rs 125,000 per song, the set designer Rs 50,000–10 lakhs per film, the music directors between 1 and 25 lakhs, a top make-up director costs between Rs 1,000–15,000 per day, while the rates for the stars are rumoured to be up to Rs 3 crore. Other costs have also increased hugely: the heroine's costumes may cost Rs 25 lakhs, an indoor set can cost up to Rs 3 crore and an overseas schedule can cost around £400,000 even after paying the Indian staff's salaries, given costs of air fares and accommodation (including various friends and family of the stars and the producer), not to mention local transport, food, location charges, local staff and so on.

The second part of the production unit is the permanent staff, who are on the pay roll at all times, such as the production manager and executive producer (Mahen Vakil), business executive (Sahdev Ghei), production executive (Sanjay Shivalkar) and other office staff. They are salaried, although their costs are written into the films' budgets.

The most important figures in film production are the immediate family who work together on the film: Pamela Chopra often writing the story and singing a song for the film, as well as managing most of the outdoor schedules; Uday working as assistant, made his acting debut in *Mohabbatein*; and the indefatigible Aditya combining the roles of director, writer and assistant. The family's role in writing the story, screenplay and dialogues is crucial as is the part they play in the critical task of deciding on the music for the film.

Yash Raj Films' music has always generated at least one major hit per film, providing some classic Hindi film songs for which the banner is celebrated. Although Shiv-Hari's music has enjoyed enormous success, other music directors were brought in to provide a different style of music for the more recent films. Uttam Singh was almost unknown outside the industry when he was hired for *DTPH*. His brief was to provide tunes for several song situations, for which he brought along more than a hundred tunes from which the Chopra family selected eight for inclusion in the film. He arranged and orchestrated the songs, then Yash Chopra booked his usual sound recordist, Daman Sood, in his regular studios, Western Outdoors, and the family took part in deciding how the arrangements were to be recorded. The singers then put their part onto the soundtrack. Most of the women's songs were sung by Lata Mangeshkar who has been singing on Yash Chopra's films since 1959. Although she sings for very few producers now, she says that she can never refuse Yash Chopra, for whom she does not charge a fee, their closeness such that he calls her 'Didi' ('older sister'). The music recordings are then used for playback (lip-synch) by the actors in the film and come into their own as part of the marketing process I describe below.

Yash Chopra usually works with established stars such as Amitabh Bachchan in the 1970s, Sridevi in the 1980s and 1990s and Shahrukh Khan in the 1990s. Prasad argues that the star text contributes to the heterogeneous mode of production of the Hindi film as it is deployed intertextually, thus disrupting the film's autonomous identity. This is another arena in which Yash Raj Films go against the grain, showing a well-known star in a way that may pick up on the star text but which ultimately subverts it. The most notable example of this is in the case of Amitabh Bachchan.[5] Yash Chopra is best known for his presentation of female stars. It is said that they have often the best role of their careers in his films and that they are presented at their most glamorous, but that this is often the last great role of their careers.

Marketing and publicity

Yash Raj Films has been at the forefront of film marketing in India, along with the Barjatyas' Rajshri Films. Sooraj Barjatya marketed his *Hum aapke hain kaun ...* ! in an innovative manner which may have brought about some of the most important changes in film-viewing practices as well as marketing. Indian cinema had perceived itself to be under threat from the video cassette in the 1980s and from the newly-arrived cable and satellite television in the 1990s. Those who could afford a VCR or the cheaper cable link stayed away from the cinema, and the cinema halls became run-down, catering to a male, lower-class audience. Barjatya astutely observed that the new media could provide useful marketing tools and he sold a programme on the making of his film to one of the new channels. The music for the film was a great hit, but rather than show the 'picturisation' of the songs, he put together a montage of a limited number of short clips from the film to the song's music, thus whetting the audience's appetite to see the song in its entirety. He instituted the practice of 'video hold-back' then released a gradually increasing but limited number of prints of the film, beginning with a single print released in Bombay's prestigious Liberty cinema, redecorated for the release and embellished with stage lights surrounding the screen which were lit sequentially for the big songs of the film. Yash Raj Films followed, making 'Making of … ' television programmes, showing montages, taking their video hold-back to the stage where *DDLJ* has still not been released on video almost five years after it was made.

Music has always been one of the strengths of Yash Raj Films, so it is not surprising that music has been at the centre of its marketing campaigns. An almost conspiratorial silence surrounds the making of a Yash Raj Film and this was certainly true of *DTPH*. The first publicity for the film was a teaser, a few seconds showing the three major stars under a spotlight, their names above them and underneath the words 'A Yash Chopra musical'. The second publicity drive began with graphics of the film's title, then the song with a montage of images, ending with the teaser. Two further songs were released in this way for television. The music was then released, the rights having been sold for an unheard of Rs 5 crore to HMV India, a wise investment in view of the phenomenal sales (four million units before the film's release and another six million afterwards). Cinema trailers were also made using montages.

The Chopras eschew personal publicity, Aditya Chopra being notoriously media-shy, although Yash Chopra does give occasional interviews. They did not hold a film première, although they could have attracted the biggest stars of all for a gala performance which would have galvanised huge media attention. Instead the advance booking for the film created its own publicity and the film, to the critics' dismay, was an instant success.

Yash Raj Films set up its own website in 1998, largely coordinated by Uday Chopra (http://www.yashrajfilms.com). The site is similar to those of the other major production houses, having information on current productions and releases in theatres and on DVD/video, alongside a special feature on a particular film, with interviews, reviews, stills and music excerpts. Other sites include information about Yash Chopra, his life and his achievements. There is an archive which features stills, video clips and music from the major films and there are e-mail cards, screensavers and interactive fan

sites. This allows the company to project its own media image and information, albeit to the limited section of the audience that has internet access
and reads English (see below for more on the audience).

To conclude, Yash Raj Films does not deploy a heterogeneous form of
production but a homogenous or serial form. It is pursuing this strategy further in its current expansion, which has involved buying the land on which
integrated offices and air-conditioned studios will be built, in order to keep
total control over all aspects of the productions, while making money in
between these productions by renting out production facilities. Other banners are perhaps in the same league, notably Subash Ghai's Mukta Arts or
R.K. Films, but there are few who follow this integrated mode of production
so thoroughly.

The Indian film industry has many organisations and guilds for the different personnel in the industry. These exist for spotboys and lightmen,
junior artistes, set workers, producers and so on. The associations fix the
length of shifts, which are observed by the entire industry. They also fix the
minimum wage at differing rates for shifts in Bombay and outdoors. The
producers' organisations have the most complicated history, which I can
barely begin to unravel and may well have confused.[6] The oldest association
is the IMPPA (Indian Motion Pictures Producers' Association) which is over
60 years old, but is not regarded as distinguished. In the 1950s an elite
group of directors and studio owners as well as producers (including Raj
Kapoor, Mehboob Khan, V. Shantaram, Sohrab Modi) formed the Film
Producers' Guild of India, of which Yash Chopra is a member. The All India
Film Producers' Council is an umbrella organisation, combining the latter
association with the Association of Motion Picture and Television
Producers. The latter organisation is the largest and Yash Chopra is associated with this only through his television company, Metavision. Other producers' organisations include the Western India Film Association
(non-Hindi films) and the Film Makers' Council, which closed at the end of
1999. In 1998, 15 top producers (including Yash Chopra, Subash Ghai,
Vinod Chopra, J.P. Dutta, F.C. Mehra, Nadiadwala, Barjatyas, Rakesh
Roshan and J. Om Prakash) formed the United Producers' Forum, a super-
league of producers, which is the most expensive and the hardest to join,

given that all members must approve a new entry. This forum meets every Saturday to discuss crucial issues and is active in promoting producers' interests. For example, led by Yash Chopra, it negotiated the government recognition of the movie business as an industry, thus allowing benefits such as access to bank finance and insurance.[7] This latter achievement shows the movie industry's determination to portray itself as a professional, organised business, capable of negotiating with the government.

Yash Raj Films is keen to be recognised by the government and to be an organisation which takes only 'white' money. This is in part because it can afford to do so, but also to avoid the association of black money with the Bombay and Gulf underworld. In other words, this production house wishes to have clearly defined relations with the state and its institutions.

Yash Raj Films is owned by the Chopra family, with Yash Chopra at the head, although his sons Aditya and Uday have equal rights in the company and are consulted regularly, Yash Chopra is very much in charge of business matters which pass through his office. The present building marks this space clearly, the ground floor being used for finance, distribution, the office manager and reception, while the first floor has the secretary's office, the subsidiary television company, Metavision, most of the floor space being given over to Yash Chopra's office. The other office and editing rooms are on the top floor.

Yash Raj Films, although an international and seemingly modern company, is still run on family principles and connections which form a variety of pre-modern networks throughout the film industry. Most powerful figures in the film industry are Punjabis, and a large number come from the Khatri caste (names include the Chopras, Kapoors, Khannas, Tandons). These caste links are subordinated to family links, with Yash Raj Films being no exception. The four immediate members of the Chopra family are involved at all levels of production, from story writing and dialogues, to music direction, to lyric writing, to marketing, to organising overseas schedules and even acting and singing for the films. Other family members are also involved, often as trainee directors (Kapil 'Junnu' Chopra, B.R. Chopra's grandson on *Mohabbatein*, while an 'almost family member', Sameer Sharma, Mukesh's[8] grandson worked on *Dil to pagal hai*). Members of the production team are treated like family members, those who are closer calling Pamela Chopra *bhabhi* ('sister-in-law'), as well as 'Pam Auntie', while many of Yash Chopra's stars call him 'Yash Uncle'. This interweaving of professional and family relationships is key to the production unit, providing a level of close-ness and understanding that helps the unit function well. This attitude to the family is seen in the films themselves, where nuclear families are shown as idealised, modern, bourgeois units, intimate and loving, with their relation-ships often expressed as friendship. Lovers are destined by fate or by the family but romance is never pursued in opposition to family values. The sanctity of the family is always upheld, while friendship becomes increas-ingly a significant part of the characters' key happiness.

The importance of the overseas market is seen within the film itself. Yash Raj Films have promoted the transnational Indian, who may enjoy for-eign travel but whose heart lies in India. Although they made one of the first NRI (Non-resident Indian) films, *Lamhe* in 1991, in which the male lead was a UK-based NRI,[9] it was *DDLJ* in 1995 that marked the high point of this (sub-)genre, the hero and heroine being UK NRIs, the first half of the film shot entirely in Europe. *DTPH* had the second heroine wearing western clothes throughout the film, the entire younger section of the cast wearing designer sportswear/dancewear in Lycra at some point.[10] Although the film did not query their Indianness, the main heroine preferred Indian clothes when not performing, unless travelling in Europe when she wore European clothes. These were among the first films to portray Indianness as some-thing inherent, not a relationship to the state nor a question of domicile.

Prasad argues that the heterogeneous mode of production in the Hindi film industry is closely related to the lack of centrality of the story, whereas the story is absolutely central to the Yash Raj Film. While a great deal of emphasis is given to the visual and the musical, which may not be 'realistic', they are embellishments of the story which set the pace for the whole film. This is clearly helped by the mode of production which develops from the initial germ of the story. Films such as *Darr* and *DDLJ* are driven by their narratives, the latter having few of the usual 'digressions' one finds in many Hindi films. Once Raj decides he is going to pursue Simran to the Punjab, the remainder of the film is about this quest.

Sooraj Barjatya, whose Rajshri banner, I believe, follows a similar mode of production, makes an entirely different style of film. His films, in particular his two later films, *Hum aapke hain kaun ... !* (1994) and *Hum saath saath hain/We Stand United* (1999), have little in the way of story at all, what plot development there is taking place well into the film, and not seemingly integrated into the song and celebratory nature of the film, bringing into question the very nature of the relation of the mode of production to the form and content of the film. Leaving this aside, I now turn to the relation between production and genre, drawing on Rick Altman's work on genre.[11] I find that Yash Raj films have many of the recognisable elements or features that would constitute a genre in Altman's definition, a combination of elements which gives rise to the 'Yash Chopra' film as almost a genre within the Indian film industry and one which is recognised by the audience.

Altman analyses the processes by which genres are conceived by the critics and by the producer,[12] arguing that critics distinguish genres synchronically, in a retrospective manner, by picking up on the idea of a genre from the industry or other critics, describing the characteristics of the films which seem to typify the genre, adding other films to this list and then beginning their analysis. Meanwhile producers use genre prospectivally by looking at a box-office success, drawing from it a formula of the elements which contributed to this success, using this in a new film, then reshaping the formula depending on the success of the new film *ad infinitum*. Altman's argument is important because he is connecting the producers' role in creating genres, in which the producer acts also as critic, to the role of the audience and the actual critics themselves, by looking at generic communication – or the lack of it. He centres his discussions on the producers, exhibitors, audiences and critics and here it becomes important to recognise the levels of control and influence that Yash Chopra wields in so many of these spheres.

The producers' game, as Altman calls it, bears striking similarities to the process Yash Chopra and other producers use in Hindi cinema. Yash Chopra has created cycles of romantic films in this way, which have then been taken up (or imitated) by other producers to form industry-wide genres, such as the NRI film, which depicts the transnational Indian, and is thus an important way of locating 'Indianness', or the romance of 'glamorous realism', films which depict what I have called the new middle classes of Bombay.[13] It is here that much of Yash Chopra's long-lived success as a film-maker lies, in his selection of generic elements, such as the star text, narratives and other features, which he reshapes and remodels in his films to such acclaim. Yash Chopra is able to recognise these cycles developing in the work of others, and it is these films which he chooses to distribute overseas, further reinforcing these incipient genres. Yash Chopra is able to take advantage of the poor generic differentiation of the Bombay cinema, using his, or his banner's name, as a genre in itself, perhaps analogous to the manner of Disney in Hollywood.

Yash Raj Films deploys a very different mode of production from that outlined by Prasad. Yash Chopra has now reached the point at which he has total control over the production processes which he is now integrating into a single unit where all business and other production activities will occur. This has been a gradual and almost imperceptible spread, with each opportunity for autonomy being taken on an *ad hoc* basis, until the company has become beholden to fewer and fewer outsiders, with control held by Yash Chopra himself, by his family and by his long-term employees. There has not been any great strategic plan, but rather a weariness with being exploited and cheated, that has led to this extension of control. A success in one area has gradually led to other areas of production coming under the control of the family. The mixture of family networks with a western plc seems to be successful, and Yash Raj Films has now become an international business.

The growth of the distribution side of the company has allowed Yash Raj Films to earn money even when not making films, as has the development of the home entertainment (DVD and VHS) side of the business. The films which the company distributes are high-quality romances, so they benefit from having the Yash Raj banner associated with them, while they provide income to the production company. This is the creation of the Yash Chopra/Yash Raj Films' brand, whose success may be seen in its public acknowledgment. The consumerist lifestyle promoted in the films works to the company's advantage as their internet pages show their marketing to be focused on the rich, English-reading, international Indian. The brand is communicated by these sites, and the crew have even begun to wear a 'uniform' of Yash Raj Films' jackets and baseball caps, with the 'Yash Raj Films' logo on the front, which may mark the beginning of a range of branding possibilities.[14]

A year later (2001), Yash perceived major changes in the industry:

We are trying for public corporate offices, now we have industry status so we can have bank finance and insurance. However 90% of producers can't make a proposal. We have to get more organised, disciplined, methodical.

The entertainment industry – films, television, music, fashion, food and beauty – is the industry on top. The future's very bright.

At home, the makers are becoming more conscious of the 'class' audience. The film must do well in A stations, where the ticket price is higher, the halls are bigger. As for overseas, we are keen to expand more into overseas markets. We must compete in the world markets, not be stopped by culture and language. Our culture may not be familiar but good music and good poetry will be accepted. Love is not old-fashioned but we have to keep pace with today. Women are shown now as more human, not just ideals. No-one can make anyone change, but I'm changing without being obvious.

Yash is a leading figure in negotiations between the film industry and the government, helping to organise conferences and overseas delegations. He has bought the land for his studio and now has architect's plans and models for it. He has also decided to expand his production by producing four films a year in order to keep his staff and his studio busy. Once again, Yash is at the forefront of those who realise that the industry has to face up to changing worldwide media and other global shifts.

Appendix
Reflections

Yash Chopra

On film-making
When I'm making films I think of story and screenplay. I close my eyes and see the whole film before me. Then I start adding colours. This scene I'd like to do like this. I don't know any art. I have to be the centre figure where artists converge. I don't know where ideas come from. The subconscious?

When I imagine a romantic scene it comes to me as a form of poetry. I think of about ten different visuals which I then try to make coherent. Every human being is a lover and wants to fall in love in his or her own way. It is the only theme in the world that can never go out of fashion. There can never be too much. Many people mix love with sex, but these are separate things. Everyone needs love, you can't live without it. Love is a very big word.

On every film I make there are many contributors. A single person can't do anything, only the art. There has to be one *malik* [boss], but it's team work. I'm the director, but the film's not just my doing. In *DTPH*, there were many of us, including Shiamak, Karisma, Adi, so many of us. There are usually five or six of us working on a scene. It's difficult to decide who's done what and when we see the final result we don't know who did it. If you take your name out of a movie, your stamp should still be there. When a film is finished it becomes everybody's film.

On work
I want to die with my boots on. Sometimes, I think we have relations with everyone but ourselves. We need moments of solitude, to do something for ourselves. Have I been happy? Am I capable of making good movies now? I think I should have done something more significant and memorable. I

would like to write something beautiful, to sing. I should have done some better work, even in direction. I am not content, I am not satisfied. I won't get the kind of respect my mother had in Jalandhar. We're dislocated here. If I had technique, I would have written poems. I feel there's much to do and there's not much time. God will give me strength to do better work. I think I could do better but I have no regrets. God is very kind to me.

When a person knows his job and is doing it well or performing then he looks beautiful. I am frustrated with cinema practices where it's the importance of money over everything. There is a lack of discipline. The working day in the industry is 9.30–6.30 although one can extend this or add a night shift. Raj Kapoor and Dilip Kumar always came late – R.K. as studio owner began with the two pm shift. The system became corrupt with artists doing multiple shifts. Anyone can produce and offer big money to actors. Banners don't matter. They went down as the actors went up.

You can't rest on your laurels. You must be active on your laurels.

On other directors

I'm a fan of Raj Kapoor. He was a very passionate film-maker. He was honest. He would put his last shirt on a film. He made films from his heart; he never calculated, whereas today everyone calculates. When he made a film, he put his whole life into that film. He was not interested in money. He was a director first and a producer afterwards. He went to functions but talked only about films, never thought of anything else. I loved *Sangam*, *Awaara/The Vagabond* (1951) and *Aag/Fire* (1949), but I didn't like *Satyam*, *Shivam*, *Sundaram* very much. I have seen his films many times. There is an *alag rup* [special form], make it in his own way, an *accha* [fine] thought.

R.K.'s sense of music is greatest. Just after marriage he heard Pam singing a Panjabi folk song: Saheliji, this is a very good song. We used it in *Kabhi kabhie* – '*Tere chere se*.../Away from your face'.

R.K.'s team was great. R.K. said, 'I am the body, Mukesh is the soul.' I have tried to do this. Sahir was great, but his best film was *Pyaasa*. Guru Dutt was very special – he came to be a dance director and the rhythm, the movements in his mind were different. He picturised songs beautifully. '*Yeh raat*/This night' was Sahir's best romantic song. (QUOTES WHOLE SONG.) The imagery is very beautiful, the basic rhythm is perfect.

Bimal Roy made very real films, they were realistic, you could believe in them. He never ran after glamour. He took very good artistes. *Koshish lagi* [I tried] to make a good film. K.L. Saigal very slow. Each scene, lacks spontaneity — *soch zyaada* [he thought too much].

Mehboob was *bilkul* [absolutely] illiterate. He was a great man, a tiger. He never bothered about anyone. What films! His *Andaz, aaj bhi modern lag rahaa* [still looks modern]. *Dosti aur ishq ki pharak kya hai?* [What's the Difference Between Friendship and Love?]

The Rajshri Company is interesting. The father was far-sighted and spread a network of distributors over the country. They made small but decent films with new artists. MPK was made as a big film with newcomers. They spent a lot of money, but the grandfather was alive and he had vision. They made no compromises on sets or money. Sooraj is a good film-maker. He has been brought up in a family of film-goers and he has no diversion other than music and scripts. Adi thinks Sooraj is god and follows his habits. They are a very good family, strictly vegetarian, they don't quarrel and they are good in business.

You can't make a film because you think the audience will like it. You should try to change the audience's taste. If we like something, maybe the audience will like it. If we don't make strong films, we'll be making a formula that we think the audience will like. People don't research when they're making films. They copy English films and videos, thinking that's research. How can you know what the audience will like? There's too much emphasis on the star cast rather than on what the film is saying, because stars mean you can sell at a high price. They are more stars than actors. They are very insecure and want to make as much money as possible rather than give a good performance. They should want to do a good role and get job satisfaction, not looking at the number of films and the amount of money they make. In *Dhool ka phool* Ashok Kumar was a guest artist. He did this to give me his blessing and there was no money involved, he worked for about ten days, yet he defined the film. Those days' affection, love and respect, such as Dadamoni showed, are gone.

On changing times and lifestyles

Sound has changed so much. *DTPH* was digital Dolby, *DDLJ* was Dolby. It was not recorded in stereo but we tried to paste a magnetic track after release. *Darr* is in stereo. *Chandni*, the music is in stereo but the background music is not.

I love old music, films made from the heart. The great directors worked then – C. Ramachandran, Madan Mohan, Shankar-Jaikishen, Naushad, S.D. Burman, Roshan – we don't hear music like that, which was simple with brilliant orchestration. Now they're trying to find a gimmick, a caption or a slogan. It should be set by situation, the writer should know which character is singing.

This was the time of the rise of middle classes. They have come to rule all the tastes of the country. They aren't *nawabi* or rich intellectuals but are new-moneyed. They have money and power but no culture. Everything has to be made for this class as they rule all fashions here in films and music. Because of them, film music and art has become very mediocre and middle class. You have to please them, their tastes govern so you need to decide what they want. It's very, very sad.

If a poet wants to write he can, but if he wants to sell he has to cater to this class. *Urdu to nikal gayi yehaan se* [Urdu's left this place]. The new generation doesn't even know it. It's a fantastic language and it shouldn't die. These people want to spend money, have luxury items and have stopped saving. We have to show this changing society in our films.

We take lifestyles from life, but society draws on the movies. If I show a marriage ceremony, such as in *Chandni*, I glamorise it, I make it beautiful so they try to copy that. North Indian marriages are said to be 'Yash Chopra' style. Some people live like this; we only make it look more beautiful. I keep in mind the things I see then add my own fantasy to them.

On attitudes to the Hindi film industry in India and abroad

It's a fashion for intellectuals to look down on our industry. We're no longer *filmi*, we've improved, grown up and are getting better every day. We don't have good critics. We have self-proclaimed box-office pundits, who have set up their own parameters and go on complaining. Sometimes we make silly movies in India, but they are very entertaining. They have music, dance and romance but they're not serious cinema. We make very basic films which are wholesome entertainment. Everyone in the world likes music, but it's only in India that we picturise songs so well.

Maybe language is a problem for some, but I think it's because Euro-American culture is so different from ours. People there are cultured, sophisticated and they suppress their emotions, whereas we're very open. The audience there understands nuances whereas here we have to lead the audience by the finger. I do think the audience is growing up here as they see different television programmes and are becoming educated. We need to work on our scripts. Our emotions are the same all over the world although we express them differently.

I don't really know as I don't know the English well. I meet them only for work. I see London as an extension of Bombay. We can be cut off from others. It's also hard for us to get into the markets there.

The most wonderful thing is watching people when they don't know you're watching them.

Yash's contemporaries on Yash

Manmohan Singh
I've made two films with Gulzar. He's more realistic, but poetic like Yashji. He hardly moves the camera. He likes long shots, slow pace and doesn't shoot overseas.

Mahesh Bhatt:
He's not where he is by chance. He has resilience, tenacity and can reinvent himself. It's no joke to be a survivor, and he's been here for more than 46 years. Here people don't like the icons they make. They want to put people down. We need to install the attitude of applauding icons. We have no appreciation. We should learn from Hollywood. He'd have had a lifetime achievement there. He's an amazing guy. A national treasure. The leadership needs to appreciate this guy is successful in the biggest industry. In India politics, cricket and cinema are the most important. It's a lasting shame that the industry doesn't give him a standing ovation.

Amitabh Bachchan

Yashji is in a league of his own, the essence of romance. He is inspired by
Raj Kapoor. His effervesence is not seen in any other film, his exuberance.
He is a poet at heart, best able to recite and to create.

Shahrukh Khan

He's mad. You can see it in his eyes. If you look deep in his eyes, he's mad.
I think he's a genius. I hate saying that word, it's very clichéd. He's mad and
I recognise his madness.

   I like his simplicity, the way he works. If someone's successful, people
will say bad things. If anyone deserves to be written about, it's Yash Chopra.

   He's an amazing guy, Yash Chopra, he's younger than me. I don't think I'll
last like this. He still loves his heroines, heroes, work, films. Best part of Yash
Chopra is he hasn't gone outdated. It's not that his children have made him
modern. His children are modern because he's not outdated. Pam and everyone keep him up with what's happening. He's a very private person. He loves
his food. He goes to sleep. He's very simple. His simplicity has kept him
updated. When you're too full of yourself you don't want to learn or accept
anything new. He accepts what happens. Very modern. Romance-wise he's
modern. This film is very modern. He's never regressive even if traditional.
How old is he? 65 years, I can't imagine. After five years I'm already staid.

Rekha

I love him.

Rajiv Rai

He has stamina. He has ended up being young and thinking young. His
drama is right for teenagers: quick, sharp-witted and he has his own style
of music. He is very original. It comes from within. He has a strong style,
emotions and music which give his films a certain aura.

Iqbal Masud

Yash Chopra has too much self-preservation for true romanticism, and is a
B 'bourgeois romantic', who styles himself 'The Great Romantic' and is

consciously and deliberately romantic. He is caught in a cultural trap between Indian romanticism and real life. He is consciously and deliberately romantic. He is the nearest to a gentleman among Bombay producers and directors, while many of the others are crude Panjabis from the streets and ghettos. Among Muslims, Dilip Kumar has aristocratic bearing while another [I don't want to name] has cultivated and bogus Nawabi manners, which make Muslims laugh. A man of Yash Chopra's age is influenced by the mystique of Urdu poetry, to which the younger generation does not have access.

Shashi Kapoor

Yash is a very disciplined director. He feels very young. He is full of excitement and enthusiasm. I sometimes think he has an extra battery. He was the only director apart from Merchant–Ivory that Jennifer would have home.

Rishi Kapoor

Raj Kapoor and Yash Chopra were great romantics. Raj Kapoor had the style of bringing out some social theme and sweetcoating with romance. Yashji, the eternal romantic. Always in love. Vision, thinking, eating, poetry, all subordinated to romance. He can make a stone cry, that guy. Later on in when Yash Chopra's films became very romantic, his heroines and Raj Kapoor's were the same. *Chandni*, I think was inspired by Raj Kapoor, a woman in white. It could have come from there, not sure. They both had different kinds of romance and I gelled with both.

Yash Chopra has changed with the times. He made socially-reflective films with B.R., with *Daag* he became a romantic, depicting bold themes, then *Kabhi kabhie* and then into violent period, where the woman was not very much in evidence. He got his form back, his heroine was there, projected in *Chandni* as a form of beauty then became more hero-oriented with *Darr*.

Sridevi

He's extraordinary. He's one of the best directors in country. Though he's such an experienced director, his thoughts are very fresh, very young.

There is no tension at all working with him. There is not even one day we cancelled the shooting, or something has not come. Very well organised, so much fun, so relaxed. He knows exactly what he is doing. He's a very fast director. I remember *Lamhe* – he had to finish, only three days left for one and half songs. Any other pictures I would have felt strain, but here I didn't even realise he'd done it. Joking mood, making artistes comfortable.

Juhi Chawla

He makes lovely films. *Chandni* is one of my favourite films. Very lovely, very romantic, classy, dream-like kind of films. He presents his heroines very beautifully. He makes them very rare, everyone wants to work with him. Everyone wants to be presented by him.

Jatin Lalit

Yashji has a very visualising mind. He knows what sort of look his film should have. Very talented family. All sit together for music. They're very much involved. They have a typical taste of music, very Indianised, and very Panjabi.

M.F. Husain

His films are purely Indian. Remarkable. Roots of our culture. Yash makes highly romantic films, entertaining films. He has a style of his own to make a good film, blockbuster. There is a language of cinema which Yash has; the way he portrays women, even in *Chandni*, Sridevi, a powerful portrayal. He has great visual imagery, sheer beauty, sheer grace.

Yash and poetry

Yash Chopra once told me that an Urdu poem summarised his life. He quoted a few lines from '*Umar gurezaan ke naam/*To the elusive life', by Akhtar ul-Iman, a member of B.R. Films' Story Department:

> *Subh uTh jaataa huuN jab murG azaaN dete haiN*
> *Aur roTii ke ta'aaqub meN nikal jaataa huuN*
> *Shaam ko Dhor palaTte haiN chaaragaahoN se jab*
> *Shab guzaarii ke liye maiN bhii palaT aataa huuN*

Qatra qatraa jo kareN jam'a to daryaa ban jaae
Zarrah zarraa jo baham kariyaa to sahraa hotaa
Apnii naadaanii se anjaam se Gaafil ho kar
MaiN ne din raat kiye jam'a xusaara baiThaa.

I get up in the morning when the cock crows
And I go out in search of my daily bread
In the evening when the cattle turn home from the pastures
I too come home to pass the night.

If we collect (water) drop by drop, an ocean is formed
Were I to gather (sand) piece by piece, there would be a desert.
In my stupidity, careless of my end
I have turned the accumulation of days and night into loss.

NOTES

Preface

1. See Dwyer (2000a), Chapter 3, for an analysis of these terms.
2. Dwyer (2000a).
3. For example 'Your mobile is bajing' ('ringing' from Hindi *bajna* 'to ring'); 'I feel silly' ('I don't feel too good').

1 – Yash Chopra: Cinema and Biography

1. See Dwyer (2000a), Chapter 2.
2. See Dwyer (2000b).
3. For example, compare the biographies of Ghalib by Hali (1990) and Russell and Islam (1994), written in the nineteenth and twentieth centuries.
4. The Indian equivalent to the *Dictionary of National Biography* is recent in origin (Sen, 1972).
5. For example, see Ray's biography, Robinson (1989); Kabir (1996).
6. See below.
7. For example, see the work of Mohan Deep or Bunny Reuben. For discussion of film magazines and their gossip see Dwyer (2000a), Chapter 6.
8. On 'auteur' theory see, for example, Wollen (1972), Buscombe (1973), Heath (1973), Barthes (1977), and Foucault (1977). Many of these papers are collected in Caughie (1981).
9. By Salim-Javed.
10. Autobiography became a productive genre in India from the nineteenth century. See for example Gandhi (1982).

11. Bhisham Sahni wrote a biography of his brother: Sahni (1981).
12. Tandon (1961), see also Tandon (1981).
13. See Chapter 7.
14. See Chapter 6.
15. See Chapter 6.
16. See Fox (1985).
17. For a detailed study of the movement see Jones (1976) and Jordens (1997).
18. Rather than the traditional 'arranged marriage'.
19. Dass (1998), p. 7.
20. I have been unable to trace this journal in India or Pakistan. A page is reproduced in Chanana (1998), p. 5.
21. Often referred to as 'Lollywood'.
22. Photograph in Chanana (1998), p. 3.
23. Chanana (1998), p. 10.
24. He says he did not study at the Arya Samaj college in Jalandhar as it was too far from the family house.
25. See Jaffrelot (1996), p. 33f. on this movement.
26. Quoted by Jaffrelot (1996), p. 38. Jaffrelot comments that this motivation is rare nowadays.

2 – From Assistant to Director

1. See Gazdar (1997), p. 24 for a longer list of migrants.
2. Both these men wrote about their lives in the Bombay film world. Manto, famous for his short stories about the Partition, also wrote about the Bombay film industry in the 1940s (Manto, 1998) while Hangal (1999)

describes his experiences of Partition in great detail.

3. This has been depicted in films, notably in *Garam hawa/Hot Storm* (M.S. Sathyu, 1973).

4. Valicha (1996), p. 62.

5. Valicha (1996), p. 107.

6. For a more vivid account of these events, see Reuben (1993), pp. 165–79. For a lurid account, see Deep (1996), pp. 71–5.

7. This is the ambition that Lal Kedarnath has for one of his sons in Yash Chopra's *Waqt*.

8. *Khuda ki amaanat.*

9. Prasad (1998), p. 79.

10. Rajadhyaksha and Willemen (1999), p. 358.

11. It is notoriously difficult to find accurate box-office statistics. I am using the terms 'hit' and 'flop' somewhat loosely in this book, based on the general consensus both contemporary to the release and also subsequent assessments.

12. When Meena presents their child to Mahesh he says '*Main izzatdar aadmi hun. Mera duniya men naam hai. Ye mujhe badnam kar dega.* I am a respectable man with a reputation in the world. This will ruin my reputation.' Even though he has recently become the proud father of another child, he tells Meena to throw their child away: '*Fenk do isse*'.

13. Bhatt (1993), p. 113.

14. Bhatt (1993), p. 112.

15. Meena: '*Ye hum se bari bhool ho gai. Ye paap hai*/We have made a big mistake. This is a sin.'
Mahesh: '*Tum thik kah rahi ho, Meena. Hamen aisi galti nahi karni chahiye thi. Hum dono samaj ki nazar men guhehgar hain*/You are right, Meena. We shouldn't

have done such a wrong thing. We are both sinners in the eyes of society.'

16. Meena uses this word in the film in a song to the baby Roshan, where she says '*Tu mere pyaar ka phool hai ki meri bhool hi kuch kah nahi sakti*/I cannot say whether you are the flower of my love or my mistake.'

17. See below on *Kabhi kabhie.*

18. Butalia (2000).

19. Rossellini's *India* (1958) has a story of construction workers on dams as one of its major themes.

20. See Dwyer (2000a), p. 137.

3 – The Founding of Yash Raj Films

1. Reuben (1993), p. 141.

2. *Screen*, XIX, 49, 21 August, 1970, p. 12.

3. *Screen*, XIX, 49, 21 August, 1970, p. 8.

4. In India the film is often associated more closely with the producer than the director, so the films which Yash directed for B.R. Films are often remembered as B.R.'s rather than Yash's films.

5. *Screen*, XXI, 32, 23 April, 1971, p. 16.

6. *Johny mera naam* ('I'm Called Johnny', Vijay Anand, 1970), *Joshila, Deewaar, Trishul, Vidhaata/The Creator*, (Subhash Ghai, 1982), *Yudh/The Fight* (1985), *Tridev/The trinity* (1989), *Vishwatma/ The Universal Soul* (1992), *Mohra/The Pawn* (1994), *Gupt/The Secret* (1997) (all Rajiv Rai, Gulshan Rai's son).

7. The entry in *The Time Out Film Guide* on *Sunflower (I girasoli)* says: 'excruciating tosh'. Pym (2001), p. 1069.

8. See Dwyer (2000b).

9. *Screen*, XXII, 33, 27 April, 1973, p. 5.

10. The programme shows a screening of the film in a rural area, where it did not go down too well, probably because of the risqué storyline.

11. *Screen*, XXII, 39, 11 May, 1973, p. 4.

12. *Screen*, XXIII, 6, 19 October, 1973, p. 16.

13. *Screen*, XXIII, 6, 19 October, 1973, p. 16.

14. *Screen*, XXIII, 6, 19 October, 1973, p. 16.

15. From the archive section of www.yashrajfilms.com.

16. *Screen*, XXII, 33, 27 April, 1973, p. 18.

17. *Screen*, XXII, 33, 27 April, 1973, p. 18.

18. Gerow (1974), pp. 216–17.

19. For futher analysis of *rasa* see De (1963), Gerow (1974) and (1977) among others.

20. McGregor (1995), p. 855.

21. Cooper (2000), Mishra (1989), Thomas (1985).

22. Notably in Cooper (2000).

23. See Solomon (1997).

24. See Bourdieu (1984) and Dwyer (2000a).

25. Carroll (1998), p. 64.

26. Bordwell (1989); Smith (1995).

27. Carroll (1998), p. 284.

28. Carroll (1998), p. 248.

29. D.G. Phalke filmed his daughter Mandakini enacting a range of emotions.

30. Carroll (1998), p. 249.

4 – The Amitabh Bachchan Films

1. Valicha (1988).

2. Dyer (1979), pp. 34–7.

3. See also Gledhill (1991), p. 214.

4. Gledhill (1991), p. 215.

5. There is more on the stars of south India such as Pandian (1992), Dickey (1993a and b), (2000).

6. On the concept of hero and heroine in a wider range of Indian texts see Dwyer (2000a), pp. 119–20.

7. See Dwyer (2000a), p. 118.

8. See Dwyer (2000a), Chapter 6.

9. See Babb (1981) and Eck (1985).

10. Prasad (1998), pp. 74–8.

11. Vasudevan (2000) queries this understanding of *darshana* saying that it may have enabling as well as authoritative functions.

12. See Somaaya (2000) for an archive of material on Bachchan; Sharma (1993) looks at Bachchan's performance in *Agneepath/Path of Fire* (1990), but does not engage with his stardom. Bachchan has proved such a figure of fascination that several English novels about the Hindi film industry have a character who bears more than a passing resemblance to him, such as Dé (1991) and Tharoor (1994).

13. For a series of interviews about script-writing and other topics see Kabir (1999).

14. Kabir (1999), p. 75.

15. Prasad (1998), Chapter 6.

16. Prasad (1998), p. 271.

17. Kabir (1999), p. 88.

18. See below on *Kabhi kabhie* and *Silsila*.

19. Kabir (1999), p. 75.

20. *Screen*, XXIV, 19, 31 January 1975, pp. 3–4.

21. *Mother India*, like other major Hindi films, also flaunts the conventions of Hindi films, as it has an unhappy ending and a mother, abandoned by her husband, who kills her own child.

22. *Screen*, XXVII, 34, 12 May, 1978, p. 3.

23. *Screen*, XXVII, 34, 12 May, 1978, p. 3.

24. Kabir (1999), p. 68.

25. Kabir (1999), p. 98.

26. For more on these films see Dwyer 2000a, Chapter 5.

27. *Screen*, XXV, 24, 5 March, 1976, p. 1.

28. See below for a discussion of the poetry.

29. See below.

30. 'You, grief for you, desire for you no longer exist. My life seems to be drifting along, without the need for companionship. No path, no goal, no light is necessary. In this dark void, my life stumbles along. And some day in this very darkness, I shall lose myself.'

31. 'Mere ghar aayi ek nanhi pari/A small fairy came to my house'.

32. Shashi and Rishi both feel that their characters were very similar to that of Yash himself. [Interviews with the author.]

33. As their other two songs: 'Tere chehre se/From your face' and 'Tere shish jaise ang/Your body is like glass'.

34. Screen, XXV, 24, 5 March, 1976, p. 6.

35. Screen, XXV, 24, 5 March, 1976, p. 6.

36. Screen, XXV, 24, 5 March, 1976, p. 6.

37. Filmfare, 16–31 January, 1981, p. 9.

38. Filmfare, 1–15 July, 1981, pp. 17 & 19.

39. Filmfare, 1–15 July, 1981, pp. 17 & 19.

40. Filmfare, 1–15 July, 1981.

41. Screen, XXX, 44, 17 July, 1981, p. 7.

42. In particular, a long speech which forms an important part of Amitabh Bachchan's stage shows in Europe and North America: 'Love is a relationship of hearts; a relationship cannot be divided like the earth by boundaries. You may be the moonlight of another's nights, but you are the pivot of my world.'

43. Early examples include Andaz/Style (Mehboob Khan, 1949); Kaagaz ke phool/Paper Flowers (Guro Dutt, 1959). The depiction of premarital sex has become widespread by this time: an early example was Yash Chopra's directorial debut, Dhool ka phool

(1959). Intercourse is symbolised by a thunderstorm: in 1975 in Deewaar, he shows the couple in bed having a post-coital cigarette.

44. This makes Amit look all the more sleazy, that he continues to have sex with his wife while he is having an affair.

45. Filmfare, 16–30 April, 1987.

46. Kabir (1999), p. 100.

47. Patrice Lumumba, leader of the breakaway state of Katanga (in Congo). Some say he was murdered by the CIA. He was a proto-African nationalist and left-winger, still much admired.

5 – The Lean Years

1. See Rajiv Menon's Kandukondain Kandukondain/I Have Found It (2000), which looks at these issues through one of the central characters played by Mammooty, a veteran wounded in the conflict.

2. See Dwyer (2000a), Chapter 3.

3. Shyam Benegal used mainstream stars and even some songs to provide a sort of crossover in films such as Mandi (1983), while the Gujarati Bhavni bhavai/Bhavai of the World (Ketan Mehta, 1980), used a mixture of local theatre (bhavai), Brechtian distancing and slapstick.

4. Raj Kapoor's Prem rog/Love Fever (1982) on widow remarriage, B.R. Chopra's Nikaah/Marriage (1982) on divorce and Muslim women, and Andha kanoon/Blind Justice (T. Rama Rao, 1983).

5. Such as two Amitabh films Aakhri raasta/The Ultimate Path (K. Bhagyaraj, 1985) and Shahenshah/King of Kings.

6. Umrao Jaan, (Muzaffar Ali, 1981).

7. Iqbal Masud in interview.

8. Pendakur (1989).

9. Pendakur (1989).

10. Pendakur (1989).

11. *Filmfare*, June 16–30, 1987, pp. 17–21.

12. *Filmfare*, June 16–30, 1987, p. 21.

13. See Chapter 6.

14. See below.

15. Directors always give oral narrations to their cast and producers, usually on a one-to-one basis. This often leads to claims by stars that they were misled as to the size and scope of their roles.

16. *Screen*, XXXIII, 23, 3 February, 1984, p. 7.

17. *Screen*, XXIV, 20, 3 February, 1985, p. 7.

18. *Screen*, XXXV, 1, 20 September, 1985, p. 1.

19. See Manuel 1993 for details.

6 – Romantic Films

1. Personal e-mail.

2. Personal e-mail.

3. We did this interview in a car.

4. NRI or Non-resident Indian, originally a legal term, is used colloquially to mean any person of South Asian origin living overseas.

5. I have focused on the British Asian community with which I am most familiar.

6. See Smith (1995).

7. Quoted in Rajadhyaksha and Willemen (1999), p. 226.

8. I am grateful to Balvender Hothi for informing me that she and many young British Asians, grew up believing that these earthly paradises were actually located in India.

9. Uberoi (1998).

10. See Stuart Hall (1991b), on this strange ethnicity.

11. In this film, actual hotels are used for his homes: Nunsmere Hall in Cheshire for the UK; the Rambagh Palace in Jaipur for India.

12. See Dwyer (2000a), Chapter 7.

13. Sardar 1998 describes his own family's Hindi moving-viewing practices in London from the 1960s, showing how he adopted attitudes of love and romance from these movies.

14. On British South Asians, see Ballard (1994).

15. See Appadurai (1996).

16. Appadurai (1996), p. 8.

17. Anderson (1983).

18. Appadurai (1996).

19. See Chapter 1, where I mention three moments, all song sequences, which are particularly striking.

20. This review of the film I wrote about a year after the release for the Yash Raj website.

21. See Dwyer (2000a).

22. See Dwyer (2000c) on fashion in the Hindi movies.

23. See Sardar (1998).

24. The so-called Hindi film is often in a form of language closer to Urdu, in particular in the song lyrics.

25. This is a reversal of a trend seen in India, where popular magazines in English are read as part of a self-help way of learning English.

26. See Dwyer (2000a), Chapter 6.

27. See Rushdie (1991).

28. This was true of the US to a lesser extent. See, for example, *Vogue* (US edition), June 1999, which featured a fashion shoot in India, using a western model alongside MTV VJ, actor Rahul Khanna, and various 'Bollywood' celebrities, including Yash Chopra.

29. See Dwyer (2000c).

30. See Stacey (1993).

31. See Appadurai (1996).

32. See Illouz (1997).

33. See Dwyer (2001a).

34. Shively (1992), in an audience ethnography, found that Native Americans identify with the 'cowboy' rather than the 'Indian' when watching Hollywood Westerns.

35. Raj Kapoor famously raised the issue of clothing (consumerism) and Indianness in 1955 in the song *Mera joota hain japani...Phir bhi dil hai Hindustani*/My shoes are Japanese ... but my heart is still Indian, a refrain which remains popular even today. See Dwyer (2000c).

36. See Barthes (1990) and Dwyer (2001c).

37. See Hall (1991a and b).

7 – Production

1. Prasad (1998).

2. Prasad (1998), p. 30.

3. Prasad (1998), pp. 31–2.

4. Prasad (1998), p. 32.

5. See Chapter 6.

6. I wish to thank Yash Johar for trying to guide me through some of these complexities. My apologies if I have misrepresented the situation.

7. Yash Raj Films took insurance from the United India Insurance Co. for *Mohabbatein.*

8. One of India's greatest playback singers, who sang *Kabhi kabhie*'s title song.

9. See Chapters 8 and 9.

10. While men have been wearing western clothes in film for years, the acceptance of 'westernised' women is new. See Dwyer (2000c).

11. Altman (1999).

12. Altman (1999), pp. 38f.

13. Dwyer (2000a).

14. I wrote this chapter when I was a guest of Yash Raj Films during their shoot for *Mohabbatein* in the west of England in March 2000. The days were gloriously sunny, but the nights were bright with frost, while winds whipped around the water that the fire brigade was pumping onto the sets for 'rain sequences'. Exhausted by the long schedules and the cold, I looked with astonishment at Yash Chopra, in his 68th year, as he charged around the sets like a teenager, among his staff, some of whom have worked with him for 35 years. I saw for the first time the slogan on the back of his jacket: 'Yash Raj Films, The crew that never tires'. 'True enough.' I said. Yash laughed and responded, 'This is not only the crew that never tires, we are the crew that never retires!'

BIBLIOGRAPHY

Ahmad, Aijaz (ed.). *Ghazals of Ghalib* (New York: Columbia University Press, 1971).

Alter, Joseph S. *The Wrestler's Body: Identity and Ideology in North India* (New Delhi: Munshiram Manoharlal, 1997).

Altman, Rick. *Film/Genre* (London: BFI, 1999).

Anderson, Benedict. *Imagined Communities: Reflections on the Origin and Spread of Nationalism* (London: Verso, 1983).

Appadurai, Arjun. *Modernity at Large: Cultural Dimensions of Globalization* (Minneapolis: University of Minnesota Press, 1996).

Babb, Lawrence A. 'Glancing: visual interaction in Hinduism'. *Journal of Anthropological Research*, vol. 37, no. 4, 1981, pp. 387–401.

Ballard, Roger (ed.). *Desh Pardesh: the South Asian Experience in Britain* (London: C. Hurst & Co, 1994).

Barthes, Roland. *Image, Music, Text*. Essays selected and trans. Stephen Heath (London: Fontana, 1977).

Bharatan, Raju. *Lata Mangeshkar: A Biography* (New Delhi: UBSPD, 1995).

Bhatt, Mahesh. 'Sex in Indian cinema: only bad people do it', in K. Singh and S. Dé (eds), *Uncertain Liaisons: Sex, Strife and Togetherness in Urban India* (New Delhi: Viking, 1993), pp. 109–26.

Bhattacharya, Rinki. *Bimal Roy: Man of Silence* (New Delhi: Indus, 1994).

Bhimani, Harish. *In Search of Lata Mangeshkar* (New Delhi: Indus, 1995).

Bordwell, David. *Making Meaning: Inference and Rhetoric in the Interpretation of Cinema* (Cambridge, MA: Harvard University Press, 1989).

Bordwell, David and Noel Carroll (eds). *Post-theory: Reconstructing Film Studies* (Madison, WI: University of Wisconsin Press, 1996).

Bourdieu, Pierre. *Distinction: A Social Critique of the Judgement of Taste* Trans. Richard Nice (Cambridge, MA: Harvard University Press, 1984).

Breckenridge, Carol (ed.). *Consuming Modernity: Public Culture in a South Asian World* (Minneapolis and London: University of Minnesota Press, 1995).

Brooks, Peter. *The Melodramatic Imagination: Balzac, Henry James, Melodrama and the Mode of Excess* (New Haven, CT: Yale, [1976] 1995).

Bruzzi, Stella. *Undressing Cinema: Clothing and Identity in the Movies* (London: Routledge, 1997).

Buscombe, Ed. 'Ideas of authorship'. *Screen*, vol. 14, no. 3, Autumn 1973, pp. 75–85.

Butalia, Urvashi. *The Other Side of Silence: Voices from the Partition of India* (London: C. Hurst & Co, 2000).

Carroll, Noel. *A Philosophy of Mass Art* (Oxford: Oxford University Press, 1998).

Caughie, John (ed.). *Theories of Authorship: a Reader* (London: BFI, 1981).

Chanana, Opender (ed.). *A Living Legend, B.R. Chopra: 50 Years of Creative Association with Cinema* (Mumbai:

Indian Film Directors' Association, 1998).

Coakley, Sarah (ed.). *Religion and the body. Cambridge studies in religious traditions, 8* (Cambridge: Cambridge University Press, 1997).

Cooper, Darius. *The Cinema of Satyajit Ray* (Cambridge: Cambridge University Press, 2000).

Dass, Janki. (1998) 'Little-known facts about well-known film people', in O. Chanana (ed.) *A Living Legend, B.R. Chopra: 50 Years of Creative Association with Cinema.*

De, S. K. *Sanskrit Poetics as a Study of Aesthetic.* (Notes by Edwin Gerow) (Berkeley: University of California Press, 1963).

Dé, Shobha. *Starry Nights* (New Delhi: Penguin, 1991).

Deep, Mohan. *The Mystery and Mystique of Madhubala* (Bombay: Magna Books, 1996).

Deep, Mohan. *Simply Scandalous: Meena Kumari* (Mumbai: Magna Books, 1998).

Deep, Mohan. *EuRekha! The Intimate Life Story of Rekha* (Mumbai: Shivani Publications, 1999).

Dickey, Sara. *Cinema and the Urban Poor in South India* (Cambridge: Cambridge University Press, 1993a).

Dickey, Sara. 'The politics of adulation: cinema and the production of politicians in South India'. *Journal of Asian Studies*, vol. 52, no. 2, May 1993b, pp. 340–72.

Dickey, Sara. (2000) 'Opposing faces: film star fan clubs and the construction of class identities in South India'. In R.

Dwyer and C. Pinney (eds), *Pleasure and the Nation: The History, Consumption and Politics of Public Culture in India*, pp. 212–46.

Dwyer, Rachel. *All You Want is Money, All You Need is Love: Sex and Romance in Modern India* (London: Cassell, 2000a).

Dwyer, Rachel. 'The erotics of the wet sari in Hindi films'. *South Asia*, vol. XXIII, no. 2, December 2000b, pp. 143–59.

Dwyer, Rachel. 'Bombay ishtyle' in S. Bruzzi and P. Church Gibson (eds), *Fashion Cultures: Theories, Explorations and Analysis* (London: Routledge, 2000c), pp. 178–90.

Dwyer, Rachel. ' "Indian values" and the diaspora: Yash Chopra's films of the 1990s'. *West Coast Line*, Autumn 2000 and in Parthiv Shah (ed.), *Figures, facts, feelings: a direct diasporic dialogue –* catalogue to accompany a British Council exhibition, November 2000 (London: British Council, 2000d).

Dwyer, Rachel. *The Poetics of Devotion: The Gujarati Lyrics of Dayārām, 1777–1852* (London: Curzon, 2001a).

Dwyer, Rachel. '*Angrezii men kahte hain ke "Aay lav yuu"*…: The kiss in the Hindi film'. Unpublished paper presented at the workshop 'Love in South Asian Traditions', University of Cambridge, May 2001 (2001b).

Dwyer, Rachel. 'Representing the Muslim: the "courtesan film" in Indian popular cinema', in T. Parfitt (ed.), *Imagining the Other: Representations of Jews, Muslims and Christians in the Media* (London: Curzon, forthcoming).

Dwyer, Rachel and Christopher Pinney (eds). *Pleasure and the Nation: The*

History, Consumption and Politics of Public Culture in India (Delhi: Oxford University Press, 2000).

Dyer, Richard. Stars (London: BFI, 1979).

Dyer, Richard. (1982) 'Don't look now: the male pin-up'. Screen, vol. 23, no. 3–4, Sept–Oct 1982, pp. 61–73.

Dyer, Richard. Heavenly Bodies: Film Stars and Society (London: BFI, 1986).

Dyer, Richard. Stars (Supplementary chapter by Paul McDonald) (London: BFI, 1998).

Eck, Diana L. Darsan: Seeing the Divine Image in India (2nd edn). (Chambersburg: Anima, 1985).

Ekman, Paul and Richard J. Davidson. The Nature of Emotion: Fundamental Questions (New York: Oxford University Press, 1994).

Elsaesser, Thomas. (1985) 'Tales of sound and fury: observations on the family melodrama', in Christine Gledhill (ed.), Home is Where the Heart Is (London: BFI, 1985).

Elster, Jon. Alchemies of The Mind: Rationality and the Emotions (Cambridge: Cambridge University Press, 1999).

Foucault, Michel. Language, Counter-memory, Practice Ed. D. F. Bouchard (Oxford: Basil Blackwell, 1977).

Fox, Richard G. Lions of the Punjab: Culture in the Making (Berkeley: University of California Press, 1985).

Gandhi, M. K. An Autobiography (Harmondsworth: Penguin, 1982).

Gazdar, Mushtaq. Pakistani Cinema 1947–1997 (Karachi: Oxford University Press, 1997).

George, T. J. S. The Life and Times of Nargis (New Delhi: Indus, 1994).

Gerow, Edwin. 'The rasa theory of Abhinavagupta and its application', in Edward C. Dimock et al. (eds), The Literatures of India: An Introduction (Chicago, IL: University of Chicago Press, 1974), pp. 216–27.

Gerow, Edwin. Indian Poetics in series J. Gonda (ed.), A History of Indian Literature, V. 3 (Wiesbaden: Oto Harrassowitz, 1977).

Ghosh, Nabendu. Ashok Kumar: His Life and Times (New Delhi: Indus, 1995).

Gledhill, Christine (ed.). Home is Where the Heart is: Studies in Melodrama and the Woman's Film (London: BFI, 1987).

Gledhill, Christine (ed.). Stardom: Industry of Desire (Routledge: London, 1991).

Haggard, Stephen. 'Mass media and the visual arts in twentieth-century South Asia: Indian film posters, 1947–present'. South Asia Research, vol. 8, no. 2, May 1988, pp. 78–88.

Hali. Yadgar-e Ghalib: A Biography of Ghalib by Maulana Altaf Hussain Hali Trans. K. H. Qadiri (Delhi: Idraha-i Adabiyat-i Delli, 1990).

Hall, Stuart. 'The local and the global: globalization and identity', in A. King (ed.), Culture Globalization and the World-System (London: Macmillan, 1991a), pp. 19–40.

Hall, Stuart. 'Old and new identities, old and new ethnicities', in A. King, (ed.) Culture Globalization and the World-System (London: Macmillan, 1991b), pp. 41–68.

Hangal, A. K. *Life and Times of A. K. Hangal* (New Delhi: Sterling, 1999).

Heath, Stephen. 'Comment on "the idea of authorship"'. *Screen*, vol. 14, no. 3, Autumn 1973, pp. 86–91.

Hjort, Mette and Sue Laver (eds). *Emotion and the Arts* (Oxford: Clarendon Press 1997).

Illouz, Eva. *Consuming the Romantic Utopia: Love and the Cultural Contradictions of Capitalism* (Berkeley: University of California Press, 1997).

Jaffrelot, Christophe. *The Hindu Nationalist Movement and Indian Politics, 1925 to the 1990s* (London: C. Hurst & Co, 1996).

Jones, Kenneth W. *Arya Dharm: Hindu Consciousness in Nineteenth-Century Punjab* (Berkeley: University of California Press, 1976).

Jones, Kenneth W. *Socio-religious reform movements in British India. The New Cambridge History of India, III.1* (Cambridge: Cambridge University Press, 1989).

Jordens, J. T. F. *Dayananda Sarasvati: His Life and Ideas* (Delhi: Oxford University Press, 1997. [Orig. 1978]).

Kabir, Nasreen (ed.). *Les Stars du Cinéma Indien* (Paris: Centre Georges Pompidou/Centre Nationale de la Cinématographie, 1985).

Kabir, Nasreen Munni. *Guru Dutt: A life in Cinema* (Delhi: Oxford University Press, 1996).

Kabir, Nasreen Munni. *Talking Films: Conversations on Hindi Cinema with Javed Akhtar* (Delhi: Oxford University Press, 1999).

Kakar, S. *The Inner World: a Psycho-analytic Study of Childhood and Society in India* (2nd ed) (Delhi: Oxford University Press, 1981a).

Kakar, Sudhir. 'The ties that bind: family relationships in the mythology of Indian cinema'. *India International Quarterly, Special Issue: Indian Popular Cinema: Myth, Meaning and Metaphor*, vol. 8, no. 1, 1981, pp. 11–21.

Kakar, Sudhir. *Intimate Relations: Exploring Indian Sexuality* (New Delhi: Viking, 1989a).

Kakar, Sudhir. 'The maternal-feminine in Indian psychoanalysis'. *International Review of Psycho-analysis*, 16. Reprinted in his (1997) *Culture and Psyche* (Delhi: Oxford University Press, 1989b), pp. 60–73.

Kakar, Sudhir. *Culture and Psyche: Selected Essays* (Delhi: Oxford University Press, 1997).

Karanjia, B. K. 'Le star-système', in R. Vasudeva and P. Lenglet (eds), *Les Cinémas Indien*, 1984, pp. 150–57.

King, Barry. 'The social significance of stardom' unpublished ms, quoted in Dyer 1998 (1974).

Lynch, Owen (ed.). *Divine Passions: The Social Construction of Emotion in India* (Delhi: Oxford University Press, 1990).

Manto, Saadat Hasan. *Stars from Another Sky: The Bombay Film World of the 1940s* Trans. Khalid Hasan (New Delhi: Penguin Books, 1998).

Manuel, Peter. *Cassette Culture: Popular Music and Technology in North India* (Chicago, IL: University of Chicago Press, 1993).

McGregor, Stuart R. *Hindi-English Dictionary* (Delhi: Oxford University Press, 1995).

Metcalf, Thomas R. *Ideologies of the Raj. The New Cambridge History of India, III.4* (Cambridge: Cambridge University Press, 1995).

Mishra, Vijay, Peter Jeffery and Brian Shoesmith. 'The actor as parallel text in Bombay cinema'. *Quarterly Review of Film and Video*, no. 11, 1989, pp. 49–68.

Nanda, Ritu. *Raj Kapoor: His Life and Films Presented by his Daughter* (Bombay: R.K. Films and Studios, 1991).

Nandy, A. *The Intimate Enemy: Loss and Recovery of Self under Colonialism* (Delhi: Oxford University Press, 1983).

Nandy, Ashis. in Ashis Nandy (ed.), *The Secret Politics of our Desires: Innocence, Culpability and Indian Popular Cinema* (Delhi: Oxford University Press, 1998), pp. 19–91.

Nesbitt, Eleanor. 'The body in Sikh tradition', in Coakley (ed.) 1997, pp. 289–305 (1997).

Nichols, Bill. *Movies and Methods, Vol II* (Berkeley: University of California Press, 1985).

Oatley, Keith and Jennifer M. Jenkins. *Understanding Emotions* (Oxford: Blackwell, 1996).

O'Flaherty, Wendy Doniger. *Asceticism and Eroticism in the Mythology of Siva* (London: Oxford University Press, 1973).

O'Flaherty, Wendy Doniger. *Women, Androgynes, and Other Mythical Beasts* (Chicago, IL: University of Chicago Press, 1980).

Pandian, M. S. S. *The Image Trap* (Delhi: Sage Publications, 1992).

Pendakur, Manjurath. 'India', in John A. Lent, *The Asian Film Industry* (Bromley: Christopher Helm, 1990), pp. 229–52.

Pinney, Christopher. *Camera Indica: The Social Life of Indian Photographs* (London: Reaktion Books, 1997).

Prasad, M. Madhava. *Ideology of the Hindi Film: A Historical Construction* (Delhi: Oxford University Press, 1998).

Pym, John. *The Time Out Film Guide* (9th edn) (London: Penguin, 2001).

Rajadhyaksha, Ashish and Paul Willemen. *An Encyclopaedia of Indian Cinema* (2nd edn) (London: BFI, 1999).

Reuben, Bunny. *Follywood Flashback: A Collection of Movie Memories* (New Delhi: Indus, 1993).

Reuben, Bunny. *Mehboob ... India's DeMille: The First Biography* (New Delhi: Indus, 1994).

Reuben, Bunny. *Raj Kapoor: The Fabulous Showman* (New Delhi: Indus, 1995).

Robinson, Andrew. *Satyajit Ray: The Inner Eye* (London: André Deutsch, 1989).

Rushdie, Salman. 'Outside the whale', in *Imaginary Homelands* (London: Granta, 1991), pp. 87–101.

Russell, Ralph and Khurshidul Islam. *Ghalib: Life and Letters* (Delhi: Oxford University Press, 1994).

'Ruswa', Muhammad Hadi. (Mirza Mohammad Hadi Ruswa) *Umrao Jan Ada.* Trans. David Matthews (New Delhi: Rupa, 1996), [1899].

Sahni, Balraj. *Balraj Sahni by Balraj Sahni* (New Delhi: Hind Pocket Books, 1979).

Sahni, Bhisham. *Balraj, my Brother* (New Delhi: National Book Trust, 1981).

Sardar, Ziauddin. (1998) 'Dilip Kumar made me do it', in Ashis Nandy (ed.), pp. 19–91.

Scherer, K. R, H. G. Wallbott and W. B. Sommerfield (eds). *Experiencing Emotion: A Cross-cultural Study* (Cambridge: Cambridge University Press, 1986).

Sen, S. P. *Dictionary of National Biography* (Calcutta: Institute of Historical Studies, 1972).

Sharma, Ashwini. 'Blood sweat and tears: Amitabh Bachchan, urban demi-god', in P. Kirkham and J. Thumim (eds), *You Tarzan: Masculinity, Movies and Men* (London: Lawrence and Wishart, 1993), pp. 167–80.

Shively, Jo Ellen. 'Cowboys and Indians: Perceptions of Western Films among American Indians and Anglos'. *American Sociological Review*, no. 57, 1992, pp. 725–34.

Smith, Murray. *Engaging Characters: Fiction, Emotion and the Cinema* (Oxford: Clarendon Press, 1995).

Solomon, Robert C. 'In defence of sentimentality', in M. Hjort and S. Laver (eds) *Emotion and the Arts* (Oxford: Oxford University Press, 1997), pp. 225–45.

Somaaya, Bhavna. *Amitabh Bachchan: The Legend* (New Delhi: Macmillan India, 1999).

Srivatsan, R. 'Looking at film hoardings: labour, gender, subjectivity and everyday life in India'. *Public Culture*, vol. 4, no. 1, Autumn 1991, pp. 1–23.

Stacey, Jackie. *Star Gazing: Hollywood Cinema and Female Spectatorship* (London: Routledge, 1993).

Tandon, Prakash. *Punjabi Century, 1857–1947* (London: Chatto and Windus, 1961).

Tandon, Prakash. *Return to Punjab* (Berkeley: University of California Press, 1981).

Tharoor, Shashi. *Showbusiness* (London: Picador, 1994).

Thomas, Rosie. 'Indian cinema: pleasures and popularity: an introduction'. *Screen*, vol. 26, no. 3–4, 1985, pp. 61–131.

Thomas, Rosie. 'Melodrama and the negotiation of morality in mainstream Hindi film', in Breckenridge 1995, pp. 157–82.

Turner, Bryan S. *The Body and Society: Explorations in Social Theory* (2nd edn) (London: Sage, 1996).

Uberoi, Patricia. 'The diaspora comes home: disciplining desire in *DDLJ*'. *Contributions to Indian Sociology*, vol. 32, no. 2, 1998, pp. 305–36.

Valicha, Kishore. *Kishore Kumar: the Definitive Biography* (New Delhi: Viking, 1988).

Valicha, Kishore. *Dadamoni: The Authorized Biography of Ashok Kumar* (New Delhi: Viking, 1996).

Vasudeva, Aruna and Philippe Lenglet (eds). (1984) *Les Cinémas Indiens. CinémAction 30* (Paris: Editions du Cerf, 1984), pp. 150–57.

Vasudevan, Ravi. 'The melodramatic mode and commercial Hindi cinema'. *Screen*, vol. 30, no. 3, 1989, pp. 29–50.

Vasudevan, Ravi. (2000) 'The politics of cultural address in a "transitional" cinema: a case study of popular Indian cinema', in C. Gledhill and L. Williams (eds) *Reinventing Film Studies* (London: Arnold), pp. 130–64.

Wollen, Peter. *Signs and Meaning in the Cinema* (2nd edn) (London: Secker and Warburg, 1972).

Wollheim, Richard. *On the Emotions* (London: Yale University Press, 1999).

FILMOGRAPHY

Dhool ka phool (Blossom of Dust, Love Child, 1959)

Screenplay/Dialogue/Story: Pandit
    Mukhram Sharma
Editor: Pran Mehra
Director of Photography: Dharam Chopra
Sound: J. S. Worlikar
Song recording: Kaushik
Music: N. Datta
Playback Singers: Lata Mangeshkar,
    Asha Bhosle, Mohammed Rafi,
    Mahendra Kapoor, Sudha Malhotra
Lyrics: Sahir Ludhianvi
Choreographer: Gopi Kishan, Prem Dhawan
Selected Cast: Ashok Kumar,
    Rajendra Kumar, Mala Sinha, Nanda
Production Company: B.R. Films
Running Time: 153 minutes
Black and White

Dharamputra (Son of Faith, 1962)

Screenplay: B.R. Films' Story Dept
Dialogue: Akhtar ul-Iman
Based on the novel by
    Acharya Chatursen Shastry
Editor: Pran Mehra
Director of Photography: Dharam Chopra
Sound: J. S. Worlikar
Music: N. Datta
Playback Singers: Asha Bhosle,
    Mohammed Rafi, Mahendra Kapoor,
    Balbir
Lyrics: Sahir Ludhianvi
Selected Cast: Ashok Kumar, Shashi Kapoor,
    Mala Sinha, Nirupa Roy

Production Company: B.R. Films
Running Time: 154 minutes
Black and White

Waqt (Time, 1965)

Story: F. A. Mirza
Screenplay: B.R. Films' Story Dept
Dialogue: Akhtar ul-Iman
Editor: Pran Mehra
Director of Photography: Dharam Chopra
Sound: Yashwant Mitkar
Song recording: Kaushik
Music: Ravi
Playback Singers: Asha Bhosle, Manna Dey,
    Mahendra Kapoor, Mohamed Rafi
Lyrics: Sahir Ludhianvi
Selected Cast: Sunil Dutt, Raj Kumar,
    Shashi Kapoor, Sadhana, Sharmila
    Tagore, Balraj Sahni, Shashikala,
    Rehman, Achla Sachdev
Production Company: B.R. Films
Running Time: 206 minutes
Colour

Admi aur Insaan (Man and Human, 1969)

Screenplay: C.J. Pavri
Dialogue: Akhtar ul-Iman
Story: Akhtar Mirza
Editor: Pran Mehra
Director of Photography:
    Dharam Chopra
Sound: Vasant Mudaliar, M. A. Shaikh
Music: Ravi
Playback Singers: Asha Bhosle,
    Mohammed Rafi, Mahendra Kapoor

Lyrics: Sahir Ludhianvi
Choreographer: P. L. Raj
Selected Cast: Saira Banu, Dharmendra,
    Feroz Khan, Mumtaz, Johnny Walker,
    Ajeet
Production Company: B.R. Films
Running Time: 181 minutes
Colour

Ittefaq
(*Coincidence*, 1969)
Screenplay: B.R. Films' Story Dept
Dialogue: Akhtar ul-Iman
Editor: Pran Mehra
Director of Photography: Kay Gee
Sound: M. A. Shaikh
Music: Salil Choudhury
Selected Cast: Rajesh Khanna, Nanda,
    Iftekar
Production Company: B.R. Films
Running Time: 104 minutes
Colour

Daag (*The Stain*, 1973)
Screenplay: Yash Chopra,
    Gulshan Nanda
Story: Gulshan Nanda
Dialogue: Akhtar ul-Iman
Editor: Pran Mehra
Director of Photography: Kay Gee
Sound: M. A. Shaikh
Music: Laxmikant Pyarelal
Playback Singers: Lata Mangeshkar,
    Kishore Kumar, Minoo Purushottam
Lyrics: Sahir Ludhianvi
Choreographer: Suresh Bhatt
Selected Cast: Rajesh Khanna, Sharmila
    Tagore, Raakhee, Prem Chopra
Running Time: 139 minutes
Colour

Joshila
(*The Passionate One*, 1973)
Screenplay:
    C. J. Pavari, Akhtar Mirza
Dialogue: Akhtar ul-Iman
Story: Gulshan Nanda
Editor: Pran Mehra
Sound: M. A. Shaikh
Music: R. D. Burman
Playback Singers:
    Lata Mangeshkar, Asha Bhosle,
    Kishore Kumar
Lyrics: Sahir Ludhianvi
Choreographer: Suresh Bhatt, P. L. Raj
Selected Cast: Dev Anand, Hema Malini,
    Raakhee, Pran, Bindu, Madan Puri,
    I. S. Johar
Production Company: Trimurti Films
Running Time: 175 minutes
Colour

Deewaar
(*The Wall*, 1975)
Story/Screenplay/Dialogue:
    Salim-Javed
Editor: Pran Mehra
Director of Photography: Kay Gee
Sound: M. A. Shaikh
Music: R. D. Burman
Playback Singers: Asha Bhosle,
    Kishore Kumar, Manna Dey,
    Bhupinder, Ursula
Lyrics: Sahir Ludhianvi
Choreographer: Suresh Bhatt
Selected Cast: Shashi Kapoor,
    Amitabh Bachchan, Parveen Babi,
    Neetu Singh, Nirupa Roy
Production Company: Trimurti Films
Running Time: 175 minutes
Colour

Kabhi kabhie
(Sometimes, 1976)
Screenplay: Yash Chopra, Sagar Sarhadi
Story: Pamela Chopra
Dialogue: Sagar Sahardi
Editor: Pran Mehra
Director of Photography: Kay Gee
Sound: M. A. Shaikh
Music: Khayyam
Playback Singers: Lata Mangeshkar,
    Mukesh, Kishore Kumar
Lyrics: Sahir Ludhianvi
Choreographer: Suresh Bhatt, Naidu
Selected Cast: Amitabh Bachchan, Shashi
    Kapoor, Waheeda Rehman, Raakhee,
    Neetu Singh, Rishi Kapoor, Naseem,
    Simi Garewal, Parikshit Sahni
Production Company: Yash Raj Films
Running Time: 177 minutes
Colour

Trishul (The Trident, 1978)
Story/Screenplay/Dialogue:
    Salim-Javed
Editor: B. Mangeshkar
Director of Photography: Kay Gee
Sound: M. A. Shaikh
Music: Khayyam
Playback Singers: Lata Mangeshkar,
    Kishore Kumar, Yesudas, Nitin Mukesh,
    Pamela Chopra
Lyrics: Sahir Ludhianvi
Choreographer: Suresh Bhatt
Selected Cast: Shashi Kapoor, Sanjeev
    Kumar, Raakhee, Amitabh Bachchan,
    Hema Malini, Prem Chopra, Poonam
    Dhillon, Waheeda Rehman, Sachin
Production Company: Trimurti Films
Running Time: 167 minutes
Colour

Kaala patthar
(Black Rock or Coal, 1979)
Screenplay/Dialogue: Salim-Javed
Editor: B. Mangeshkar
Director of Photography: Kay Gee
Sound: M. A. Shaikh
Music: Rajesh Roshan
Playback Singers: Lata Mangeshkar, Kishore
    Kumar, Mohammed Rafi, Mahendra
    Kapoor, S. K. Mahaan, Pamela Chopra
Lyrics: Sahir Ludhianvi
Selected Cast: Amitabh Bachchan,
    Shatrughan Sinha, Shashi Kapoor, Parveen
    Babi, Neetu Singh, Sanjeev Kumar
Production Company: Yash Raj Films
Running Time: 176 minutes
Colour

Silsila
(The Affair, 1981)
Screenplay: Yash Chopra
Dialogue: Sagar Sarhadi
Story: Preeti Bedi
Editor: Keshav Naidu
Director of Photography: Kay Gee
Sound: M. A. Shaikh
Music: Shiv-Hari
Playback Singers: Lata Mangeshkar,
    Kishore Kumar, Amitabh Bachchan,
    Pamela Chopra
Lyrics: Javed Akhtar, Rajendra Krishan,
    Hassan Kamal, Nida Fazli,
    Harivanshrai Bachchan
Choreographer: Suresh Bhatt
Selected Cast: Amitabh Bachchan,
    Sanjeev Kumar, Shashi Kapoor,
    Jaya Bachchan, Rekha
Production Company: Yash Raj Films
Running Time: 182 minutes
Colour

Mashaal
(The Torch, 1984)

Story/Screenplay/Dialogue: Javed
Editor: Keshav Naidu
Director of Photography: Kay Gee
Sound: M. A. Shaikh
Music: Hridaynath Mangeshkar
Playback Singers: Lata Mangeshkar,
   Kishore Kumar, Mahendra Kapoor,
   Shailendra Singh, Suresh Wadkar,
   Hariharan, Anup Jalota
Lyrics: Javed Akhtar
Choreographer: Suresh Bhatt
Selected Cast: Dilip Kumar,
   Waheeda Rehman, Anil Kapoor, Rati
   Agnihotri, Amrish Puri, Saeed Jaffrey,
   Nilu Phule, Madan Jain
Production Company: Yash Raj Films
Running Time: 173 minutes
Colour

Faasle *(Distances, 1985)*

Story/Screenplay: Sachin Bhowmick
Dialogue: Sagar Sarhadi
Editor: Keshav Naidu
Director of Photography:
   Manmohan Singh
Sound: Ramesh Yadav, M. A. Shaikh
Music: Shiv-Hari
Playback Singers: Lata Mangeshkar, Asha
   Bhosle, Kishore Kumar, Pamela Chopra,
   Shobha Gurtu
Lyrics: Shahryar
Choreographer: Suresh Bhatt
Selected Cast: Sunil Dutt, Rekha, Rohan
   Kapoor, Farah, Raj Kiran, Deepti Naval,
   Farooque Sheikh
Production Company: Yash Raj Films
Running Time: 136 minutes
Colour

Vijay [1988]

Story/Screenplay: Sachin Bhowmick
Dialogue: Akhtar ul-Iman,
   Surendra Prakash
Editor: Keshav Naidu
Director of Photography:
   Manmohan Singh
Sound: Vasant Mudaliar
Music: Shiv-Hari
Playback Singers: Lata Mangeshkar,
   Mahendra Kapoor, Asha Bhosle,
   Suresh Wadkar, Vinod Kumar Rathod,
   Anupam Kher, Pooja Chopra
Lyrics: Nida Fazli
Choreographer: Suresh Bhatt
Selected Cast: Rajesh Khanna, Hema Malini,
   Anil Kapoor, Rishi Kapoor, Meenakshi
   Sheshadri, Sonam, Shakti Kapoor,
   Gulshan Grover, Anupam Kher
Production Company: Yash Raj Films
Running Time: 174 minutes
Colour

Chandni [1989]

Screenplay: Umesh Kalbag,
   Arun Kashyap
Dialogue: Sagar Sarhadi
Story: Kamna Chandra
Editor: Keshav Naidu
Director of Photography:
   Manmohan Singh
Sound: Vasant Mudaliar
Music: Shiv-Hari
Playback Singers: Lata Mangeshkar,
   Asha Bhosle, Nitin Mukesh,
   Suresh Wadkar, Pamela Chopra, Babla
   Mehta, Vinod Rathod, Jolly Mukherji,
   Sridevi
Lyrics: Anand Bakshi
Choreographer: Saroj Khan

Selected Cast: Sridevi, Rishi Kapoor,
  Vinod Khanna, Waheeda Rehman,
  Anupam Kher
Production Company: Yash Raj Films
Running Time: 186 minutes
Colour

Lamhe (Moments, 1991)

Story/Screenplay: Honey Irani
Dialogue: Dr Rahi Masoom Reza
Editor: Keshav Naidu
Director of Photography:
  Manmohan Singh
Sound: Anuj Mathur
Music: Shiv-Hari
Playback Singers: Lata Mangeshkar,
  Suresh Wadkar, Hariharan, Ila Arun,
  Moinuddin, Pamela Chopra,
  Sudesh Bhonsale
Lyrics: Anand Bakshi
Choreographer: Saroj Khan
Selected Cast: Anil Kapoor, Sridevi,
  Anupam Kher, Waheeda Rehman
Production Company: Yash Raj Films
Running Time: 192 minutes
Colour

Parampara (Tradition, 1992)

Story/Screenplay: Honey Irani
Dialogue: Dr Rahi Masoom Reza
Editor: Keshav Naidu
Director of Photography:
  Manmohan Singh
Sound: Anuj Mathur
Music: Shiv-Hari
Playback Singers: Lata Mangeshkar, Suresh
  Wadkar, Abhijeet, Vinod Rathod, Devki,
  Anupama Deshpande
Lyrics: Anand Bakshi

Choreographer: Saroj Khan
Selected Cast: Sunil Dutt, Vinod Khanna,
  Aamir Khan, Saif Ali Khan, Raveena
  Tandon, Neelam, Anupam Kher,
  Ramaiya, Ashvini Bhave
Production Company: AF Films (P) Ltd.
Running Time: 154 minutes
Colour

Darr (Fear, 1993)

Story/Screenplay: Honey Irani
Dialogue: Javed Siddiqui
Editor: Keshav Naidu
Director of Photography:
  Manmohan Singh
Sound: Anuj Mathur
Music: Shiv-Hari
Playback Singers: Lata Mangeshkar,
  Pamela Chopra, Alka Yagnik, Kavita
  Krishnamurthy, Udit Narayan, Sudesh
  Bhosale, Vinod Rathod, Abhijeet,
  Hariharan, Devki Pandit
Lyrics: Anand Bakshi
Choreographer: Saroj Khan,
  B. H. Tarun Kumar
Selected Cast: Sunny Deol, Juhi Chawla,
  Shahrukh Khan, Anupam Kher
Production Company: Yash Raj Films
Running Time: 178 minutes
Colour

Dil to pagal hai (The Heart is Crazy, 1997)

Story: Pamela Chopra
Screenplay: Yash Chopra, Pamela Chopra,
  Uday Chopra
Dialogue: Aditya Chopra
Editor: V. V. Karnik
Director of Photography:
  Manmohan Singh

Sound: Anuj Mathur
Music: Uttam Singh
Playback Singers: Lata Mangeshkar, Asha
    Bhosle, Udit Narayan, Hariharan
Lyrics: Anand Bakshi
Choreographer: Shiamak Davar, Farah Khan
Selected Cast: Shahrukh Khan,
    Madhuri Dixit, Karisma Kapoor,
    Akshay Kumar
Production Company: Yash Raj Films
Running Time: 182 minutes
Colour

INDEX